Demand Systems Estimation

Demand Systems Estimation

METHODS AND APPLICATIONS

STANLEY R. JOHNSON
PROFESSOR OF ECONOMICS AND AGRICULTURAL ECONOMICS
UNIVERSITY OF MISSOURI, COLUMBIA

ZUHAIR A. HASSAN
CHIEF, DEMAND AND PRICE ANALYSIS,
MARKETING AND ECONOMICS BRANCH, AGRICULTURE CANADA

RICHARD D. GREEN
ASSOCIATE PROFESSOR OF ECONOMICS
UNIVERSITY OF CALIFORNIA, DAVIS

The Iowa State University Press / Ames

Printed by The Iowa State University Press
Ames, Iowa 50010

First edition, 1984

Library of Congress Cataloging in Publication Data

Johnson, Stanley R., 1938–
Demand systems estimation.

Includes bibliographical references and index.
1. Demand (Economic theory)—Mathematical models. 2. Consumption (Economics)—Mathematical models. I. Hassan, Zuhair A. II. Green, Richard D. (Richard Dale), 1943– . III. Title.
HB801.J653 1984 338.5′212 83-12816
ISBN 0-8138-0431-0

The text in this book was printed from camera-ready copy provided by the authors.

E R R A T U M

Demand Systems Estimation

P. 138-- In space at bottom of page, insert the following:

$$\gamma_{it} = \gamma_i^* + \beta_i q_{it-1} \quad (8.1)$$

S

Preface

The research on which this book is based was initiated at Agriculture Canada in 1972. The objective was to provide a set of demand parameter estimates for Canada that made use of the more recent developments in theory for specifying and estimating demand systems. Until the early 1970s, the demand parameters used for forecasting and policy exercises by Agriculture Canada had not utilized fully the prior information available with demand systems methods. A monograph, Consumer Demand for Major Foods in Canada, from this early study was published by Agriculture Canada, and has gone through two printings. The apparent interest in these basic parameters and their use in policy contexts lead to a continuation of support for demand systems research at Agriculture Canada.

During the 1970s, a number of demand systems specifications were developed and applied for Canada and other countries. These included the linear expenditure system, the Rotterdam model, and the indirect addilog system among the static representations. Demand systems designed to provide explanations for persistence in consumption behavior and other dynamic features of the available time series data emerged, also. These included the dynamic linear expenditure system, the stock adjustment model of Houthakker and Taylor and others. The availability of these alternative systems representations raised important questions for applied analyses of consumption behavior. How sensitive would the resulting price and income elasticity estimates be to differences in systems specifications? What factors should guide choices between static and dynamic systems? How should these choices be influenced by assumptions on persistence in the error terms for the statistical models?

Based on these and other questions, the initial demand research at Agriculture Canada moved to an empirical examination of results from alternative demand systems representations. Available empirical results for evaluating implications of alternative demand systems specifications were not from similar data bases in terms of commodity definitions, time periods, or even countries. Thus, for specifying systems to be used in applied forecasting and policy contexts, the available literature provided only limited information on the empirical consequences of choosing among the alternative demand systems specifications. Evaluating the alternative systems required a review of the theory supporting the specifications, designing appropriate estimation procedures, usually nonlinear; and applications in comparable time series data. In the process of assembling this information a number of reports, monographs and journal papers were developed to present different aspects of these comparisons of empirical results.

The collection of the already published and new results on demand systems into this short and concise book occurred as a natural extension of our research activity. The major purpose for the book is to provide those who are reviewing and evaluating results of applied demand systems analyses or undertaking demand systems research with a consistently developed summary of the theory leading to the systems specifications, appropriate estimation methods and a comparable set of empirical results. This information is intended to serve as a basic introduction to demand systems theory as well as to aid in the selection of systems specifications for use in applied studies.

We expect the individuals who use this book to employ the contents much as we have in our own demand research. That is, the readers should view the book as an introduction to demand systems and as a basis for comparing demand systems results. For this reason, the theoretical treatment of the background for the demand systems specifications has been developed traditionally. Beginning with utility maximization, the systems specifications are rationalized and compared for their implications regarding the Slutsky relationships. To assist in understanding the nonlinear estimation methods necessary for applying the systems, a review of the basics for these estimation approaches has been included. Finally, following from the evaluation and results for static and dynamic demand systems, a chapter has been included showing that hypotheses on persistence and habits have important impacts for the selection of demand systems specifications and for interpretations of empirical findings.

The development of the manuscript occurred over a number of years. During this period it benefited from support of a number of institutions and constructive comments from several individuals. The institutions from which we obtained direct or indirect support are Agriculture Canada, University of Missouri, Columbia; University of California, Davis; and University of California, Berkeley. Also, two USDA grants for analyses of cross section food consumption data (USDA-53-32U4-0-194 and USDA-53-32U4-9-188) contributed to the development of some of the theoretical background. The individuals we gratefully acknowledge for assistance with drafts of the manuscript are

Ramon Lopez, Jean-Paul Chavas, and Rulon Pope. Preliminary discussions with John Nash were very helpful in the development of the chapter on nonlinear estimation. Also, he adapted computer programs for estimating most of the demand systems models. Finally, in the winter of 1982, a graduate class at the University of Missouri, Columbia, used a version of the manuscript and helped, through their suggestions and questions, to improve the exposition. These individuals and institutions should of course not share our responsibility for errors of commission or omission that remain.

The process of producing the book heightened our horizons regarding the difficulties of such undertakings. Our editor, Carol Sanderson, did much to improve the style and exposition in the book. R. P. LaFrance of Agriculture Canada developed the graphics. Beverly Baker, who typed all the drafts and even the final copy, demonstrated great skill and even greater patience, understanding, and most of all good nature during the whole process.

Demand Systems Estimation

1 • Consumption Behavior

Consumption behavior is the focus of continuing emphasis in applied economic research. In some respects this emphasis may be attributed to the relatively strong theoretical basis for the various consumption hypotheses and an interest in empirical tests of the underlying propositions. However, it is difficult to separate these interests from more problematic concerns with refinements of structural relationships used in economic models designed for application in policy analysis and forecasting. Since major economic questions of the day provide priorities for refinement and specialization of the theory, such a separation would appear to be difficult and highly artificial. Policy issues, applied work, and theoretical advances are more productively viewed as outcomes of an interdependent system.

Aspects of consumption behavior that have attracted the attention of economists include (1) consumer demand, (2) Engel curve analysis, and (3) consumption functions in more aggregated contexts. All are important components of more complex economic policy and forecasting models and also are applicable to address testable propositions from the theory of consumer behavior. For example, in the case of demand analysis, price and income elasticities are the important policy parameters, while restrictions or hypotheses that follow from the formulation of the consumer allocation problem and specialized utility functions are important for tests of the theory.

Engel curves can be employed to estimate income or expenditure elasticities. Questions of how these parameter estimates change with income levels, across commodity groups, and among sample partitions generated by socioeconomic characteristics are important in both theoretical and applied work. Also, Engel curves can be viewed as demand functions with prices held constant. However, their development has been largely empirical and the hypotheses tests they afford are of greater interest from an applied perspective.

Finally, the aggregate consumption function has microeconomic foundations in the theory of consumer behavior. Expressions relating household consumption to income and socioeconomic characteristics provide at least an informal link between microtheory and the aggregate consumption function, advanced largely as an empirically robust behavioral proposition.

In this book, the theory of consumer demand is synthesized and applied to time series data for the Canadian economy to estimate the parameters for alternative static and dynamic demand systems models. The dynamic demand systems are viewed in a habit formation context, and statistical tests are conducted to discriminate between these and other hypotheses for representing persistence in consumption patterns.

Results are interesting for testing the theory, for the relatively complete comparisons among demand systems specifications they permit, and for policy and forecasting. Synthesis and exposition of the theory is provided as a reference in itself, a framework for specifying the econometric models and advancing duality concepts, and a basis for an enriched interpretation of the empirical results. Tests for habit formation attempt to deal directly and in a full demand systems framework with the persistence in consumption patterns observed in this and similar data bases.

1.1 DEVELOPMENT

Analysis of consumer demand has historically occupied a central role in economic theory, evidenced by the extensive literature on demand and utility and by the fact that many concepts crucial to modern work in theory and demand systems estimation have their origins in writings that might be considered dated by those without an appreciation for this rich tradition. In the present context, this historical development is reviewed with special reference to demand systems and their estimation. This orientation distinguishes the current treatment from those available elsewhere (e.g., Katzner 1970; Ekelund et al. 1972). The objective of the review is to provide a perspective for demand systems theory and the applied results subsequently reported.

The discussion is organized to permit separate consideration of the static and dynamic systems, and a distinction is made between applied and theoretical results. The intent of the organization is, however, to give the review structure more than to imply that the topics are completely separate. Since the dynamic theory has been more recently developed and applications of static models are more extensive, the review proceeds from the static framework.

1.1.1 Static Demand Models

Static demand models and the associated theory are a product of two important lines of economic inquiry; see Fig.

1.1. Demand and utility theory were not integrated until the seminal work of Slutsky (1915). Before then, demand analysis was descriptive in nature and utility theory addressed problems of measurement and definition more than implications for observed consumption behavior.

After this integration (see the first shaded block in Fig. 1.1), demand and utility or preference theory again tended to proceed somewhat separately. Developments in utility were focused to a major extent on problems of reconciling assumptions of marginal analysis with primitive conditions on preference orderings. Demand studies remained more empirical; they evolved with increasingly ambitious attempts to introduce the structure imposed by the theory in estimation and hypotheses testing contexts.

Recently the two areas of inquiry have had a more common focus because of the development of demand systems representations and their estimation; see second shaded block in Fig. 1.1. Separability conditions have suggested approaches for specifying empirically tractable systems; directly specified demand systems have been explored simultaneously for their implications in terms of utility functions and separability, resulting in increased applied work and in a substantial extension of the propositions for empirical testing. Ideas of revealed

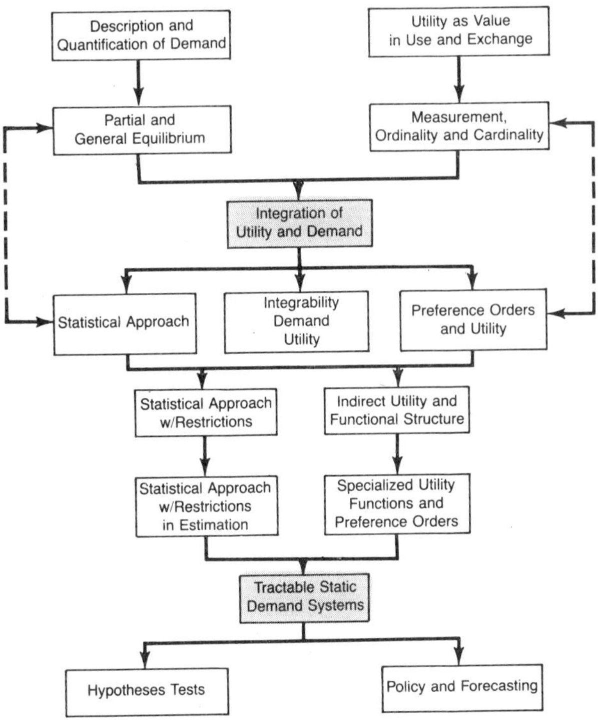

FIG. 1.1. Static demand and utility theory.

preference and indirect utility have been incorporated in applications to add to the empirical substance of the demand systems approach.

1.1.1.1 Static theory. This review of static demand theory is organized to emphasize the developments noted in the left side of Fig. 1.1; that is, it follows the evolution of the theoretical results on demand beginning with the early descriptive work and moving to the present demand systems concepts. Reference to the right side of Fig. 1.1 is more abbreviated and features the contributions of utility and preference ordering to the advancement of demand specifications for empirical application. Readers more interested in utility and preference theory may wish to consult Katzner (1970) as a supplement to this review.

The initial "descriptive and quantification" phase (see Fig. 1.1) of the development is difficult to date or to attribute to a particular author or authors. The inverse relationship between market price and the quantity of a commodity available within a particular time frame is directly observable; thus (with the generosity of hindsight) it is not difficult to read recognition of the so-called law of demand into early writings. To link these observations to the more systematic thought on the law of demand it has been useful to omit reference to the ancients and to initiate the discussion with a very perceptive piece by King (Stigler 1950a, b; Ekelund et al. 1972). King (1696) attempted to formulate a numerical relationship between a defect in the harvest and a corresponding increase in the price of corn. He computed a demand schedule for corn and developed King's law, based on the inverse relationship between price and quantity.

This "law" was considerably refined later by Davenant (1771), who referred to deviations from an assumed normal price if the harvest fell short of expectations. For shortages of 0.1, 0.2, 0.3, 0.4, and 0.5, Davenant argued the price would rise above a normal value by 0.03, 0.08, 0.16, 0.28, and 0.45, respectively. Although the "law of demand" remained a descriptive hypothesis, this treatment and systematic work with the concept was important for the present theory of consumer demand.

Another noteworthy contribution in this phase was that of Verri (1771), who postulated a demand function. Price and the quantity demanded were inversely related with the relationship proportional (Manfra 1932). Paolo Frisi gave this hypothesis an algebraic formulation, specifying $pq = c$ with p indicating price, q quantity, and c a constant. That is, the demand function was hyperbolic with unit elasticity (Robertson 1949).

The next phase identified in Fig. 1.1, "partial and general equilibrium," represents a considerable leap in time to the period of Cournot, Walras, and Marshall. Although extensive discussions of demand and price-quantity relationships by the classical economists occurred in England prior to this period, there was little progress in refining the concept of consumer demand (Stigler 1950a, b; Ekelund et al. 1972). Exceptions to such broad statements exist and those who would argue with this claim would likely point to the work of Malthus (1836) and Mill (1965).

Early continental writers of the classical period made substantial advances in the refinement and application of the demand concept (Cournot 1838; Dupuit 1844; Bordas 1847). These authors were concerned with clarifying the conditions under which the law of demand as observed in a partial equilibrium context is conditioned by other factors. Cournot rigorously stated the concept of demand, indicating that sales or the annual demand q for each article is a particular function f(p) of its price p. He further argued that this function should be known as the law of demand or of sales. Mathematically, Cournot's law was expressed as $q = f(p)$. Cournot drew this demand curve as negatively sloped and assumed that demand was continuous. Besides this law and a numerical application, Cournot introduced the differential and integral calculus into economic theory and recommended improvements in statistics of production, trade, consumption, and prices for more accurate estimates of demand parameters.

Dupuit identified utility with demand and provided a clear explanation of the relationships between marginal utility, total utility, and price. He also described the concept of "consumer surplus," which was measured by the area under the demand curve minus the expenditure on the commodity. Dupuit constructed a demand curve and, like Cournot, gave the equation for the demand function as $q = f(p)$. Graphically, the independent variable price was placed on the horizontal axis and the dependent variable quantity on the vertical axis. Finally, Bordas is identified with early thinking on real and nominal income and apparently made the first reference to an <u>income effect</u> in the discussion of demand functions.

Although Jevons (1871) had useful insights regarding the relationship between utility and demand, not until the time of Walras (1954) and Marshall (1890) did systematic and cumulative work on demand theory begin. Walras succeeded in linking utility to demand and provided a substantial elaboration of the concept advanced by Cournot. He also visualized the general interdependence of all economic variables and posited a system of equations to depict a general equilibrium of prices and quantities in interrelated markets. In this system the quantity demanded of any commodity was expressed as a function of the prices of all commodities with money income and tastes (utility function) held constant.

Marshall, on the other hand, elaborated on the concept of market demand in a partial equilibrium context. These partial equilibrium demand functions depended upon the price of the commodity in question and upon the income of the consumer. All other prices and marginal utility for income were assumed constant. In fact, the much used concept <u>ceteris paribus</u>

emerged in full force with Marshall. The partial equilibrium demand analysis, along with a constant marginal utility for income and the usual curvature properties for the utility function, imply a downward sloping demand curve. Another of Marshall's major contributions was the clarification and extension of the concept of elasticity of demand.

The theory of consumer demand was refined by Pareto (1906), who extended Walras's earlier work and showed that the major results from theory of consumer behavior could be rationalized under the assumption of ordinal rather than cardinal properties and diminishing marginal rates of substitution rather than diminishing utilities (Brown and Deaton 1972). Pareto is also credited with demonstrating that demand curves can be derived theoretically from information furnished by introspective reasoning. The originality and analytical richness of Pareto's works can be traced further into the modern theory of consumer behavior to the current concepts of economic equilibrium (Wold and Jureen 1953).

Utility by this time occupied an important role in the theory of demand. But these developments in utility theory were not all demand oriented. Smith (1776) and others dealt with the discrepancy between value to the individual (in use) and market price (in exchange). Bernoulli (1738), independently; Smith; and the others were expressing in different ways the concept of diminishing marginal utility. These concepts found refinement in the work of Edgeworth (1881), who introduced indifference curves and defined a cardinal utility function to analyze barter in a nonadditive case. However, it remained to Fisher (1892) and Pareto to show that maximization of the utility function involves only ordinal properties.

With these utility concepts, the stage was set for the full "integration of utility and demand" in Fig. 1.1 by Slutsky (1915). His major conclusions were related to the now famous inequality, stating that the compensated direct price derivative is negative, and to the Slutsky equation, stating that compensated cross price derivatives are symmetric. The distinction between income and substitution effects is also attributed to him. During this period Hicks and Allen (1934) extensively reviewed and refined the work of Marshall and also isolated income and substitution effects of price changes with money income held constant. Although not formulated with the special purpose of generating implied restrictions for empirical estimation, these results are important in theory and current applications. They are developed in detail subsequently.

The next level of Fig. 1.1 identifies three areas of activity: "statistical approach," "integrability," and "preference orders and utility." In utility theory, the third area of activity occupied a prominent role in the period after the merging of utility theory and demand. Important contributors include Wold (1943-1944) and Debreu (1954). These results developed and refined conditions under which a real valued utility function could represent a preference ordering. "Integrability" in Fig. 1.1 is used in a less than completely technical context and refers to the interconnections between demand equations and utility functions. The completion of the correspondence between utility and demand (Samuelson 1947; Houthakker 1950) and the attention it generated was important in impressing upon careful applied researchers the cost of ad hoc specifications to potential generality and the hypotheses provided by the theory.

The statistical approaches to demand (see Fig. 1.1) are discussed in Chap. 6 in the section on applications because of the importance of treating them in detail.

The major concepts of utility theory involved the recognition of "indirect utility and functional structure" and the clarification of separability concepts for preference orders and utility functions. In the former case, the results have culminated in the modern theory of duality; Hotelling, Roy, Court, McKenzie, Shephard, Diewert, Hanoch, and Weymark have been instrumental in extending the theory of consumer demand using duality and functional structure.

Hotelling (1932) derived indirect utility as a function of prices and income. Roy (1947) showed that the indirect utility function leads to an explicit expression for the demand functions; in particular, he demonstrated that demand functions can be expressed as ratios of the partial derivatives of the indirect utility function with respect to prices and income. Court (1941) showed that maximizing the direct utility function with respect to quantities and subject to the budget constraint is equivalent to maximizing the indirect utility function with respect to prices and income and subject to the budget constraint. McKenzie (1957) derived the cost function by inverting the indirect utility function and solving for income in terms of a level of utility and a set of prices. A fourth alternative for characterizing the consumer optimization problem is the transformation function (Shephard 1953; Diewert 1978; Hanoch 1978; Weymark 1980), which can be interpreted as an indirect cost function and gives the minimum cost of achieving a level of utility and a set of quantities.

The final theoretical results preceding modern demand systems in Fig. 1.1 are "specialized utility functions and preference orders." In the present context, these results relate to separability concepts. Theoretical implications of the separability concepts introduced by Leontief (1947) and Sono (1961) have been elaborated upon by Strotz (1957), Goldman and Uzawa (1964), and Blackorby et al. (1978). Separability generally restricts the structure of the preference ordering and the utility functions, implying special conditions for the Slutsky equation in the consumer allocation problem; they reduce the structural parameters for the demand system parameters to the point that the allocation problem is empirically tractable.

The culmination of the advances on utility and preferences

and the applied work after the integration of utility and demand (Fig. 1.1) resulted in the flurry of empirical analysis on demand systems that has occurred during the last 15 years. It has been encouraged by advancements in computational technology that make the parameter estimation problem feasible and of interest for hypotheses testing.

1.1.1.2 Static applications. Applications of demand theory are highly varied, ranging from the intuitive analyses of firms and individuals creating markets to behavioral concepts used in formalized analytical models. Our discussion of applications can be confined to the statistical estimation of parameters of demand systems and occurs in four components: "statistical approaches," "statistical approach with restrictions," "statistical approach with restrictions in estimation," and "tractable static demand systems." For the first the work was statistical but with little more guidance from the theory than to suggest that price, quantity, and income were the appropriate variables to include in demand expressions. The theory, in the sense that the analysis was rigorous, was statistical.

Statistical studies using time series data and attempting to measure demand functions are generally thought to have originated with estimates by Benini (1907) of the elasticity of demand for cotton in Italy and estimates by Lehfeldt (1914) of the elasticity of demand for wheat in England. According to Stigler (1954), two significant initial statistical results on demand curves are due Lenoir and Moore. Lenoir, in a published piece (Stigler 1954), was the first to discuss the identification problem in estimating demand and supply curves from observed price and quantity data; Moore (1914) made a major attempt to combine economic theory and statistical techniques in the estimation of demand parameters. In Economic Cycles: Their Law and Cause, Moore estimated statistical demand curves for corn, hay, oats, and potatoes.

The careful linking of theory with data and statistical methods, although simple by modern standards, gave Moore's work the major impact it has had on applied demand theory. In 1919 Moore introduced the concept of the flexibility of price defined as the reciprocal of the elasticity of demand. He observed that for many agricultural products the quantity supplied is generally unaffected by current price--the supply curve is assumed to be perfectly inelastic. In estimating demand parameters under these circumstances, price is the dependent variable; quantity supplied and selected demand shifts are the independent variables. Resulting estimates of price flexibility proved and continue to be useful for judging the effect of a change in quantity on the commodity price, particularly for agricultural and other seasonal commodities.

The next step in the more systematic application of demand concepts was to introduce into the analysis some of the theoretical restrictions "statistical approach with restrictions" in Fig. 1.1. The major work leading to these advances is attributed to Schultz (1938). The statistical methods Schultz employed are now superseded, but the approach integrating the restrictions from theory into a systems representation is a forerunner of current demand systems applications. He first took a number of precautions to adjust for demand shift factors in the time series data and then employed an ordinary least squares method with quantity demanded expressed as a function of prices and income to obtain estimates of demand parameters.

Empirical applications of demand theory expanded rapidly after World War II. Wold and Jureen (1953) published an exposition of Paretian demand theory and of the theory of stationary random processes as related to the analysis of economic time series. Stone (1954a) also published a significant empirical work in demand analysis. These two contributions consolidated the theoretical and empirical work on static demand models in the first half of this century (Brown and Deaton 1972, p. 1148).

Some of these studies were examining the idea of directly estimating a demand system, but the estimation methods and restrictions imposed to obtain estimable demand functions were limiting in a number of respects. More recent studies in statistical literature show that estimates of demand equation systems can be improved by simultaneously considering the complete set of commodities. The link making this possible involved the results on specialized utility functions. In addition, the development and use of separability concepts made it possible to specify and estimate theoretically plausible demand systems (see Fig. 1.1, "statistical approach with restrictions in estimation").

The earliest example of the specification and estimation of complete demand systems is by Leser (1941). Stone (1954b) estimated the linear expenditure system that satisfied various theoretical restrictions, Frisch (1959) developed a scheme for computing all price elasticities in a systems context, Houthakker (1960) studied the theoretical and empirical implications of direct and indirect additivity, and Brandow (1961) used Frisch's assumption of "want independence" and constructed for 24 foods and 1 nonfood commodity group a matrix of price and income elasticities of demand at retail level. These contributions mark the beginnings of complete demand systems approach applications.

This book, in particular Chaps. 3 and 4, reviews the major static demand systems and associated separability concepts. The discussion of "tractable static demand systems" (Fig. 1.1) is deferred. The object is to estimate systems that obey the restrictions on the consumer allocation problem and that incorporate specialized interpretable behavioral assumptions.

The final two blocks in Fig. 1.1 refer to extensions through "policy and forecasting" and "hypotheses tests." The hypotheses tests are largely associated with the translog utility function approximation and its empirical applications.

The potential for testing is developed in Chaps. 4 and 5.

1.1.2 Dynamic Demand

The treatment of dynamic demand systems is considerably less extensive than that for static systems because most of the significant work on the subject has been recent and much of it is developed in considerable detail here. However, it is useful to give even this relatively complete development of dynamic demand systems a historical perspective.

Dynamic demand systems are shown schematically in Fig. 1.2. First came the idea of time in allocation problems, discounting, and time preference. Then came analysis of the multiperiod maximization and, finally, two separate threads of thought merging applied and theoretical results. The first involves the use of modern demand systems ideas in dynamic contexts; the second addresses directly the habit formation or persistence problem with various hypothesized adjustment mechanisms in the structure and on the disturbances.

Since applied and theoretical work on dynamic demand systems are so highly integrated, the theory-application distinction made in the case of the static systems is not retained. A more manageable task is to view both empirical and

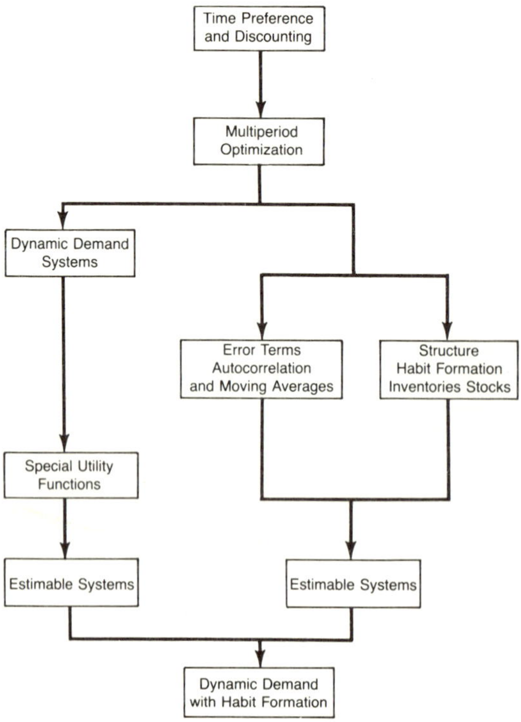

FIG. 1.2. Dynamic demand systems.

applied results as extensions of the static formulations.

Ideas of impatience and time discounting have been familiar in economic analysis since von Bohm-Bawerk (1912, pp. 257-289); however, the dynamic theory of economic behavior emphasizing the sequential nature of intertemporal consumption decisions is only evolving now. Milestones in this process have been the time preference analysis of Fisher (1930), the use of variational methods in multiperiod maximization formulations by Ramsey (1928), and the development of a framework for analysis of dynamic processes by Samuelson (1947). At this point the split indicated in Fig. 1.2 occurs.

The left side of the figure is the less interesting, largely because it represents only an extension of the results on demand systems formulated in a static setting. These studies discount sequences of static systems; as indicated by the left-hand blocks, these estimates can be computed with systems methods and no specialized restrictions on utility functions. Temporally linked static models or more integrated dynamic systems incorporate a fuller explanation for intertemporal choice, and the distinction from the habit formation options indicated in the right side of Fig. 1.2 is simply a matter of degree.

For habit formation, two themes have occurred. The first is the treatment of the persistence phenomenon as an error term problem and the use of various autoregressive and moving average processes to represent it. The second and more interesting approach has been to make the systems dynamic, at least in an exploratory way, and to try to incorporate explanations for persistence and other intertemporal patterns in consumption behavior. Models that incorporate habit formation (Pollak and Wales 1969), stock adjustment (Houthakker and Taylor 1970) and related types of adaptive behavior (Phlips 1972; Lluch 1974; Klijn 1977) are best viewed as provisional structural specifications. Any completely dynamic theory must more fully incorporate the sequential nature of the decision process (Strotz 1956). The introduction of additional information into the consumer decision is difficult because the problem must be realistically modeled (Theil 1967).

From an applied viewpoint these systems, though exploratory in their relationships to time dimensional utility functionals, have been attractive because of the highly confining assumptions of the static models. Such models have allowed for both habit formation and the presence of durable goods in the explanation of consumer behavior. The major theoretical and empirical contributions to the estimation of demand parameters under the assumption of endogenously changing preferences are by Houthakker and Taylor (1970), Phlips (1972, 1974), Taylor and Weiserbs (1972), Lluch (1974), and Klijn (1977). Interesting tests of one of these models against a naive autocorrelation hypothesis are also indicative of future studies in the applied field (Green et al. 1980). Chapter 5 presents some of these contributions.

1.2 CONTENT ORGANIZATION

Applied results are preceded by an exposition of relevant theory in Chaps. 2 and 3. Chapter 2 provides a review of the static theory of consumer demand, beginning with a formulation of the utility maximization problem. Restrictions on the demand functions following from the model and behavioral assumptions underlying the curvature conditions on the utility functions are identified and interpreted. A discussion of duality theory and its application in representing the consumer allocation problem is followed by specific examples that illustrate these more modern duality concepts.

Chapter 3 discusses alternative separability concepts as sources of restrictions that can be applied in the estimation of demand relationships. The major separability assumptions are defined and various types of separable utility functions are presented and compared. The consequences of different separability concepts are investigated using the Slutsky terms from the basic demand theory model. The separability concepts are related to the various functional forms that have been used in representing the consumer decision problem. An example relating separability to the optimization formulations utilized in duality is provided.

Selected algebraic forms for static utility functions and/or demand systems are considered in Chap. 4. These range from ad hoc double-log systems to systems more consistent with the restrictions implied by the theory, including those associated with direct algebraic specifications of the demand functions and those arising from specific forms for the utility function. All represent methods that have as their primary motivation the achievement of economies in parameter estimation. The objective is to make the demand models tractable for applied work with the use of behaviorally attractive assumptions. The linkages between applied systems models and the behavioral aspects of the specialized utility functions they imply or explicitly incorporate are identified.

Chapter 5 provides a review and integration of three dynamic demand systems: state adjustment, a dynamic version of the linear expenditure, and intertemporal. They are frameworks through which questions of adjustment and the persistence of consumption patterns can be investigated. Habit formation, durable goods purchase, and consumer reactions to new household and market information can be accommodated in these more general demand models.

Statistical procedures required for estimation of demand systems models are reviewed in Chap. 6. These systems formulations typically require nonlinear estimation of the parameters. The chapter reviews various techniques for obtaining linear and nonlinear estimators for parameters of demand systems. Using the linear pseudomodel, these estimation methods are linked. The advantage is to separate numerical analysis problems from problems concerned with inference in nonlinear models and to provide a means for solving nonlinear problems with simple capital intensive methods.

Empirical results for a number of static and dynamic demand systems models are reported in Chap. 7 after a discussion of the error processes generating the residuals and the data and commodity groupings. Reasons for presenting the results of several demand systems are largely empirical. Applications of demand systems to Canadian and other data bases have been limited so alternative results should be especially useful in appraising the consequences of the different systems and empirical implications for the various systems formulations. The comparison of results should be helpful in assessing the appropriateness of the differing behavioral assumptions and structures on which the estimates are based.

Chapter 8 summarizes tests for habit formation, autocorrelation, and regularity conditions using the likelihood ratio procedure in order to provide a basis for clarifying applications of static demand systems and an evaluation of alternative characterizations for persistence in consumption patterns. Chapter 9 briefly summarizes the empirical results and delineates important issues for applied work raised by the empirical comparisons and tests of restrictions implicit in the alternative systems specifications.

REFERENCES

Benini, R. 1907. Sull'uso delle formole empiriche nell'economia applicata. Giornale Degli Economisti, 2d ser. Vol. 35.

Bernoulli, Daniel. 1738. Specimen theoriae novae de mensura sortis. In Commentarii Academemiae Scientiarum Imperialis Petropolitanae. English transl. L. Sommer, Exposition of a new theory of the measurement of risk. Econometrica 22 (1954):23-36.

Blackorby, C.; Primont, D.; and Russell, R. R. 1978. Duality, Separability, and Functional Structure: Theory and Economic Applications. New York: Elsevier-North Holland.

Bordas, M. 1847. Of the measurement of the utility of public works. Transl. Eleonar Evans, ed. R. B. Ekelund, Jr. In Annales des Ponts et Chaussees, 2d ser. Vol. 13.

Brandow, G. E. 1961. Interrelationships among demands for farm products and implications for control of market supply. Pennsylvania State University, Agricultural Experiment Station Bulletin 680, University Park.

Brown, A., and Deaton, A. 1972. Surveys in applied economics: Models of demand behaviour. Economic Journal 82 (Dec.):1145-1236.

Cournot, A. 1838. Researches into the mathematical principles of the theory of wealth. Paris: Huchette. Transl. N. Bacon, 1897. New York: Macmillan.

Court, 1941. Entrepreneurial and consumer theories for commodity spectra. Econometrica 9 (Apr.):135-62.
Davenant, C. 1771. The political and commercial works of Charles D'Avenant, L.L.D. Vol. 2. Collected and revised by Sir Charles Whitworth. 5 vol. London.
Debreu, G. 1954. Representation of a preference ordering by a numerical function. In Decision Processes, ed. R. M. Thrall, C. H. Coombs, and R. L. Davis, pp. 159-65. New York: John Wiley.
Diewert, W. E. 1978. Duality approaches to microeconomic theory. University of British Columbia, Department of Economics, Discussion Paper 78-09, Vancouver.
Dupuit, Jules. 1844. On the measurement of the utility of public works. Annales des Ponts et Chaussees, 7. Transl. R. H. Barback, 1952, in International Economic Papers, 2. London: Macmillan.
Edgeworth, F.Y. 1881. Mathematical Psychics. London: Paul Kegan.
Ekelund, R. B., Jr.; Furubotn, E. G.; and Granin, W. P. 1972. The Evolution of Modern Demand Theory. Lexington, Mass.: D. C. Heath.
Fisher, Irving. 1930. The Theory of Interest. New York: Macmillan.
Fisher, Irving. 1892. Mathematical investigations in the theory of value and prices. Transactions of the Connecticut Academy of Arts and Sciences. 9 (1892):1-24. New York: Augustus M. Kelly, Inc., 1965.
Frisch, R. A. 1959. A complete scheme for computing all direct and cross demand elasticities in a model with many sectors. Econometrica 27 (Apr.):177-96.
Frisi, Paolo. 1772. Mathematical commentaries in Pictro Verri. Meditazioni sull' economia politica, 6th ed., Livorno, pp. 37-39, 43, 84, 92, 97-98, 134, 152, 232-33 and 237-53.
Goldman, S. M., and Uzawa, H. 1964. A note on separability in demand analysis. Econometrica 32 (July):387-98.
Green, R.; Hassan, Z.; and Johnson, S.R. 1980. Testing for habit formation, autocorrelation, and theoretical restrictions in linear expenditure systems. Southern Economic Journal 47 (Oct.): 433-43.
Hanoch, G. 1978. Symmetric duality and polar production functions. In Production Economics: A Dual Approach To Theory and Applications, Vol. I, ed. D. McFadden and M. Fuss, pp. 111-31. Amsterdam: Elsevier-North Holland.
Hicks, J. R; and Allen, R. G. D. 1934. A reconsideration of the theory of value. Economica 1 (Feb.):52-75.
Hotelling, H. 1932. Edgeworth's taxation paradox and the nature of demand and supply functions. Journal of Political Economy 40 (Oct.):577-616.
Houthakker, H. S. 1950. Revealed preference and the utility function. Journal of Econometrics 17:159-74.
———. 1960. Additive preferences. Econometrica 28

(Apr.):244-57.
Houthakker, H. S., and Taylor, L. D. 1970. Consumer Demand in the United States, 2d ed. Cambridge, Mass.: Harvard University Press.
Jevons, W. S. 1871. The Theory of Political Economy. London: Macmillan.
Katzner, D. W. 1970. Static Demand Theory. New York: Macmillan.
King, Gregory. 1696. Natural and Political Observations and Conclusions upon the State and Condition of England. Reprint. In Two Tracts by Gregory King, ed. George E. Barnett. 1936. Baltimore, Md.: Johns Hopkins Press.
Klijn, N. 1977. Expenditure, savings, and habit formation: A comment. International Economic Review 18 (Oct.):771-78.
Lehfeldt, R. A. 1914. The elasticity of demand for wheat. Economic Journal 24 (June):212-17.
Leontief, W. W. 1947. Introduction to a theory of the internal structure of functional relationships. Econometrica:361-73.
Leser, C. E. V. 1941. Family budget data and price elasticities of demand. Review of Economic Studies 9 (Nov.):40-57.
Lluch, C. 1974. Expenditure, savings and habit formation. International Economic Review 15 (Oct.):786-97.
McKenzie, L. W. 1957. Demand theory without a utility index. Review of Economic Studies 24:185-89.
Malthus, T. R. 1836. Principles of Political Economy Considered with a View of Their Practical Application, 2d ed. Reprint, 1964. New York: Augustus M. Kelley.
Manfra, Modestino Remigio. 1932. Pictro Verrie i Problemi Economici del Tempo Suo. Milano: Albrighi, Segati.
Marshall, A. 1890. Principles of Economics. London: Macmillan.
Mill, J. S. 1965. Principles of Political Economy with Some of Their Applications to Social Philosophy. Ed. Sir W. J. Ashley. New York: Augustus M. Kelley.
Moore, H. L. 1914. Economic Cycles: Their Law and Cause. New York: Macmillan.
———. 1919. Empirical laws of demand and supply and the flexibility of prices. Political Science Quarterly 34 (Dec.):556-67.
Pareto, V. 1906. Manuale di Economia Politica. Milan: Societa Editrice Libraria.
Phlips, L. 1972. A dynamic version of the linear expenditure model. Review of Economics and Statistics 54 (Nov.):450-58.
———. 1974. Applied Consumption Analysis. Amsterdam: North Holland.
Pollak, Robert A., and Wales, Terence J. 1969. Estimation of the linear expenditure system. Econometrica 37 (Oct.):611-28.
Ramsey, F. P. 1928. A mathematical theory of saving. Economic

Journal 38 (Oct.):109-20.
Robertson, Ross M. 1949. Mathematical economics before Cournot. Journal of Political Economy 57 (Dec.):523-36.
Roy, R. 1947. La distribution du revenu entre les divers biens. Econometrica 15 (July):205-25.
Samuelson, P. A. 1947. Foundations of Economic Analysis. Cambridge, Mass.: Harvard University Press.
Schultz, H. 1938. The Theory and Measurement of Demand. Chicago: University of Chicago Press.
Shephard, R. W. 1953. Cost and Production Functions. Princeton: Princeton University Press.
———. 1970. Theory of Cost and Production Functions. Princeton: Princeton University Press.
Slutsky, E. 1915. On the theory of the budget of the consumer. Engl. transl. in Readings in Price Theory pp. 27-56. ed. G. J. Stigler and K. E. Boulding. Homewood, Ill.: Irwin, 1952.
Smith, Adam. 1937. An Inquiry into the Nature and Causes of the Wealth of Nations. New York: Random House, Modern Library Ed.
Sono, M. 1961. The effect of price changes on the demand and supply of separable goods. International Economic Review 2 (Sept.):239-71.
Stigler, G. J. 1954. The early history of empirical studies of consumer behavior. Journal of Political Economy 62 (Apr.):95-113.
Stigler, G. J. 1950a. The development of utility theory. 1 Journal of Political Economy 58 (Aug.):307-27.
———. 1950b. The development of utility theory. 2 Journal of Political Economy 58 (Oct.):371-96.
Stone, R. 1954a. The Measurement of Consumers, Expenditure and Behaviour in the United Kingdom, 1920-1938. Vol. I. Cambridge: Cambridge University Press.
———. 1954b. Linear expenditure systems and demand analysis: An application to the pattern of British demand. Economic Journal 64 (Sept.):511-27.
Strotz, R. H. 1956. Myopia and inconsistency in dynamic utility maximization. Review of Economic Studies 23:165-80.
———. 1957. The empirical implication of a utility tree. Econometrica 25:269-80.
Taylor, D., and Weiserbs, D. 1972. On the estimation of dynamic demand functions. Review of Economics and Statistics 54 (Nov.):459-65.
Theil, H. 1967. Economics and Information Theory. Amsterdam: North-Holland.
Verri, Pietro. 1771. Meditazioni Sull' Economia Politica. Republished in the Custodi Collection, Milano, Italy.
Von Bohm-Bawerk, E. 1959. Positive Theoriedes Kapitals, Dritte Auflage, especially Buch IV, Abschnitt I, Genenwart and Zukunft in der Wirtschaft, pp. 426-86. Engl. transl. in

Capital and Interest 2, Positive Theory of Capital. Book 4, sec. 1, pp. 257-89. South Holland, Ill.: Libertarian.

Walras, L. 1954. Elements d'economie politique pure. L. Corbas et Cie Lausanne. Engl. transl. Elements of Pure Economics. W. Jaffe, 1954. London: Allen and Unwin.

Weymark, J. A. 1980. Duality results in demand theory. European Economic Review 14 (Nov.):377-95.

Wold, H., and Jureen, L. 1953. Demand Analysis. New York: John Wiley.

2 • Theory of Consumer Demand

Systems of demand equations are estimated by applying the theory of consumer demand with additional assumptions that relate to the problem at hand. These assumptions are usually motivated by empirical considerations; that is, they are plausible restrictions resulting in systems of demand equations that can be estimated with existing time series data on prices, incomes, and consumption levels. To understand the behavioral implications of these assumptions and their empirical consequences, it is thus important to have a fundamental grasp of the basics of the theory of consumer demand.

The theory of consumer demand is well documented in a number of readily available sources. Hicks (1946) and Samuelson (1947) are the more commonly known of the early and complete treatments. More recent expositions that are pedagogically more attractive include Goldberger (1967), Phlips (1974), Powell (1974), Theil (1975, 1976), Barten (1977), and Deaton and Muellbauer (1980).

A review and synthesis of the theory of consumer demand in this chapter has two purposes. (1) It provides a backdrop for the subsequent results on systems of demand equations. Standard testable propositions obtained from the theory are important for the work on systems of demand equations, since they verify that the systems investigated are consistent with the theory. (2) The review is of value in itself as a primer on demand analysis that is enhanced by following the results utilizing the direct utility maximization approach with similar derivations based on more modern concepts of duality. The latter have great advantages from a pedagogical viewpoint.

The formulation of the utility maximization problem presumes the existence of a utility function with a number of convenient analytical properties. As such, interesting aspects of the theory of consumer behavior relating to conditions on preferences and preference orderings that can generate these functions or (more properly) for which these functions are correspondences have been omitted (for example, see Katzner 1970, Phlips 1974 and Silberberg 1978). The object is to proceed from the utility function to the demand functions and the conditions they exhibit. After these derivations and results are summarized, the major propositions for the demand functions are restated in terms of elasticities; then the comparative statics for effects of price and income changes are reviewed. Integrability as a concept for relating demand systems to utility functions is briefly discussed. Finally, duality concepts are used to obtain the standard results by a more direct and analytically convenient method.

2.1 UTILITY MAXIMIZATION AND DEMAND FUNCTIONS

Assumptions about consumer behavior are introduced into the theory of demand through the specification of a utility function. The utility function measures the level of satisfaction an individual experiences as a result of consuming a particular bundle of goods and services, or as termed hereafter, commodities. Implicit in this definition is a time dimension; that is, consumption is measured as a flow, the amounts of the commodities consumed per unit of time. The utility function is denoted

$$u = u(q) \tag{2.1}$$

where $q = (q_i)$ is taken to be an n-element vector whose elements are levels of the commodities consumed per unit of time. The commodities are assumed to be defined so that the representation is complete with respect to the choice set of the consumer.

The utility function (2.1) is assumed to be strictly increasing, strictly quasi-concave, and twice continuously differentiable. A function $f(x)$ is said to be strictly increasing on the interval (a, b) if $f(x_2) > f(x_1)$ whenever $x_2 > x_1$; it is strictly decreasing if $f(x_2) < f(x_1)$ whenever $x_2 > x_1$. A function $f(x)$ is quasi-concave over the interval (a, b) if $f[\lambda x_1 + (1 - \lambda)x_2] \geq \min[f(x_1), f(x_2)]$ for all x_1, x_2 in (a, b) and all $0 \leq \lambda \leq 1$; the function $f(x)$ is strictly quasi-concave if the strict inequality ($>$) holds. A function $f(x)$ is continuous at the point $x = a$ if the following conditions are fulfilled: $\lim_{x \to a} f(x)$ and $f(a)$ exist and $\lim_{x \to a} f(x) = f(a)$. Interpretations of these conditions are easily made with the aid of indifference curves, which are contours of the utility surface. For two commodities, q_1 and q_2, an indifference curve u_0u_0 is plotted in Fig. 2.1. The indifference curve represents combinations of q_1 and q_2 that yield the same utility level.

Strict quasi-concavity of the utility function (2.1) prevents the indifference surfaces or contours from containing linear segments or bending back on themselves. The indifference curve depicted in Fig. 2.1 is consistent with this assumption on utility function (2.1). The increasingness assumption implies that the consumer prefers more to less, even if confined to only small changes in the consumption bundle. In the context of Fig. 2.1, indifference curves for higher levels of utility than u_0 must lie to the right of u_0u_0 and the indifference curves cannot cross. Continuity ensures that the difference curves are well defined. Finally,

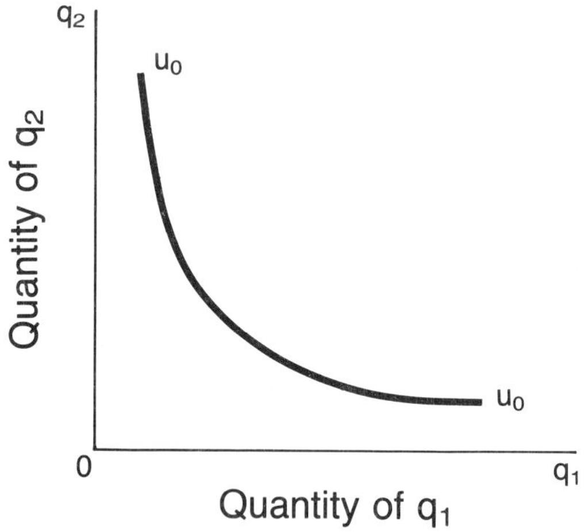

FIG. 2.1. A representative indifference curve for the utility function (2.1).

the differentiability assumption assures that the indifference curves are not kinked, as the derivatives describing the curvature of the indifference surface are themselves well defined and not kinked.

These conditions all imply behaviorally a consistency of choice by the consumer they represent. They also ensure that the consumer will not become so endowed with a particular commodity that it creates disutility. These consistency assumptions on choice render the utility maximization problem tractable in the context of a relatively simple application of the calculus, as is now shown.

First partial derivatives of the utility function are interpreted as marginal utilities; that is, they show the increment to total utility that occurs as a result of consuming an additional amount of the commodity per unit of time. These derivatives of the utility function are represented by

$$u_i = \frac{\partial u}{\partial q_i} > 0 \qquad (i = 1, 2, \ldots, n) \tag{2.2}$$

and, as indicated, are positive. Because of the continuity and differentiability assumptions, the second partial derivatives of the utility surface are symmetric by Young's theorem, i.e.,

$$u_{ij} = \frac{\partial^2 u}{\partial q_i \partial q_j} = \frac{\partial^2 u}{\partial q_j \partial q_i} = u_{ji} \qquad (i, j = 1, 2, \ldots, n) \tag{2.3}$$

The second derivatives describe the rates of change of the first derivatives and thus the behavior of the marginal utility for each of the commodities. Obviously, for the description to be complete it must include how the marginal utilities change with consumption levels of other commodities, u_{ij} $(i \neq j)$. The strict quasi-concavity assumption implies that the marginal rate of substitution is diminishing.

The utility function (2.1) is maximized subject to a budget constraint, which specifies that available income is exactly spent:

$$p'q = m \tag{2.4}$$

where $p = (p_i)$ is the n-element column vector of prices and m is consumer income. For this analysis both p and m are assumed to be positive and, from the standpoint of the consumer, they are regarded as given; that is, we are studying the consumption decision for the situation in which the consumer is not at liberty to alter the level of income.

Maximization of the utility function (2.1) subject to the budget constraint (2.4) is carried out by the Lagrangian method. According to this procedure, form the expression

$$L(q, \lambda) = u(q) - \lambda(p'q - m) \tag{2.5}$$

where λ is the Lagrangian multiplier interpreted as the marginal utility of income. Differentiating the Lagrangian equation (2.5) with respect to each of the arguments, q_i and λ, yields the first order conditions

$$u_q - \lambda p = 0, \qquad p'q - m = 0 \tag{2.6}$$

where u_q is the vector of derivatives of the utility function with respect to the quantities, q_i $(i = 1, 2, \ldots, n)$.

The second order conditions for a maximum can be written as

$$x'Ux \leq 0 \quad \text{for all } x \text{ such that } p'x = 0 \tag{2.7}$$

The matrix U is called the Hessian and denoted

$$U = \begin{bmatrix} u_{11} & u_{12} & \cdots & u_{1n} \\ u_{12} & u_{22} & \cdots & u_{2n} \\ \vdots & \vdots & & \vdots \\ u_{n1} & u_{n2} & \cdots & u_{nn} \end{bmatrix} \tag{2.8}$$

Condition (2.7) is assured by the assumption that the utility function u is strictly quasi-concave.

The system of equations obtained from the first order conditions (2.6) provides n + 1 equations in 2n + 2 variables: the n prices, the n quantities, λ, and income. Applying the implicit function theorem (Apostol 1957, p. 146), system (2.6) can be solved uniquely for $q_1, \ldots, q_n$ and λ in terms of prices and income. The resulting expressions are

$$q_i = q_i(p_1, \ldots, p_n, m) \tag{2.9a}$$

$$\lambda = \lambda(p_1, \ldots, p_n, m) \tag{2.9b}$$

The demand function q_i is important in both theory and practice because it describes how the consumer will behave when confronted with alternative sets of prices and a particular income. The term λ shows that the marginal utility of income, that is, consumer evaluation of increments to income, is governed by commodity prices and the existing income level. The value of these functional relationships is increased because the curvature restrictions on the utility function result in a number of potentially testable propositions.

2.2 PROPERTIES OF THE DEMAND FUNCTIONS

Restrictions on consumer demand functions or, alternatively, their properties, are obtained from manipulating the first order conditions specified in (2.6). Specifically, they are developed by considering the consequences of parametric shifts in the first order conditions with respect to prices and income. Results of these parametric shifts are described by the partial derivatives of the first order conditions for both prices and income.

Partially differentiating the equations in the system represented by (2.6) with respect to income m (all prices held constant) yields

$$\sum_j \frac{\partial^2 u}{\partial q_i \partial q_j} \frac{\partial q_j}{\partial m} = p_i \frac{\partial \lambda}{\partial m} \qquad (i = 1, 2, \ldots, n)$$

$$\sum_j p_j \frac{\partial q_j}{\partial m} = 1$$

These expressions can be more conveniently written using matrix and vector notation:

$$UQ_m = \lambda_m p \quad \text{and} \quad p'Q_m = 1 \tag{2.10}$$

where $Q'_m = (\partial q_1/\partial m, \ldots, \partial q_n/\partial m)$ is an n-component vector with elements defined as the partial derivatives of the n demand functions with respect to income m, $\lambda_m = \partial\lambda/\partial m$ is the change in the marginal utility of income as its level changes, and U is the Hessian defined in (2.8).

Partially differentiating system (2.6) with respect to the price for an arbitrary commodity k, p_k, yields

$$\sum_j \frac{\partial^2 u}{\partial q_i \partial q_j} \frac{\partial q_j}{\partial p_k} = p_i \frac{\partial \lambda}{\partial p_k} \qquad (i = 1, 2, \ldots, n;\ i \neq k)$$

$$\sum_j \frac{\partial^2 u}{\partial q_i \partial q_j} \frac{\partial q_j}{\partial p_k} = \lambda + p_i \frac{\partial \lambda}{\partial p_i} \qquad (i = k)$$

$$\sum_j p_j \frac{\partial q_j}{\partial p_k} = -q_k$$

All other prices and income m are held constant. As before the expressions can be written in matrix and vector notation, i.e.,

$$UQ_p = p\lambda'_p + \lambda I \quad \text{and} \quad p'Q_p = -q' \tag{2.11}$$

where

$$Q_p = \begin{bmatrix} \frac{\partial q_1}{\partial p_1} & \frac{\partial q_1}{\partial p_2} & \cdots & \frac{\partial q_1}{\partial p_n} \\ \frac{\partial q_2}{\partial p_1} & \frac{\partial q_2}{\partial p_2} & \cdots & \frac{\partial q_2}{\partial p_n} \\ \vdots & & & \vdots \\ \frac{\partial q_n}{\partial p_1} & \frac{\partial q_n}{\partial p_n} & \cdots & \frac{\partial q_n}{\partial p_n} \end{bmatrix}, \qquad \lambda'_p = \left[\frac{\partial \lambda}{\partial p_1}, \ldots, \frac{\partial \lambda}{\partial p_n}\right]$$

Thus, Q_p is an n x n matrix with the ith row given by partial derivatives of the demand function for commodity i with respect to each of the n prices, and λ'_p is a row vector that describes how the marginal utility of income changes for changes in each of the n prices.

Combining the expressions contained in (2.10) and (2.11) gives the so-called fundamental matrix equation for consumer demand theory (Barten 1969, p. 2),

$$\begin{bmatrix} U & P \\ p' & 0 \end{bmatrix} \begin{bmatrix} Q_m & Q_p \\ -\lambda_m & -\lambda'_p \end{bmatrix} = \begin{bmatrix} 0 & \lambda I \\ 1 & -q' \end{bmatrix} \tag{2.12}$$

To obtain an explicit solution for the derivatives of the demand equations with respect to the variables p_i and m (namely Q_m, Q_p, λ_m, and λ_p), the first term in the left-hand side of (2.12) the bordered Hessian, is inverted. Since U is nonsingular this inverse exists (see Goldberger 1964, p. 27). The result, which is easily verified by multiplication, can be written

$$\begin{bmatrix} U & p \\ p' & 0 \end{bmatrix} = \frac{1}{p'U^{-1}p} \begin{bmatrix} (p'U^{-1}p)U^{-1} - (U^{-1}p)(U^{-1}p)' & (U^{-1}p) \\ (U^{-1}p') & -1 \end{bmatrix}$$

Applying the expression for the inverse of the bordered Hessian, the solution of system (2.12) can be expressed term by term:

$$\lambda_m = (p'U^{-1}p)^{-1} \tag{2.13a}$$

$$Q_m = \lambda_m U^{-1} p \tag{2.13b}$$

$$\lambda_p = -\lambda Q_m - \lambda_m q \tag{2.13c}$$

$$Q_p = \lambda U^{-1} - \frac{\lambda}{\lambda_m} Q_m Q'_m q' \tag{2.13d}$$

The restrictions on demand parameters implied by the theory are derived from the solution of the fundamental demand equations, (2.13). In particular, these restrictions are the Engel aggregation:

$$p'Q_m = p'\lambda_m U^{-1} p = \lambda_m p'U^{-1} p = 1 \tag{2.14a}$$

or $\Sigma_i\, p_i\, (\partial q_i/\partial m) = 1$; the Cournot aggregation,

$$p'Qp = p'\lambda U^{-1} - p'(\lambda/\lambda_m)Q_m Q_m' - p'Q_m q'$$

$$= (\lambda/\lambda_m)Q_m' - (\lambda/\lambda_m)Q_m' - q' = -q' \tag{2.14b}$$

or $\Sigma_i p_i(\partial q_i/\partial p_j) = -q_j$ $(j = 1, 2, \ldots, n)$; the symmetry condition,

$$(Q_p + Q_m q') = Q_p + Q_m q' \tag{2.14c}$$

or $\partial q_i/\partial p_j + (\partial q_i/\partial m)q_j = \partial q_j/\partial p_i + (\partial q_j/\partial m)q_i$ $(i, j = 1, 2, \ldots, n)$ or $k_{ij} = k_{ji}$; and the homogeneity condition,

$$Q_p p = \lambda U^{-1} p - (\lambda/\lambda_m)Q_m Q_m' p - Q_m q'\, p$$

$$= (\lambda/\lambda_m)Q_m - (\lambda/\lambda_m)Q_m - Q_m m = -Q_m m \tag{2.14d}$$

or $\Sigma_j p_j(\partial q_i/\partial p_j) + m(\partial q_i/\partial m) = 0$ $(i = 1, 2, \ldots, n)$. Section 2.3 provides a more detailed interpretation.

The Engel aggregation is obtained by premultiplying (2.13b) by the transpose p' of the price vector and using the result in (2.13a); it provides one restriction on the coefficients of demand equations. The Cournot aggregation is similarly obtained by premultiplying (2.13d) by the transpose p' of the price vector, applying (2.13b), and using (2.14a). Like the Engel aggregation restriction, the Cournot aggregation restrictions come directly from the budget constraint. Since there are n prices, the Cournot aggregation result specifies n conditions that the parameters of demand equations must satisfy.

The symmetry condition follows by noting that the inverse U^{-1} of the Hessian, which in (2.3) is symmetric, is itself symmetric. Since U^{-1} is symmetric it follows that $\lambda U^{-1} - (\lambda/\lambda m)Q_m Q_m'$ is also symmetric; since the difference in two symmetric matrices is symmetric, (2.14c) is obtained. The terms k_{ij} implicitly defined by (2.14c) represent the well-known "substitution effects," of which there are $n^2 - n$. The symmetry relation between the substitution effects reduces the number of independent terms, k_{ij} $(i \neq j)$, to $(n^2 - n)/2$.

Finally, the homogeneity condition is obtained by postmultiplying (2.13d) by p and using (2.13b) and (2.4). In other words, if we multiply p_1, p_2, ..., p_n and m by any constant t in (2.6), the optimal quantities consumed will remain unchanged. This result is important because it states that the consumption decision is made in response to relative price and income levels; alternatively, it shows that the demand functions are homogeneous of degree zero in income and prices. Traditionally, this homogeneity condition has been shown to exist using Euler's theorem (see Allen 1964, p. 319). The homogeneity condition does not impose further restrictions on the demand equations, since it is simply derived from the other constraints and (2.4).

2.3 ELASTICITIES

Economists find it convenient and more useful to express the restrictions on the demand system in elasticities rather than derivatives. Therefore, a restatement of the restrictions in Sec. 2.2 is presented. Let

$$E = \bar{q}^{-1} Q_p \bar{p} \qquad (2.15)$$

be an n x n matrix of direct and cross price elasticities of demand. In (2.15) $\bar{q}$ denotes an n x n diagonal matrix, with the values on the diagonal given by the elements of the vector q. The diagonal matrix $\bar{p}$ is similarly defined. Algebraically the demand elasticities for prices are

$$e_{ij} = \frac{\partial q_i}{\partial p_j} \frac{p_j}{q_i} \qquad (i, j = 1, 2, \ldots, n)$$

The n-element column vector of income elasticities is also easily obtained using the notational convention just developed; that is, the income elasticities for the n commodities are

$$\eta = \bar{m}^{-1} Q_m \qquad (2.16)$$

In particular, for the ith commodity the income elasticity is, more familiarly,

$$\eta_i = \frac{\partial q_i}{\partial m} \frac{m}{q_i} \qquad (i = 1, 2, \ldots, n)$$

One additional expression useful in subsequent derivations is the expenditure proportion; that is, the part of income m that the individual spends on each commodity. Accordingly, define

$$w = m^{-1}\bar{p}q = m^{-1}\bar{q}p \tag{2.17}$$

as the n-element column vector of expenditure proportions. Observe that the elements of the vector w are simply the ratios

$$w_i = m^{-1}(p_i q_i) = p_i q_i/m \qquad (i = 1, 2, \ldots, n)$$

Finally, as a convenience, a column vector $\int$ consisting of n unit elements is introduced: $\int' = [1, 1, \ldots, 1]'$. With these definitions, the restrictions on the demand functions in Sec. 2.2 can be expressed using elasticities. Corresponding to (2.14a) is the Engel aggregation:

$$w'\eta = (m^{-1}p'\bar{q})(m\,\bar{q}^{-1}Q_m) = p'Q_m = 1 \tag{2.18a}$$

or $\Sigma_i w_i \eta_i = 1$. In this more intuitive form, the Engel aggregation condition states that the weighted (by the expenditure proportions) sum of the income elasticities is unity. In (2.17) these weights are the relative shares of each commodity in total expenditure.

The Cournot aggregation, using (2.14b) and (2.17), is

$$w'E = (m^{-1}p'\bar{q})(\bar{q}^{-1}Q_p\bar{p})$$

$$= m^{-1}p'Q_p\bar{p} = m^{-1}(-q')\bar{p} = -w' \tag{2.18b}$$

or $\Sigma_i w_i e_{ij} = -w_j$ $(j = 1, 2, \ldots, n)$. Again, in this more commonly used notation, the Cournot aggregation condition expresses the weighted column sum of the price elasticities (the jth column of E) as the negative of the expenditure proportion on the jth commodity. The symmetry relation, using (2.14c) and (2.17) again, is

$$[w(E + \eta w')] = (E' + w\eta')\bar{w}$$

$$= [\bar{p}Q_p'\bar{q}^{-1} + m^{-1}\bar{p}q)(mQ_m'\bar{q}^{-1})]\ m^{-1}\bar{q}\bar{p}$$

$$= m^{-1}\bar{p}Q_p'\bar{p} + m^{-1}\bar{p}qQ_m'\bar{p}$$

$$= m^{-1}\bar{p}(Q_p + Q_m q')\bar{p} = \bar{w}(E + \eta w') \tag{2.18c}$$

or $w_i(e_{ij} + \eta_i w_j) = w_j(e_{ji} + \eta_j w_i)$ $(i, j = 1, 2, \ldots, n)$ or alternatively,

$$e_{ij} = w_j/w_i\ e_{ji} - w_j(\eta_i - \eta_j) \qquad (i, j = 1, 2, \ldots, n)$$

TABLE 2.1 Matrix of demand elasticities: Percentage changes in quantities demanded resulting from 1% change in price or income

Quantity q_i	Price, p_j: p_1	p_2	. . .	p_n	Income m
q_1	e_{11}	e_{12}	. . .	e_{1n}	η_1
q_2	e_{21}	e_{22}	. . .	e_{2n}	η_2
⋮	⋮			⋮	⋮
q_n	e_{n1}	e_{n2}	. . .	e_{nn}	η_n
Expenditure proportion					
w_i	w_1	w_2	. . .	w_n	

$\sum_i w_i \eta_i = 1$ (Engel aggregation)

$\sum_i w_i e_{ij} = -w_j$ $(j = 1, 2, \ldots, n)$ (Cournot aggregation)

$e_{ij} = (w_j/w_i)e_{ji} - w_j(\eta_i - \eta_j)$ $(i, j = 1, 2, \ldots, n)$ (Symmetry)

$\Sigma\, e_{ii} = -\eta_i$ $(i = 1, 2, \ldots, n)$ (Homogeneity)

Simply stated, the matrix of cross price elasticities is symmetric.

Finally, for the homogeneity condition from (2.14d),

$$E\int = \bar{q}^{-1} Q_p \bar{p}\int = \bar{q}^{-1} Q_p p = \bar{q}^{-1}(-Q_m m) = -\eta \tag{2.18d}$$

or $\Sigma_j e_{ij} = -\eta_i$ $(i = 1, 2, \ldots, n)$. The homogeneity condition implies that the consumer does not exhibit money illusion; that is, decisions on the purchases of commodities are made on the basis of relative prices and income. The restrictions implicit in the demand model are summarized, using demand elasticities and expenditure proportions, in Table 2.1.

2.4 SUBSTITUTION AND INCOME EFFECTS OF PRICE CHANGES

One of the important uses of estimated demand systems is the evaluation of changes in income and prices. These independent variables for the demand system cannot be viewed independently. The decomposition of these changes is accomplished using the results of Slutsky (1915) and Hicks (1946).

2.4.1 Slutsky Equation

Consider a typical element of (2.13d) in more detail:

$$\frac{\partial q_i}{\partial p_j} = \lambda u^{ij} - \frac{\lambda}{\partial\lambda/\partial m}\frac{\partial q_i}{\partial m}\frac{\partial q_j}{\partial m} - q_j\frac{\partial q_i}{\partial m} \quad (i, j = 1, 2, \ldots, n) \quad (2.19)$$

where u^{ij} is the (i, j)th element of U^{-1}, the inverse of the Hessian. The first term on the right-hand side, u^{ij}, is known as the specific substitution effect. It notes that goods i and j occur as an indecomposable pair in u^{ij} (Theil 1975, p. 18). Alternatively, the utility a consumer receives from commodity i is a function of the consumption level for commodity j.

The second term on the right-hand side of (2.19) is the general substitution effect. It shows that all goods are competing for an increment in the consumer budget (Houthakker 1960). The last term is the income effect. The total effect of a price change $\partial q_i/\partial p_j$ has been partitioned into a specific substitution effect, a general substitution effect, and an income effect.

Note that $u^{ij} - [\lambda/(\partial\lambda/\partial m)](\partial q_i/\partial m)(\partial q_j/\partial m) = k_{ij}$ is the substitution term (see 2.14c). Using this notation, (2.19) can be rewritten

$$\partial q_i/\partial p_j = k_{ij} - q_j(\partial q_i/\partial m) \quad (i, j = 1, 2, \ldots, n) \quad (2.20)$$

which is the famous Slutsky equation (1915), or the fundamental equation of value (Hicks 1946, p. 309). According to this result, the total effect of a price change $\partial q_i/\partial p_j$ shown in (2.20) can be expressed as the sum of two components, a substitution effect k_{ij} and an income effect $-q_j(\partial q_i/\partial m)$.

These results regarding the decomposition of the total effect of a price change can be illustrated graphically. Fig. 2.2 demonstrates the Hicks and Slutsky methods of isolating substitution and income effects. According to the method proposed by Hicks, the price change is accompanied by an income change and leaves the consumer on the initial indifference curve. The Slutsky method is somewhat different because it defines income in terms of the original bundle of goods; specifically, the price change is accompanied by an income change that enables the consumer to purchase the original consumption basket at the new or changed prices.

In Fig. 2.2, the total effect of the price change for q_1 is represented by the change in the consumption level for q_1 indicated by the projection of points a and b to the horizontal axis. The pure substitution effect with the Hicks definition of constant income is ac and the income effect associated with the price change is cb. The related decomposition using the Slutsky

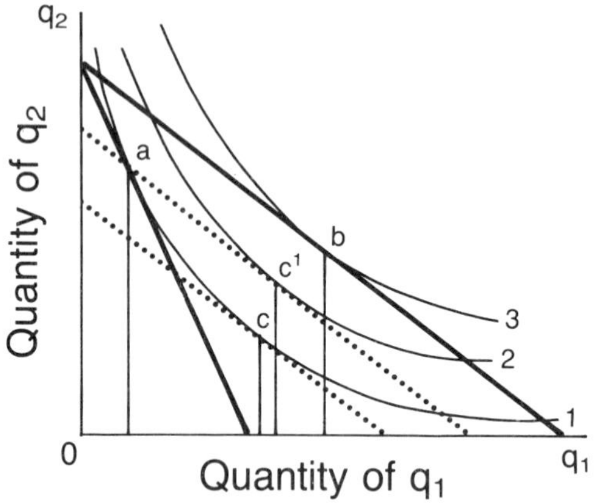

FIG. 2.2. Substitution and income effects, normal good, price decline, and Hicks and Slutsky decompositions.

approach is that ac' is the substitution effect and c'b the income effect. Thus the decompositions differ on the basis of how the initial income level is defined--as a bundle of goods apart from perceptions of the consumer or as a utility level internal to the calculus and preferences of the consumer.

Equations (2.19) and (2.20) develop the basis for this decomposition of the total price effect and can be expressed using elasticities. Multiplying (2.19) or (2.20) throughout by p_j/q_i and multiplying the income term, $q_j(\partial q_i/\partial m)$ by m/m gives

$$e_{ij} = e^*_{ij} - w_j \eta_i \qquad (i, j = 1, 2, \ldots, n) \tag{2.21}$$

where * indicates the compensated effect.

2.4.2 Properties of the Substitution Term

The substitution term k_{ij} can be shown (Phlips 1974, p. 51) to satisfy the symmetry relation (2.14c), the homogeneity condition, and the negativity condition. The homogeneity and the negativity conditions can be written as

$$\sum_j k_{ij} p_j = 0 \qquad (i = 1, \ldots, n) \tag{2.22a}$$

$$k_{ii} < 0 \qquad (i = 1, \ldots, n) \tag{2.22b}$$

In (2.22a) the sum of substitution terms for one commodity multiplied by the appropriate prices is zero. Consequences of the negativity condition (2.22b) are (1) the total effect of a price change $\partial q_i/\partial p_i$ is negative if $\partial q_i/\partial m \geq 0$ or if $\partial q_i/\partial m <$ 0 and $|q_i(\partial q_i/\partial m)| < |k_{ii}|$; and (2) the total effect of a price

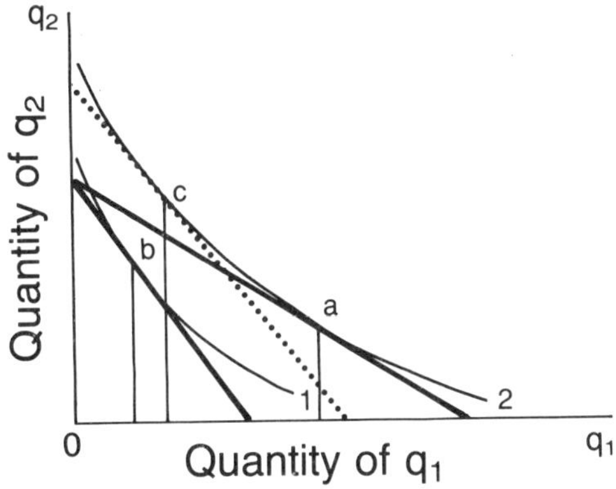

FIG. 2.3. Substitution and income effects, normal good, price rise, and Hicks decomposition.

change $\partial q_i/\partial p_i$ can be positive if $\partial q_i/\partial m \geq 0$ and $|q_i(\partial q_i/\partial m)| > |k_{ii}|$, which is the case of Giffen's paradox. Accordingly, a good is defined as normal if $\partial q_i/\partial p_i < 0$, Giffen if $\partial q_i/\partial p_i > 0$, superior if $\partial q_i/\partial m > 0$, and inferior if $\partial q_i/\partial m < 0$. Hence a Giffen good must be inferior (Intriligator 1971, p. 159).

Figures 2.3, 2.4, and 2.5 and Table 2.2 illustrate these results. Figure 2.3 shows the Hicks decomposition for the income and substitution effects in the case of a normal good and is chosen to illustrate the Hicks and Slutsky decompositions in Fig. 2.2. For the normal good both the income and substitution effects, bc and ca, respectively, are positive. The decomposition for the inferior good in Fig. 2.4 uses the Hicksian decomposition. The income effect cb is negative. The Giffen good is illustrated in Fig. 2.5, with the income effect negative and greater than the substitution effect ca which is positive. As a result, a decrease in the price of q_1 reduces the consumption level. Table 2.2 shows the conditions delineating these cases algebraically.

Alternatively, using the elasticities, superior commodities are those with income elasticities that are positive. Commodities with income elasticities less than unity but positive are necessities and those with elasticities greater than unity are luxuries. Inferior commodities have negative income elasticities, normal goods have negative own price elasticities, and those with positive own price elasticities are Giffen.

2.4.3 Substitutes and Complements

The specific substitution term λu^{ij} in (2.19) provides a

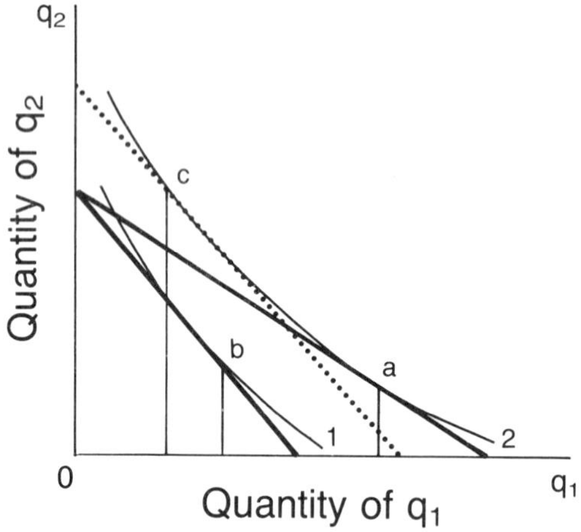

FIG. 2.4. Substitution and income effects, inferior good, price rise, and Hicks decomposition.

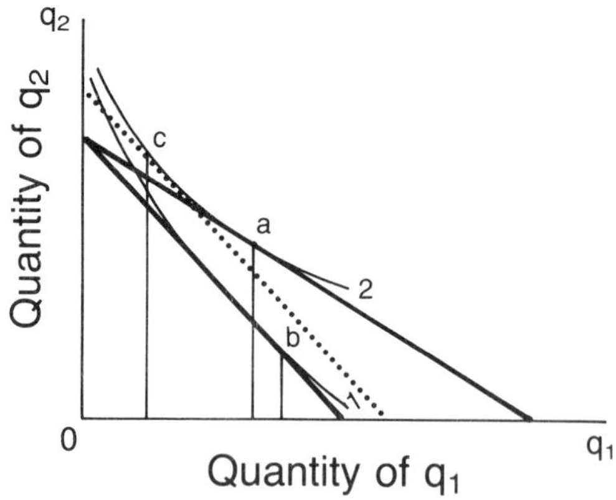

FIG. 2.5. Substitution and income effects, Giffen food, price rise, and Hicks decomposition.

TABLE 2.2 Classes of goods and services

Total Effect of Change in Own Price ($\partial q_i/\partial p_i$)	$\partial q_i/\partial m \geq 0$ (superior)	$\partial q_i/\partial m < 0$ (inferior), $\lvert q_i(\partial q_i/\partial m)\rvert < \lvert k_{ii}\rvert$	$\partial q_i/\partial m < 0$ (inferior), $\lvert q_i(\partial q_i)/\partial m\rvert > \lvert k_{ii}\rvert$
< 0 (normal)	normal, superior	normal, inferior	
> 0 (Giffen)			Giffen

See Intriligator (1971, p. 160).

clear basis for classifying substitute, complementary, and independent commodities. Houthakker (1960, p. 248) suggests that commodities ($i \neq j$) be classified as substitutes, independents, or complements as the terms $\lambda u^{ij} = \lambda u^{ji}$ are positive, zero, or negative, respectively.

This definition differs from Hicks's, which is based on the total substitution effect k_{ij}. Goods i and j are classified as substitutes, complements, or independent as $k_{ij} = k_{ji}$ is positive, negative, or zero, respectively (Hicks 1946, p. 311).

2.5 INTEGRABILITY

Sections 2.1-2.4 deal with properties of demand functions derived from a constrained utility maximization process. If the consumer is represented by a utility function adhering to the assumptions indicated and maximizes utility subject to a budget constraint, then certain characteristics of consumption behavior are implied that can be substantiated or refuted by observation. The integrability problem concerns the converse of the above proposition; that is, if the demand relations possess certain properties, namely those obtained from the utility maximization framework, then do they imply that the consumer is a utility maximizer or behaves as a utility maximizer? This second question represents a difficult mathematical proposition (see Silberberg 1978, pp. 335-42).

Suppose, in a two-commodity case, there exist two demand functions

$$q_i = m/(2p_i) \qquad (i = 1, 2) \tag{2.23}$$

where the p_i are prices and m is income. As shown by Henderson and Quandt (1971, p. 23), the utility function $u = q_1q_2$ generates the above two demand relations. The demand system is integrable; however, for expository purposes the utility function is derived from the demand functions.

If a utility function $u(q_1, q_2)$ exists, then along any indifference curve it must be true that

$$du = u_1dq_1 + u_2dq_2 = 0 \tag{2.24}$$

where the u_i ($i = 1, 2$) are again marginal utilities and du is the total differential. Equation (2.24) can be rewritten as

$$-\frac{dq_2}{dq_1} = \frac{u_1}{u_2} \tag{2.25}$$

But since at the equilibriums described by the demand functions (see Fig. 2.2) $u_2/u_1 = p_1/p_2$ and $p_1 = m/(2q_1)$, $p_2 = m/(2q_2)$ from (2.23), (2.25) can be rewritten as

$$\frac{dq_2}{dq_1} = -\frac{q_2}{q_1} \tag{2.26}$$

or $dq_2/q_2 = -dq_1/q_1$. Integrating (2.26) gives (2.27) or (2.28):

$$\ell n\ q_2 = -\ell n\ q_1 + \ell n\ u \tag{2.27}$$

$$u = q_1 q_2 \tag{2.28}$$

where u is the constant of integration corresponding to the indifference level associated with dq_2/dq_1. Thus, for this example a utility function exists that gives rise to the two demand functions specified in (2.23).

These results hold in general for the two-commodity situation. In (2.24) it can be shown that a function $u(q_1, q_2)$ exists such that $du = u_1 dq_1 + u_2 dq_2$ if $\partial u_1/\partial q_2 = \partial u_2/\partial q_i$; that is, there exists a function $u(q_1, q_2) = c$ that is the general solution to (2.24). This result follows from a standard theorem in differential equations. It can be stated as follows (see Rainville 1964, p. 32): If u, $\partial u/\partial q_1$, and $\partial u/\partial q_2$ are continuous functions of q_1 and q_2, then a necessary and sufficient condition that $u_1 dq_1 + u_2 dq_2 = 0$ be an exact equation is that $\partial u/\partial q_1 = \partial u/\partial q_2$. However, a number of subtle mathematical problems remain. For the two-commodity situation, a utility function that generates the demand functions always exists. For the more general case, there is not necessarily a solution to the higher order differential equation corresponding to (2.24).

What conditions on the demand relations ensure integrability? Since the mathematics become rather complicated, the necessary and sufficient conditions for integrability are discussed in only a cursory manner. Samuelson (1950) uses indirect demand functions with relative prices expressed in terms of equilibrium quantities to show that if the Slutsky-Hicks substitution matrix (2.14c) is symmetric and negative semidefinite then the demand functions can be generated by the maximization of a utility function. Katzner (1970) provides an alternative proof of the integrability problem based on inverse demand functions. The symmetry conditions prevent the demand function from being such that the individual is inconsistent in selecting bundles of commodities after certain price or income changes; that is, these conditions are needed to preserve the transitivity property. Silberberg (1978, p. 339) has diagrammed this situation for the three-commodity case. He also points out that the strong axiom of revealed preference is needed to prevent a violation of the transitivity property. Thus the conditions required for integrability are closely related to the axioms underlying the revealed preference approach to consumer theory.

Hurwicz and Uzawa (1971, pp. 117-24) worked with direct demand functions with quantities expressed as functions of prices and income to show that the symmetry and negative semidefiniteness of (2.14c) combined with certain regularity properties are sufficient for the existence of a utility function to have generated the demand functions. The regularity conditions are that the whole budget is spent, the demand function is single valued and differentiable, and its derivatives with respect to income satisfy a boundedness condition.

Recently, indirect and direct translog demand functions have been used to perform empirical tests of integrability for German time series data (Conrad and Jorgenson 1979). The econometric approach employed to conduct these tests was developed by Jorgenson and Lau (1979) and begins by specifying consumer demand functions as ratios of two first order polynomials in prices, income, and time; that is, direct and indirect translog demand systems in expenditures shares are formulated. Then restrictions implied by integrability-homogeneity, summability (adding up), symmetry, nonnegativity, and monotonicity are evaluated. The likelihood ratio procedure is used to perform the tests on the various sets of restrictions. Tests of integrability can be carried out in many different sequences so the usual problems of sequential testing methods arise.

Conrad and Jorgenson (1979) indicate that the set of restrictions on parameters of the direct translog demand systems implied by integrability cannot be rejected. However, they rejected the restrictions imposed by integrability for the indirect translog demand system. More empirical work is required to evaluate this aspect of the theory, but it is important when making backward inferences on the utility function and examining its fundamental propositions.

2.6 DUALITY

In Sec. 2.1 the maintained hypothesis of demand theory is that a consumer will select from the set of affordable commodity bundles the one that yields maximum utility. Results from this behavioral proposition and assumptions underlying the utility function have been obtained in the traditional utility maximization framework. An alternative and more analytically convenient formulation of the consumer optimization problem can be constructed using duality concepts, popularized by the work of Shephard (1953) on production and cost functions and employed to advantage in the analysis of consumer demand.

2.6.1 Direct and Indirect Utility

The duality formulation of the consumer allocation problem is developed from the expression

$$v(p, m) = \max_{q} u(q) \quad \text{subject to } p'q = m \tag{2.29}$$

where v(p, m) is the indirect utility function. An equivalent expression can be obtained by substituting the demand function (2.9a) into the utility function expressed in (2.1). This substitution gives

$$u = u[q(p, m)] = v(p, m) \tag{2.29'}$$

The term indirect utility function derives from the arguments of prices and income. Expression (2.29) specifies the maximum attainable utility level for a given set of prices and a particular income.

Alternatively, the indirect utility function may be used to derive a direct utility function. In particular, if the indirect utility function v(p, m) is minimized with respect to prices and income and subject to the budget constraint, the direct utility function u(q) is obtained. This property of the direct and indirect utility functions is attractive analytically. This correspondence only occurs if the indirect utility function is continuous, decreasing in prices, increasing in income, strictly quasi-convex in prices, and homogeneous of degree zero in prices and income and if the direct utility function satisfies the regularity conditions specified in Sec. 2.1. Recall that a function f(x) is quasi-concave over the interval (a, b) if $f[\lambda x_1 + (1 - \lambda)x_2] \leq \min[f(x_1), f(x_2)]$ for all x_1, x_2 in (a, b) and all $0 \leq \lambda \leq 1$. The function f(x) is strictly quasi-convex if the strict inequality (<) holds.

The advantage of considering the consumer demand problem in this context is the ease with which the demand functions and associated conditions on the demand system can be derived. For example, the uncompensated (Marshallian) demand function for the ith commodity is obtained by differentiating the indirect utility function in (2.29) with respect to prices and income and applying Roy's identity; that is, the uncompensated demand functions can be obtained as

$$-[\partial v(p, m)/\partial p_i]/[\partial v(p, m)/\partial m] = q_i(p, m) = q_i$$

$$(i = 1, 2, \ldots, n) \tag{2.30}$$

Similarly, the inverse uncompensated demand function can be obtained by applying the Hotelling-Wold identity to the direct utility function (Hotelling 1935, p. 71; Weymark 1980)

$$\frac{(\partial u/\partial q_i)m}{\sum_j q_j \partial u/\partial q_i} = p_i(q, m) = p_i \qquad (i = 1, 2, \ldots, n) \tag{2.31}$$

2.6.2 Cost and Transformation or Distance Functions

The cost and transformation functions are closely related to the direct and indirect utility functions. The cost function is obtained by inverting the indirect utility function (2.29) and solving for m in terms of the level of utility u^0 and a set of prices p. This operation is permissible, since the indirect utility function is increasing in income. More formally, the cost of attaining utility level u^0 with prices p is

$$c(u, p) = \min_q p'q \quad \text{subject to } u(q) \geq u^0 \tag{2.32}$$

The cost function (2.32) gives the minimum cost of achieving a utility level u^0 at prices p. If the cost function (2.32) is continuous, increasing in utility, increasing, concave, and homogeneous of degree one in prices, a preference ordering (or a utility function) can be represented equivalently by a direct utility function, an indirect utility function, or a cost function (Blackorby et al. 1978). Note that a function f(x) is concave over the interval (a, b) if $f[\lambda x_1 + (1 - \lambda)x_2] \geq \lambda f(x_1) + (1 - \lambda)f(x_2)$ for all x_1, x_2 in (a, b) and all $0 \leq \lambda \leq 1$. The function f(x) is strictly concave if the strict inequality (>) holds.

The transformation function is a distance relationship implicitly defining the direct utility function. It is defined as the solution to the constrained minimization problem,

$$f(u, q) = \min_p p'q \quad \text{subject to } v(p, m) \leq u^0 \tag{2.33}$$

That is, the transformation function can be interpreted as an indirect cost function, and it gives the minimum cost of achieving a utility level u^0 at quantities q. Again, if the transformation function (2.33) is continuous; decreasing in utility; and increasing, concave, and homogeneous of degree 1 in quantities, it can be shown that the direct utility function, indirect utility function, cost function, and transformation function can be used as equivalent representations for the consumer optimization problem.

Roy's identity is applied to derive the uncompensated (Marshallian) demand functions from the indirect utility function. Similarly, the Shephard and the Shephard-Hanoch lemmas can be applied to yield the compensated demand functions and the inverse compensated demand functions from the cost and transformation functions, respectively. That is, the compensated demand functions follow from differentiating the cost function (2.32) with respect to p_i. In particular, the compensated demand functions are

$$\frac{\partial c(u, p)}{\partial p_i} = q_i^*(u, p) = q_i^* \qquad (i = 1, 2, \ldots, n) \tag{2.34}$$

Similarly, the inverse compensated demand functions can be derived by differentiating the transformation function (2.33) with respect to q; that is, from the Shephard-Hanoch lemma, the inverse compensated price functions are

$$\frac{\partial f(u, q)}{\partial q_i} = p_i^*(u, q) = p_i^* \qquad (i = 1, 2, \ldots, n) \tag{2.35}$$

2.6.3 Illustration

It is useful to illustrate the duality results using the Cobb-Douglas utility function. Let the algebraic form for the direct utility function be

$$u(q) = q_1q_2 \tag{2.36}$$

Maximizing the utility function (2.36) subject to the budget constraint $p_1q_1 + p_2q_2 = m$ yields the two demand functions

$$q_i = m/(2p_i) \qquad (i = 1, 2) \tag{2.37}$$

The indirect utility function is obtained by substituting the demand functions (2.37) into the utility function (2.36). As in (2.29'), it is a function of prices and income, that is,

$$v(p, m) = [m/(2p_1)][m/(2p_2)] = m^2/(4p_1p_2) \tag{2.38}$$

The uncompensated demand functions are generated by applying Roy's identity (2.30) to the indirect utility function (2.38). Specifically, partially differentiating (2.38) with respect to p_1, p_2, and m and substituting into (2.30) provides the expression

$$-\frac{\partial v/\partial p_1}{\partial v/\partial m} = \frac{m^2/(4p_2)}{2m/(4p_1p_2)} = \frac{m}{2p_1} = q_1 \tag{2.39}$$

A similar substitution for $\partial v/\partial p_2$ gives the uncompensated demand function for the second commodity, $q_2 = m/(2p_2)$.

The cost function is constructed by completing the minimization problem in (2.32). Here the minimization is carried out using the Lagrangian expression

$$L' = p_1q_1 + p_2q_2 - \lambda(q_1q_2 - u^0) \qquad (2.40)$$

For simplicity and convenience in representing the solution to the first order conditions, it is assumed that the inequality in (2.32) holds as an equality. Differentiating L' partially with respect to q_1, q_2 and λ yields a set of first order conditions that can be solved for the cost function. Standard manipulation of these equations, gives $\lambda = (p_1p_2/u^0)^{1/2}$ and $p_i = \lambda q_i$ (i = 1, 2). Substituting these expressions into the objective function for the minimization problem (2.40) the cost function becomes

$$c(p, u) = 2u^{1/2}p_1^{1/2}p_2^{1/2} \qquad (2.41)$$

Compensated demand functions in (2.34) can be produced by employing the Shephard lemma; that is,

$$\frac{\partial c}{\partial p_1} = u^{1/2}(p_2/p_1)^{1/2} = q_1 \qquad (2.42)$$

and a corresponding expression for q_2.

The result that completes the duality possibilities is the transformation function (2.33). The Lagrangian for this problem is

$$L'' = p_1q_1 + p_2q_2 + \lambda[m^2/(4p_1p_2) - u^0] \qquad (2.43)$$

using (2.33). Again, the solution is obtained with the constraint expressed as an equality. Solving the first order conditions for p_1, p_2, and λ (not a simple algebraic task) gives

$$p_1 = [\lambda m^2q_2/(4q_1^2)]^{1/3}, \qquad p_2 = [\lambda m^2q_1/(4q_2^2)]^{1/3}$$

$$\lambda = m(q_1q_2)^{1/2}/(2u^0)^{3/2}$$

Substituting these expressions into the objective function for the transformation problem (2.43) yields, after considerable simplification,

$$f(u, q) = m(q_1q_2/u)^{1/2} \qquad (2.44)$$

Alternatively, setting m = 1, normalizing income, we obtain

$$f(u, q) = (q_1q_2/u)^{1/2}$$

Note that the expression uses u instead of u^0, since it could in principle be obtained for any such assumed constant utility level.

By applying the Shephard-Hanoch lemma (2.35) the inverse compensated demand functions can be obtained:

$$\frac{\partial f}{\partial q_1} = (1/2)\ [q_2/(uq_1)]^{1/2} = p_1 \tag{2.45}$$

A similar application produces the other inverse compensated demand function. Setting the transformation function (2.44) equal to one and inverting the expression in u yields

$$u(q) = q_1 q_2 \tag{2.46}$$

which is, the direct utility function. By applying the Hotelling-Wold identity (2.31) to the direct utility function, the inversed uncompensated demand functions are obtained:

$$p_i = m/(2q_1) \qquad (i = 1,\ 2) \tag{2.47}$$

The above example shows that with appropriate regularity conditions the direct utility, indirect utility, cost, and transformation functions can be used as equivalent representations for characterizing the consumer optimization problem.

EXERCISES

1. Consider $u = \alpha_1 q_1 + \alpha_2 q_2 + (1/2)(\alpha_{11} q_1^2 + 2\alpha_{12} q_1 q_2 + \alpha_{22} q_2^2)$, a quadratic utility function. The budget constraint is $p_1 q_1 + p_2 q_2 = m$.
   (a) Derive the demand functions associated with this utility function. (To simplify the algebra you may want to set $\alpha_{12} = 0$. In this special case the utility function is additive.) Hint: The demand equation for q_1 is

$$q_1 = \frac{\alpha_{22} p_1 m}{\alpha_{22} p_1^2 + \alpha_{11} p_2^2} + \frac{\alpha_2 p_1 p_2 - \alpha_1 p_2^2}{\alpha_{22} p_1^2 + \alpha_{11} p_2^2}$$

   (b) Show that the demand functions in (a) satisfy the Engel, Cournot, symmetry, and homogeneity conditions.
   (c) Obtain the income and price elasticities of demand for the functions derived in (a).
   (d) Derive the indirect utility function for the direct quadratic utility function in (a). (Again, assume that $\alpha_{12} = 0$.)

(e) Apply Roy's identity to the indirect utility function found in (d) to obtain the uncompensated demand functions.

(f) Obtain the inverse uncompensated demand functions by applying Hotelling-Wold's identity to the direct utility function in (a).

(g) Derive the cost function associated with the utility function in (a).

(h) Using Shephard's lemma, obtain the compensated quantity demand functions from (g).

(i) Find the transformation function corresponding to the direct utility function in (a).

(j) Using the Shephard-Hanoch lemma, find the inverse compensated demand functions. Hint: Use the results obtained in (i).

2. Repeat Ex. 1 for the Klein-Rubin utility function $u = \mu_1 \cdot \ell n(q_1 - \gamma_1) + \mu_2 \ell n(q_2 - \gamma_2)$.

3. For the utility function used in the illustrations of Chap. 2, $u = q_1 q_2$:

(a) Derive the price and income elasticities.

(b) Are the results in (a) what you expected? Are they realistic?

(c) Do the results found in (a) hold for the Klein-Rubin utility function?

4. Prove Roy's identity, (2.29).

5. Prove the Hotelling-Wold identity, (2.31).

REFERENCES

Allen, R. G. D. 1964. Mathematical Analysis for Economists. New York: St. Martin's Press.

Apostol, T. M. 1957. Mathematical Analysis. Reading, Mass.: Addison-Wesley.

Barten, A. P. 1969. Consumer demand functions under conditions of almost additive preferences. Econometrica 32 (Jan.-Apr.):1-38.

———. 1977. The systems of consumer demand functions approach: A review. Econometrica 45 (Jan.):23-51.

Blackorby, C.; Primont, D.; and Russell, R. R. 1978. Duality, Separability, and Functional Structure: Theory and Economic Applications. New York: Elsevier-North Holland.

Conrad, K., and Jorgenson, D. W. 1979. Testing the integrability of consumer demand functions. European Economic Review 12 (Apr):149-69.

Deaton, A., and Muellbauer, J. 1980. Economics and Consumer Behavior. Cambridge: Cambridge University Press.

Goldberger, A. S. 1964. Econometric Theory. New York: John Wiley.

———. 1967. Functional form and utility: A review of

consumer demand theory. Social Systems Research Institute, University of Wisconsin: Systems Formulation, Methodology, and Policy Workshop Paper 6703 (Oct.).
Henderson, J. M., and Quandt, R. E. 1971. Microeconomic Theory. New York: McGraw-Hill.
Hicks, J. R. 1946. Value and Capital, 2d ed. Oxford: Oxford University Press.
Hotelling, H. 1935. Demand functions with limited budgets. Econometrica (Jan.):66-78.
Houthakker, H. S. 1960. Additive preferences. Econometrica 28 (Apr.):244-57.
Hurwicz, L., and Uzawa, H. 1971. On the integrability of demand functions. In Preferences, Utility and Demand, ed. J. S. Chipman et al., pp. 114-48. New York: Harcourt Brace Jovanovich.
Intriligator, M. 1971. Mathematical Optimization and Economic Theory. Englewood Cliffs, N.J.: Prentice-Hall.
Jorgenson, D. W., and Lau, L. J. 1979. Integrability of consumer demand functions. European Economic Review 12 (Apr.):115-48.
Katzner, D. W. 1970. Static Demand Theory. New York: MacMillan.
Phlips, L. 1974. Applied Consumption Analysis. Amsterdam: North Holland.
Powell, A. A. 1974. Empirical Analytics of Demand Systems. Lexington, Mass.: D. C. Heath.
Rainville, E. 1964. Elementary Differential Equations, 3d ed. New York: MacMillan.
Samuelson, P. A. 1947. Foundations of Economic Analysis. Cambridge, Mass.: Harvard University Press.
———. 1950. The problem of integrability in utility theory. Economica 17 (Nov.):355-385.
Shephard, R. 1953. Cost and Production Functions. Princeton, N.J.: Princeton University Press.
Silberberg, E. 1978. The Structure of Economics: A Mathematical Analysis. New York: McGraw-Hill.
Slutsky, E. 1915. On the theory of the budget of the consumer. English transl. In Readings in Price Theory, ed. G. J. Stigler and K. E. Boulding, pp. 27-56. Homewood, Ill.: Irwin.
Theil, H. 1971. Principles of Econometrics. New York: John Wiley.
———. 1975. Theory and Measurement of Consumer Demand. Vol. 1. Amsterdam: North Holland.
———. 1976. Theory and Measurement of Consumer Demand. Vol. 2, Amsterdam: North Holland.
Weymark, J. A. 1980. Duality results in demand theory. European Economic Review 14 (Nov.):377-95.

3 • Separability: An Extension of Consumer Behavior Theory

The theory of consumer behavior provides a complete set of demand equations, (2.9a), obtained by maximizing the utility function for the consumer subject to the budget constraint, (2.4). The demand functions relate quantities consumed to all commodity prices and income. From these relationships a complete array of demand elasticities can, in principle, be estimated; that is, given n commodities, there are n direct price elasticities, $n^2 - n$ cross price elasticities, and n income elasticities describing consumption responses to possible price and income shifts. The number of coefficients to be estimated for specializing the demand system to a particular situation can be reduced by imposing the restrictions resulting from the curvature of the utility function and the model formulation. The symmetry relations reduce this number by $(1/2)(n^2 - n)$ coefficients. The Cournot and Engel aggregation equations further limit the number of independent coefficients by n + 1. Hence, $(1/2)(n^2 + n) - 1$ independent parameters remain to be estimated if the full demand system applies. Because of the shortness of economic time series and the magnitude of n, this number of parameters is usually too large to allow a direct estimation of the complete demand system. Estimable specifications of the complete demand system require additional restrictions on the consumer behavior problem.

Additional restrictions have been added to the theoretical demand system in two general ways. First, faced with a comparatively short time series and the prospect of estimating $(1/2)(n^2 + n) - 1$ parameters, a logical and pragmatic approach is to simply redefine the commodities, that is, estimate the system for a set of $S < n$ commodity aggregates. Depending upon the objectives of the empirical exercise, the use of these S commodity aggregates in place of the n specific commodities may be adequate for hypothesis testing and policy. It is attractive because if S - n = r, then the number of parameters to estimate is reduced by r(n - 1). But this approach raises important questions, including the conditions under which consumers perceive the commodities as groups or aggregates, the price that should be used for the aggregates, how consumers allocate expenditures within the aggregates and how the price and income responses estimated for S commodity aggregates correspond to those estimated for the n commodities in the initial set. These questions form the applied motivations for studying concepts of separability: the identification of restrictions on the utility function that are consistent with such practices and their behavioral implications.

The second alternative for reducing the parameter estimates is the elimination of specified price and income responses for the algebraically specified system in n commodities, involving the imposition of exclusion restrictions or other forms of prior information in the estimation problem. This practice raises questions similar to those for commodity groupings. There is also a more fundamental question of the source of these restrictions and their behavioral interpretation vis-a-vis the assumptions underlying the theory of consumer demand.

This chapter assesses the nature of the restrictions of the two approaches. Grouping commodities has the more attractive theoretical rationalization. Associated separability concepts are defined and evaluated by their behavioral underpinnings and consequences for the complete demand system parameter estimates and they are assessed for their importance in duality contexts.

3.1 SOURCES OF RESTRICTIONS

The two types of additional restrictions identified above have numerous sources, ranging from those introduced as a consequence of previous empirical investigations, to pretesting in the sample data, to the introduction of specialized utility functions. The last option is the only alternative for systematically reconciling the actual demand system parameter estimates with the theory of consumer behavior developed in Chap. 2. This section presents the statistical and behavioral limitations of these sources and directs the search for additional restrictions used to estimate demand systems to an investigation of separability concepts and their applied consequences.

A frequent method of obtaining additional restrictions necessary to make the complete system estimable is more ad hoc than systematic, with certain price variables in the demand functions omitted. Resulting demand functions include own price, prices of one or two commodities thought to be close substitutes, or complements and income. Demand systems estimated on this basis are those of Schultz (1938) and Wold and Jureen (1953). Although forerunners of modern applied work, these studies incorporate highly specialized restrictions on the demand system.

The interpretability of the results is the major problem with such restrictions and/or systems of demand functions estimated on this basis. Since these restrictions are not derived from primitive concepts regarding consumer behavior, the results are difficult to generalize and interpret; that is, the application, because of the imposed restrictions and the selection process, is identified with the researcher and/or the specialized restrictions. Therefore, generalization and comparison with other empirical results or theoretical propositions are limited.

There are also statistical problems with the incorporation of ad hoc restrictions because if they are introduced in an artificial manner, it is not clear that the statistical properties of resulting estimations are improved. Conclusions about these improvements generally require an evaluation of the bias introduced by the more restrictive specification (Judge and Bock 1978; Leamer 1978). If they are obtained by pretests in the sample data, it is likely that the statistical properties of the estimators are not as good as those which would have been obtained from the unrestricted model. Unless there is a plausible basis for the restrictions, apparent variance reduction results that follow from adding the restrictions can be interpreted with unjustified optimism.

The alternative is to extend the theory for the consumer allocation problem through additional information in the form of more simplified behavioral assumptions, that is, to incorporate the information into the consumer maximization problem more specifically with respect to the utility function. The advantage is that the resulting restrictions on the demand functions follow from a conditioning of the problem, can be interpreted behaviorally, and are not special to the particular researcher doing the empirical work. As anticipated, this involves the use of commodity aggregates and the corresponding interpretation of the results using separability concepts.

3.2 SEPARABILITY

The concept of separability, introduced independently by Leontief (1947) and Sono (1960), assumes that the set of n commodities available to the consumer can be partitioned into S mutually exclusive and collectively exhaustive subsets, $\{N_1, N_2, \ldots, N_S\}$. Each subset contains n_s $(s = 1, 2, \ldots, S)$ commodities where $n = \Sigma_{s=1}^{S} n_s$. The commodities within each subset are assumed to possess some common characteristics.

A rationale for incorporating such assumptions into the consumer allocation problem is that the consumption decision occurs in two stages (Strotz 1957). First, the consumer budgets income between subsets of commodities, $N_1, N_2, \ldots, N_S$. The second stage involves within subset or commodity group allocation decisions. Weak separability is a necessary and sufficient condition for the second stage of the two stage budgeting procedure (Deaton and Muellbauer 1980, p. 124). A necessary and sufficient condition for the budgeting procedure to be consistent with a one stage procedure is that the utility function be weakly separable and each of the category aggregator functions be homothetic (Blackorby et al. 1970). This type of hierarchical classification provides a rationalization for the grouping or aggregation of commodities suggested as an alternative for limited data.

Several types of separability have been advanced for the consumer allocation problem, especially those referred to as strong, weak, and Pearce separability (Goldman and Uzawa 1964). Strong and weak separability were coined by Strotz (1959), and Pearce separability is a complementary concept introduced by Pearce (1964).

A great deal of study concerned with concepts of separability and their implications for demand systems preceded the work by Goldman and Uzawa. Since then a number of specializations and extensions have been developed that have been summarized by Blackorby et al. (1978) and relate to two stage optimization (Gorman 1971), the utility tree (Brown and Heien 1972), duality (McFadden and Fuss 1975; Blackorby et al. 1975; Gorman 1976) and the applied demand systems developed in Chaps. 4 and 5. Treatment here is confined to the work of Green (1961) and Goldman and Uzawa (1964). These results, although generalized in subsequent work, suffice as background to interpret the behavioral conditions underlying the demand systems presented in Chaps. 4 and 5 and for evaluating the results of the associated empirical applications.

The three basic definitions for strong, weak, and Pearce separability are:

Strong separability: The utility function $u(q)$ is termed strongly separable with respect to the partition $\{N_1, N_2, \ldots, N_S\}$ if the marginal rate of substitution between two commodities i and j from different subsets I and J, respectively, does not depend upon the quantities of commodities outside of I and J. Hence

$$\frac{\partial(u_i/u_j)}{\partial q_k} = 0 \tag{3.1}$$

for all $i \in I$, $j \in J$, and $k \notin I$ and J $(I \neq J)$ and where u_i and u_j indicate partial derivatives of u with respect to q_i and q_j, respectively.

Weak separability: The utility function $u(q)$ is termed weakly separable with respect to a partition $\{N_1,$

$N_2, \ldots, N_S\}$ if the marginal rate of substitution between two commodities i and j from I is independent of the quantity of all commodities not in that subset. In other words, the ratio of their marginal utilities is independent of the quantity of any commodity outside the subset. Thus

$$\frac{\partial(u_i/u_j)}{\partial q_k} = 0 \tag{3.2}$$

for all i, j ε I, and k $\notin$ I.

Pearce separability: A utility function u(q) is called Pearce separable with respect to a partition $\{N_1, N_2, \ldots, N_S\}$ if the marginal rate of substitution between two commodities i and j from the same subset I does not depend upon the quantities of all other commodities including other commodities in the same subset; that is, the ratio of marginal utilities is independent of the quantity of any third commodity whether inside or outside the subset. Thus

$$\frac{\partial(u_i/u_j)}{\partial q_k} = 0 \tag{3.3}$$

for all i, j ε I, and k $\neq$ i, j.

3.3 SEPARABILITY AND THE UTILITY FUNCTION

These three separability definitions are related to admissible forms of utility functions, providing the basis for incorporating the restrictions implied by the behavioral assumptions into the consumer allocation problem and the corresponding demand functions. The following theorems have been developed to summarize the connections between the three separability concepts and forms of utility functions (Goldman and Uzawa 1964).

Theorem 1: A utility function u(q) is strongly separable with respect to partition $\{N_1, N_2, \ldots, N_S\}$ (S > 2) if and only if u(q) is of the form

$$u(q) = F[u^1(q^1) + \ldots + u^S(q^S)] \tag{3.4}$$

where F is a monotone-increasing function of one variable and, for each s = 1, 2, ..., S, u^s is a function of subvector q^s.

Theorem 2: A utility function u(q) is weakly separable with respect to a partition $\{N_1, N_2, \ldots, N_S\}$ if and only if u(q) is of the form

$$u(q) = F[u^1(q^1), \ldots, u^S(q^S)] \tag{3.5}$$

where F is a function of S variables and, for each s, u^s is a function of subvector q^s alone.

Theorem 3: A utility function u(q) is Pearce separable with respect to a partition $\{N_1, N_2, \ldots, N_S\}$ if and only if it is of the form

$$u(q) = F\{u^1[\sum_{i=1}^{n_1} g_i(q_i)], \ldots, u^S[\sum_{i=1}^{n_S} g_i(q_i)]\} \tag{3.6}$$

where F is a function of S variables and u^s is an additive function of q^s whenever the number of commodities in the subset N_s is greater than two. If the number of commodities in N_s is equal to two, Pearce separability reduces to weak separability.

Note that strong separability implies an additive utility function but weak separability does not. In the case of Pearce separability the utility function includes both weak and strong separability concepts; that is, it is weakly separable between groups, additive and strongly separable within groups.

3.4 SEPARABILITY AND THE SUBSTITUTION TERM

These three types of separable utility functions imply special conditions for the responses to price and to the Slutsky terms of the consumer allocation problem. As suggested, the symmetry conditions for price responses may be used as nonlinear restrictions in the estimation of complete systems of demand equations. The following theorems, abstracted from Goldman and Uzawa (1964), establish the nature of these restrictions for utility functions incorporating alternative separability assumptions and show that separability restrictions impose conditions on the demand systems in addition to those implied by symmetry. Since the symmetry restrictions can be viewed in terms of the Slutsky relationship, the interpretation of their implications is straightforward.

Theorem 4: A strictly quasi-concave utility function u(q) is strongly separable with respect to a partition $\{N_1, N_2, \ldots, N_S\}$ $(S > 2)$ if and only if the Slutsky terms k_{ij} are of the form

$$k_{ij} = \theta \frac{\partial q_i}{\partial m} \frac{\partial q_j}{\partial m} \tag{3.7}$$

for all $i \in I$, $j \in J$ $(I \neq J)$, where the factor of proportionality θ has no subscript to indicate that it is common to all subsets. By using (2.20) it follows that

$$\frac{\partial q_i}{\partial p_j} = \theta \frac{\partial q_i}{\partial m} \frac{\partial q_j}{\partial m} - q_j \frac{\partial q_i}{\partial m} \tag{3.8}$$

for all $i \varepsilon I$, $j \varepsilon J$ ($I \neq J$). Expressed in terms of elasticities, (3.8) becomes

$$e_{ij} = w_j \theta \eta_i \eta_j - w_j \eta_i \tag{3.9}$$

Theorem 5: A strictly concave utility function $u(q)$ is weakly separable with respect to a partition $\{N_1, N_2, \ldots, N_S\}$ if and only if the Slutsky terms k_{ij} are of the form

$$k_{ij} = \theta_{IJ} \frac{\partial q_i}{\partial m} \frac{\partial q_j}{\partial m} \tag{3.10}$$

for all $i \varepsilon I$, $j \varepsilon J$ ($I \neq J$), where the factor of proportionality θ_{IJ} is the same for all cross substitution effects between pairs of commodities with one member belonging to subset I and one member belonging to subset J (Phlips 1974, p. 84). Furthermore, it follows that

$$\frac{\partial q_i}{\partial p_j} = \theta_{IJ} \frac{\partial q_i}{\partial m} \frac{\partial q_j}{\partial m} - q_j \frac{\partial q_i}{\partial m} \tag{3.11}$$

for all $i \varepsilon I$, $j \varepsilon J$ ($I \neq J$). Alternatively, for elasticities and expenditure proportions the result (3.11) can be specified as

$$e_{ij} = w_j \theta_{IJ} \eta_i \eta_j - w_j \eta_i \tag{3.12}$$

Theorem 6: A strictly concave utility function $u(q)$ is Pearce separable with respect to a partition $\{N_1, N_2, \ldots, N_S\}$ if and only if the Slutsky terms k_{ij} are of the form

$$k_{ij} = \theta_{IJ} \frac{\partial q_i}{\partial m} \frac{\partial q_j}{\partial m} \tag{3.13}$$

for all $i \varepsilon I$, $j \varepsilon J$ and with the factor of proportionality θ_{IJ} defined for all I and J including I = J and depending only on the subsets involved. Under Pearce separability the corresponding demand function restriction is

$$\frac{\partial q_i}{\partial p_j} = \theta_{IJ} \frac{\partial q_i}{\partial m} \frac{\partial q_j}{\partial m} - q_j \frac{\partial q_i}{\partial m} \tag{3.14}$$

for all $i \in I$, $j \in J$. Again, the equivalent condition in elasticities is

$$e_{ij} = w_j \theta_{IJ} \eta_i \eta_j - w_j \eta_i \tag{3.15}$$

Theorems 4, 5, and 6 demonstrate the substantial reductions in parameters required to determine price and income responses for demand systems that occur from use of the alternative separability assumptions. From (3.9) it is clear that price elasticities can be determined on the basis of θ and n income elasticities. Thus, n + 1 parameters need to be estimated as a basis for fully characterizing consumer responses to price and income in such demand systems. Of course the budget proportions are observable. By similar reasoning in the context of equations (3.10) and (3.11) we can conclude that for weak separability the required parameters are $n + 1/[2(S^2 - S)]$, with no restrictions other than symmetry on the price responses between the S groups or commodity aggregates.

Separability restrictions provide a way to reduce the econometric problems associated with demand systems estimation. These results also suggest caution in the use of such models and/or assumptions. Strong consumption pattern similarities within and across commodity groups are implied, so the selection of commodity groups is a question of empirical significance in demand systems applications using separability hypotheses.

This composition problem for the commodity aggregates appears to have been solved by Hicks (1946). The composite commodity theorem develops conditions under which sets of commodities can be treated as one. Unfortunately, these conditions involve relative prices; that is, prices moving over time at proportionate rates. This is of little help in a world with substantial price fluctuations. In fact, one of the major uses of the system's parameters is to anticipate effects of changed relative prices. The appropriateness of the commodity composition used thus comes back to a behavioral rationalization.

3.5 ADDITIVITY

The three types of separability require further adaptation when they are applied in estimating the system of consumer demand functions. In particular, to apply the results and/or obtain an explicit algebraic statement of the implied restrictions, a specific class of utility functions must be assumed. Direct and block additivity, two broad classes of utility functions, are explored for their consequences relating to the separability results from Sec. 3.4.

3.5.1 Direct Additivity

Strong separability implies a utility function with an additive term as the argument of F. In the special case where each commodity group N_s contains only one element, strong separability reduces to what will be termed *point-wise strong separability*; that is, the utility function (3.4) takes the form

$$u(q) = F[u^1(q^1) + \ldots + u^S(q^S)] \tag{3.16}$$

where the argument for F includes S(= n) additive terms. A utility function u(q) is directly additive if (1) it is point-wise strongly separable and (2) F is the identity function. From (3.16) the directly additive or *want independent* utility function can be written

$$u(q) = u^1(q^1) + \ldots + u^S(q^S) \tag{3.17}$$

where each u^s is a function of q^s alone.

Direct additivity or want independence occurs when the marginal utility of good i depends on the quantity of good i and not on the quantity of any other good; that is, a good i is termed *want independent* if

$$u_{ij} = 0 \qquad (i \neq j) \tag{3.18}$$

as seen by examining the partial derivatives of (3.17). Under conditions of directly additive preferences, the substitution term k_{ij} is

$$k_{ij} = \theta^* \frac{\partial q_i}{\partial m} \frac{\partial q_j}{\partial m} \qquad (i \neq j) \tag{3.19}$$

where $\theta^* = \lambda/(\partial\lambda/\partial m)$. Notice the correspondence of this result to the expressions obtained from Theorem 4. Clearly, this want-independent utility function is a special case for (3.7). The factor of proportionality   has no subscript to indicate that it is common to all commodities. Relatedly, for the demand functions,

$$\frac{\partial q_i}{\partial p_j} = - \frac{\partial q_i}{\partial m}(q_j + \theta^* \frac{\partial q_j}{\partial m}) \qquad (i \neq j) \tag{3.20}$$

In terms of elasticities expression (3.20) becomes

$$e_{ij} = w_j \phi \eta_i \eta_j - w_j \eta_i \tag{3.21}$$

The coefficient $- m/\theta^* = 1/\phi = \omega$ has been called the *money flexibility parameter* (Frisch 1959); it describes how the level of the marginal utility of money changes in relation to its rate of change with the level of money or income m. (See Frisch 1959 and Houthakker 1960 for a more detailed discussion of these results.)

The conclusion of Sec. 3.4 suggests that all direct and cross demand elasticities can be computed from the knowledge of income elasticities, the money flexibility, ω, and expenditure proportions. Only n income elasticities and the money flexibility parameter must be estimated to compute elasticities for the entire system of demand relations. This is a drastic reduction in the parameters required for the estimation of a complete system of n demand equations when only the assumptions from Chap. 2 are imposed on the utility function.

The condition of want independence (or direct additivity) is highly restrictive; that is, the behavioral consequences of direct additivity are either that (1) all goods are normal and substitute for each other; or (2) if one good is normal and substitutes for every other good, the remaining goods are either all inferior and complementary to each other or all neutral and unrelated to each other (Green 1961). Direct additivity also eliminates the possibility of specific substitution effects, since all $u^{ij} = 0$ $(i \neq j)$ (Houthakker 1960).

Even with these restrictions, direct additivity may be appropriate for a broadly defined classification of commodities, such as food and clothing. Deaton (1974) has shown that with highly aggregated commodity groups there are added and possibly unrealistic restrictions associated with additivity. For reasonably low degrees of aggregation, additivity is an overly strong assumption. Because of these observations, somewhat weaker behavioral restrictions on the utility function have been advanced, including block additivity.

3.5.2 Block Additivity

Under this assumption the marginal utility of the ith commodity depends on the quantity of the jth commodity only if i and j belong to the same block, i.e.,

$$u_{ij} = 0 \quad \text{for all } i \in I,\ j \in J\ (I \neq J) \tag{3.22}$$

This condition on the cross partial derivatives of the utility function implies that under block additivity the Hessian matrix U and its inverse U^{-1} are block diagonal. The block utility function u(q) can be written

$$u(q) = u^1(q^1) + u^2(q^2) + \ldots + u^S(q^S) \tag{3.23}$$

where q^s is the vector of commodities in the sth block. Note that this is the definition of strong separability (3.4) with only the monotonic function F deleted. This implies that in the case of block additivity the Slutsky term is similar to that given in (3.7).

Under the assumption of block additivity, the number of parameters to be estimated in a complete system of equations depends on the number of groups and the number of commodities in each group. After the various constraints are imposed, the number reduces to $(1/2)(n + \Sigma_{s=1}^{S} n_s^2)$, where S is the number of blocks and n_s the number of commodities in the sth blocks. In contrast to direct additivity, block additivity does not exclude inferiority for those commodities that are part of a set consisting of more than one commodity (Theil 1967, p. 200). See Barten (1968) and Theil (1975) for an extended discussion of these results and their implications for consumer demand functions.

Chapter 4 discusses more examples of demand functions corresponding to a number of specific utility functions. The present discussion illustrates the consequences of direct additivity and provides a useful example for studying the consequences of the separability assumptions. These additive utility functions occupy a central position in the applied demand systems work.

3.6 SEPARABILITY IN INDIRECT UTILITY, COST, AND TRANSFORMATION FUNCTIONS

The results reported in this section are summary statements of conclusions by Blackorby et al. (1978). The algebra necessary to substantiate these claims and correspondences is outside the scope of the present demand systems treatment; but we should at least be aware that the correspondences exist.

3.6.1 Definitions of Weak Separability

Indirect utility: The indirect utility function v in (2.29) is said to be weakly separable with respect to the partition $\{N_1, N_2, \ldots, N_S\}$ if the ratio of the demand functions for commodities i and j in I is independent of the prices that are not in I. Thus

$$\frac{\partial}{\partial p_k}\left(\frac{(\partial v/\partial p_i)/(\partial v/\partial m)}{(\partial v/\partial p_j)/(\partial v/\partial m)}\right) = \frac{\partial(q_i/q_j)}{\partial p_k} = 0 \qquad (3.27)$$

for all $i, j \in I$ and $k \notin I$.

Cost function: The cost function c in (2.32) is weakly separable with respect to a partition $\{N_1, N_2, \ldots, N_S\}$ if the ratio of the compensated demand functions for commodities i and j in I is independent of prices of commodities not in I. However, the ratio depends on the level of the utility, implying that the subset I is not separable from the utility function. Thus

$$\frac{\partial}{\partial p_k}\left(\frac{\partial c/\partial p_i}{\partial c/\partial p_j}\right) = \frac{\partial(q_i^*/q_j^*)}{\partial p_k} = 0 \qquad (3.28)$$

for all i, j ε I and k $\notin$ I.

Transformation function: The transformation function f in (2.33) is said to be weakly separable with respect to the partition $\{N_1, N_2, \ldots, N_S\}$ if the ratio of the inverse compensated demand functions is independent of the quantities of commodities not in I. As for the cost function, the ratio depends on the level of the utility. Thus

$$\frac{\partial}{\partial q_k}\left(\frac{\partial f/\partial q_i}{\partial f/\partial p_j}\right) = \frac{\partial(p_i^*/p_j^*)}{\partial q_k} = 0 \qquad (3.29)$$

for all i, j ε I and k $\notin$ I.

In general, separability of u, v, and f (or u, v, and c) is implied by different conditions on the preference orderings; however, the conditions for separability in c and f are equivalent. The duality between the structure of f and c occurs because the respective functions constitute homogeneous representations of the preference ordering. This lack of correspondence in separability concepts is an advantage and not a disadvantage because the separability restrictions may be more plausible for the allocation problem expressed in alternative forms (Blackorby et al. 1978).

3.6.2 Functional Forms

In Sec. 3.3 the concepts of weak, strong, and Pearce separability are related to admissible forms of the direct utility function. We now summarize the connections between weak separability and the indirect utility, cost, and transformation functions.

Indirect utility: The indirect utility function v is weakly separable in the partition $\{N_1, N_2, \ldots, N_S\}$ if it can be written as

$$v(p, m) = F[m, v^1(p^1, m), \ldots, v^S(p^S, m)] \qquad (3.30)$$

where F is increasing in m; continuous; homogeneous of degree zero in prices and income and F(m, .) is continuous, nonincreasing, and strictly quasi-convex.

Cost function: The cost function c is weakly separable in the partition $\{N_1, N_2, \ldots, N_S\}$ if it can be written in the form

$$(u, p) = F[u, c^1(u, p^1), \ldots, c^S(u, p^S)] \qquad (3.31)$$

where F is continuous and F(u, .) is increasing and differentiable in p.

Transformation function: The transformation function f is weakly separable in the partition $\{N_1, N_2, \ldots, N_S\}$ if it can be written as

$$f(u, q) = F[u, f^1(u, q^1), \ldots, f^S(u, q^S)] \tag{3.32}$$

where f is continuous and F(u, .) is increasing and differentiable in q.

Strong separability in the indirect utility, cost, and transformation functions can be defined similarly to the strong separability in the direct utility function (Sec. 3.3). For example, if we replace the direct utility function u in (3.4) with the indirect utility function v and q by (p, m), strong separability in the indirect utility function can be defined.

3.6.3 ILLUSTRATION

The direct quadratic utility function is used to explain the various concepts of separability. Illustrations based on the definitions of strong, weak and Pearce separabiilty are provided.

The direct quadratic utility function is

$$u = \alpha_1 q_1 + \alpha_2 q_2 + \alpha_3 q_3 + (1/2)\alpha_{11} q_1^2 + (1/2)\alpha_{22} q_2^2$$

$$+ (1/2)\alpha_{33} q_3^2 + \alpha_{12} q_1 q_2 + \alpha_{13} q_1 q_3 + \alpha_{23} q_2 q_3 \tag{3.33}$$

where $q_1 = \beta_1 q_{11} + \beta_2 q_{12} + \beta_3 q_{13}$, i.e., commodity 1 is a linear combination of three less aggregated commodities (see Phlips 1974, p. 70).

Partition the commodities such that $I = \{1_1, 1_2, 1_3\}$ or $I = \{1\}$, $J = \{2\}$, and $K = \{3\}$. In (3.33) set $\alpha_{12} = \alpha_{13} = \alpha_{23} = 0$; it follows that

$$\frac{\partial u}{\partial q_{11}} = \frac{\partial u}{\partial q_1}\frac{\partial q_1}{\partial q_{11}} = (\alpha_1 + \alpha_{11} q_1)\beta_1, \qquad \frac{\partial u}{\partial q_2} = \alpha_2 + \alpha_{22} q_2$$

$$\frac{\partial u/\partial q_{11}}{\partial u/\partial q_2} = \frac{(\alpha_1 + \alpha_{11} q_1)\beta_1}{\alpha_2 + \alpha_{22} q_2}$$

Thus

$$\frac{\partial}{\partial q_3}\left(\frac{\partial u/\partial q_{11}}{\partial u/\partial q_2}\right) = \frac{\partial}{\partial q_3}\left[\frac{(\alpha_1 + \alpha_{11} q_1)\beta_1}{\alpha_2 + \alpha_{22} q_2}\right] = 0 \tag{3.34}$$

and by definition (3.1) preferences are strongly separable with respect to the given partition.

Consider the concept of weak separability for the above example, but this time do not set $\alpha_{12} = \alpha_{13} = \alpha_{23} = 0$. From (3.33) it follows that

$$\frac{\partial u}{\partial q_{11}} = \frac{\partial u}{\partial q_1}\frac{\partial q_1}{\partial q_{11}} = (\alpha_1 + \alpha_{11}q_1 + \alpha_{12}q_2 + \alpha_{13}q_3)\beta_1$$

$$\frac{\partial u}{\partial q_{12}} = \frac{\partial u}{\partial q_1}\frac{\partial q_1}{\partial q_{12}} = (\alpha_1 + \alpha_{11}q_1 + \alpha_{12}q_2 + \alpha_{13}q_3)\beta_2$$

$$\frac{\partial u/\partial q_{11}}{\partial u/\partial q_{12}} = \frac{(\alpha_1 + \alpha_{11}q_1 + \alpha_{12}q_2 + \alpha_{13}q_3)\beta_1}{(\alpha_1 + \alpha_{11}q_1 + \alpha_{12}q_2 + \alpha_{13}q_3)\beta_2} = \frac{\beta_1}{\beta_2}$$

Thus

$$\frac{\partial}{\partial q_2}\left(\frac{\partial u/\partial q_{11}}{\partial u/\partial q_{12}}\right) = \frac{\partial(\beta_1/\beta_2)}{\partial q_2} = 0, \qquad \frac{\partial}{\partial q_3}\left(\frac{\partial u/\partial q_{11}}{\partial u/\partial q_{12}}\right) = 0$$

By definition (3.2), preferences are weakly separable with respect to the given partition.

To demonstrate the idea of Pearce separability, again consider the quadratic utility function in (3.3). It follows from (3.3) that

$$\frac{\partial u}{\partial q_{13}} = (\alpha_1 + \alpha_{11}q_1 + \alpha_{12}q_2 + \alpha_{13}q_3)\beta_3$$

Hence

$$\frac{\partial}{\partial q_{13}}\left(\frac{\partial u/\partial q_{11}}{\partial u/\partial q_{12}}\right) = \frac{\partial(\beta_2/\beta_1)}{\partial q_{13}} = 0,$$

$$\frac{\partial}{\partial q_2}\left(\frac{\partial u/\partial q_{11}}{\partial u/\partial q_{12}}\right) = \frac{\partial}{\partial q_3}\left(\frac{\partial u/\partial q_{11}}{\partial u/\partial q_{12}}\right) = 0$$

By definition (3.3), preferences are Pearce separable with respect to the above partition.

The concepts of weak separability in an indirect utility function, cost function, and transformation function are left as exercises for the interested reader.

EXERCISES

1. Consider the direct quadratic function

$$u = \alpha_1 q_1 + \alpha_2 q_2 + \alpha_3 q_3 + (1/2)\alpha_{11} q_1^2 + (1/2)\alpha_{22} q_2^2$$

$$+ (1/2)\alpha_{33} q_3^2 + \alpha_{12} q_1 q_2 + \alpha_{13} q_1 q_3 + \alpha_{23} q_2 q_3$$

where $q_1 = \beta_1 q_{11} + \beta_2 q_{12} + \beta_3 q_{13}$ is an aggregate commodity. Partition the commodity space as follows: $I = \{1_1, 1_2, 1_3\}$ or $I = \{1\}$, $J = \{2\}$, and $K = \{3\}$.

(a) Derive the associated indirect utility for the direct quadratic utility function.

(b) Determine, using (3.27), whether the indirect utility function is weakly separable with respect to the given partition.

(c) Derive the cost function corresponding to the direct quadratic utility function.

(d) Determine, using (3.28), whether the cost function is weakly separable with respect to the given partition.

(e) Derive the transformation function associated with the above direct quadratic utility function.

(f) Determine, using (3.29), whether the cost function is weakly separable with respect to the given partition.

2. Consider the Klein-Rubin utility function $u = \Sigma\, \mu_i \ell n (q_i - \gamma_i)$.

(a) Show that u is additive.

(b) Derive the corresponding indirect utility function.

(c) Show that the associated indirect utility function is not additive. Hint: See Pollak (1971).

(d) How would the results change in (a) and (b) if $\gamma_i = 0$, $i = 1, 2, \ldots, n$? Is this what you expected? Explain.

3. For the utility function $u = \Pi_{i=1}^{n} q_i^{\alpha_i}$ determine whether the direct and associated indirect cost and transformation functions are weakly separable.

4. Discuss the problems, in terms of causal observations on consumption behavior, of applying demand systems that assume strong separability on a highly disaggregated basis vis-a-vis the commodity groupings.

REFERENCES

Barten, A. P. 1968. Estimating demand equations. _Econometrica_ 36 (Apr.):213-51.

Blackorby, C.; Lady, G.; Nissen, D.; and Russell, R. 1970. Homothetic separability and consumer budgeting. _Econometrica_ 38:468-72.

Blackorby, C.; Primont, D.; and Russell, R. R. 1975. Some simple remarks on duality and the structure of utility functions. Journal of Economic Theory 11 (Aug.)155-60.

———. 1978. Duality, Separability, and Functional Structure: Theory and Economic Applications. New York: Elsevier-North Holland.

Brown, M., and Heien, D. 1972. The S-branch utility tree: A generalization to the linear expenditure system. Econometrica 40 (July):737-47.

Deaton, A. 1974. A Reconsideration of the Empirical Implications of Additive Preferences. Economic Journal 84 (June):338-48.

Deaton, A., and Muellbauer, J. 1980. Economics and Consumer Behavior. Cambridge: Cambridge University Press.

Frisch, R. A. 1959. A complete scheme for computing all direct and cross-demand elasticities in a model with many sectors. Econometrica 27 (Apr.):177-96.

Goldman, S. M., and Uzawa, H. 1964. A note on separability in demand analysis. Econometrica 32 (July):387-98.

Gorman, W. M. 1971. Two stage budgeting. Unpublished paper, London School of Economics.

———. 1976. Tricks with utility functions. In Essays in Economic Analysis, ed. M. Artis and R. Nobay, pp. 211-43. Cambridge: Cambridge University Press.

Green, H. A. J. 1961. Direct additivity and consumer behavior. Oxformal Economic Papers 13 (June):132-36.

Hicks, J. R. 1946. Value and Capital, 2d ed. Oxford: Oxford University Press.

Houthakker, H. S. 1960. Additive preferences. Econometrica 28 (Apr.): 244-57.

Judge, G. G., and Bock, M. E. 1978. The Statistical Implications of Pre-Test and Stein Rule Estimators in Econometrics. New York: Elsevier-North Holland.

Leamer, E. E. 1978. Specification Searches: Ad Hoc Inference with Non-Experimental Data. New York: John Wiley.

Leontief, W. W. 1947. Introduction to the theory of internal structure of functional relationships. Econometrica 15 (Oct.):361-73.

McFadden, D., and Fuss, M. 1975. An Econometric Approach to Production Theory. Amsterdam: North Holland.

Pearce, I. F. 1964. A Contribution to Demand Analysis. Oxford: Oxford University Press.

Phlips, L. 1974. Applied Consumption Analysis. Amsterdam: North Holland.

Pollak, R. A. 1971. Additive utility functions and linear Engel curves. Review of Economic Studies 38 (Oct.):401-13.

Schultz, H. 1938. The Theory and Measurement of Demand. Chicago: University of Chicago Press.

Sono, M. 1960. The effect of price changes on the demand and supply of separable goods. International Economic Review 2 (Sept):239-71.

Strotz, R. H. 1957. The empirical implications of a utility tree. Econometrica 25 (Apr.):269-80.

———. 1975. The utility tree--a correction and further appraisal. Econometrica 27 (July):482-88.

Theil, H. 1967. Economics and Information Theory. Amsterdam: North Holland.

———. 1975. Theory and Measurement of Consumer Demand, Vol. 2. Amsterdam: North Holland.

Wold, H., and Jureen, L. 1953. Demand Analysis. New York: John Wiley.

4 • Static Demand Systems

Demand systems specifications in contemporary economic literature are developed using a utility maximization framework or are expressed directly with certain restrictions imposed. All of the systems reviewed, however, correspond to a utility maximization problem.

Each of the specifications results in a reduction of the number of coefficients in the complete system of demand functions, making joint estimation of the parameters more feasible. The resulting demand systems are attractive because they satisfy basic restrictions from the theory as reviewed in Chap. 2 and they can be estimated from available time series data. This chapter reviews these formulations, describes their similarities and relationships to the theory of consumer behavior and the separability results of Chap. 3 and provides the basis for evaluating parameter estimates from the Canadian data and for interpreting supportable comparisons.

4.1 DEMAND SYSTEMS AND UTILITY MAXIMIZATION

Three of the utility function approaches the linear expenditure, the indirect addilog, and the flexible systems have been broadly applied (Stone 1954; Frisch 1959; Houthakker 1960; Parks 1969; Yoshihara 1969; Christensen et al. 1975; Berndt et al. 1977).

4.1.1 Linear Expenditure System

The linear expenditure system (LES) is derived from a utility function suggested by Klein and Rubin (1947-1948):

$$u = \mu' \log(q - \gamma) \tag{4.1}$$

where $\mu = [\mu_i]'$ is the n-component vector of marginal budget shares and $\gamma = [\gamma_i]'$ is the n-component vector of quantities interpreted as minimum consumption levels. This interpretation holds only when γ_i is assumed positive. The parameter vectors μ and γ are estimated subject to the restrictions $0 < \mu_i < 1$ (i = 1, 2, ..., n), $\iota'\mu = 1$, and $(q - \gamma) > 0$. Maximizing the utility function expressed in (4.1) subject to the budget constraint $p'q = m$ yields as first order conditions

$$(\bar{q} - \bar{\gamma})^{-1}\mu - \lambda p = 0 \qquad (4.2a)$$

$$p'q - m = 0 \qquad (4.cb)$$

where, according to the convention introduced in Chap. 2, $\bar{q}$ and $\bar{\gamma}$ denote n x n diagonal matrices with nonzero elements given by the vectors q and γ. To obtain the demand functions implied by the first order conditions, first solve (4.2) for the vector μ,

$$\mu = \lambda(\bar{q} - \bar{\gamma})p = \lambda\bar{p}(q - \gamma) \qquad (4.3)$$

where $\bar{p}$ is defined to be related to p as $\bar{q}$ is to q. Premultiplying (4.3) by the sum vector ι' and making use of the conditions $\iota'\mu = 1$ and $p'q = m$ gives, after rearranging the terms,

$$\lambda = (m - p'\gamma)^{-1} \qquad (4.4)$$

Inserting (4.4) into (4.3) and solving for q yields

$$q = \gamma + (m - p'\gamma)\bar{p}^{-1}\mu \qquad (4.5)$$

It is easily verified that demand functions in this system are homogeneous of degree zero in prices and income, they satisfy the adding-up criterion, and the matrix of substitution terms is symmetric and negative semidefinite (Yoshihara 1969, p. 263).

The system of expenditure equations corresponding to the demand system expressed in (4.5) can be written as

$$\bar{p}q = \bar{p}\gamma + (m - p'\gamma)\mu \qquad (4.6a)$$

The individual expenditure functions contained in the system represented in (4.6a) take the form

$$p_iq_i = p_i\gamma_i + \mu_i(m - \sum_j p_j\gamma_j) \qquad (i = 1, 2, ..., n) \qquad (4.6b)$$

Expenditure functions of this type have been widely used and can be interpreted as implying a sequence of actions. First, the consumer may purchase minimum required quantities of each commodity, γ_i (i = 1, 2, ..., n). At the current market prices these quantities cost $\Sigma\, p_j\gamma_j$. The consumer then distributes the remainder of the available income $(m - \Sigma\, p_j\gamma_j)$ over all commodities in fixed proportions, μ_i $(i = 1, 2, \ldots, n)$. Hence $\Sigma\, p_j\gamma_j$ and $(m - \Sigma\, p_j\gamma_j)$ can be considered subsistence and supernumerary incomes, respectively.

From the system of equations represented by (4.5) the income elasticities are

$$\eta_i = \mu_i/w_i \tag{4.7a}$$

where w_i is the expenditure proportion, $w_i = p_iq_i/m$. Since $\mu_i >$ 0, all income elasticities are positive, implying that all goods are normal. Own price elasticities are

$$e_{ii} = -1 + (1 - \mu_i)(\gamma_i/q_i) \tag{4.7b}$$

With $0 < \mu_i < 1$ and $q_i - \gamma_i > 0$, it follows that all own price elasticities are negative. Expressions for the cross price elasticities are similarly obtained, that is,

$$e_{ij} = -\mu_i[p_j\gamma_j/(p_iq_i)] \qquad (i \neq j) \tag{4.7c}$$

All uncompensated cross price elasticities are negative, indicating that all goods are gross complements. However, the compensated cross price elasticities are positive, suggesting that all goods are net substitutes. If the associated γ_i is negative, then all price elastic goods are gross substitutes for all price inelastic goods.

Inferior goods are excluded by the linear expenditure system and if γ_i is negative, the demand for the ith good is elastic. This system has only 2n - 1 independent parameters, the n - 1 parameters of μ_i and the n parameters of γ_i.

A generalization of the linear expenditure system developed and used by Lluch (1973) is called the <u>extended linear expenditure system</u> (ELES) and is based on an intertemporal maximization of the Klein-Rubin utility function. The typical ELES equation can be written as

$$p_iq_i = p_i\gamma_i + \beta^*\mu_i(m - \sum_j p_j\gamma_j)$$

where β^* is the marginal propensity to consume and the remaining terms are defined as in (4.6b). The system is distinguished from the LES by the inclusion of the savings-consumption decision. Observe that for $\beta^* = 1$ or zero savings propensity, the equation above is equivalent to (4.6b).

A more detailed discussion of the linear expenditure system is available in Stone (1954).

4.1.2 Indirect Addilog System

Houthakker (1960) has derived a set of demand equations that is termed the indirect addilog demand system. The approach is based on the idea of an indirect utility function, $v = v(p, m)$. In particular, the indirect utility function specified by Houthakker is

$$v(p, m) = \sum_i a_i (m/p_i)^{b_i} \tag{4.8}$$

where a_i and b_i are parameters with $a_i b_i \geqq 0$ and $b_i \geqq -1$, the equality holding for at most one commodity (Murty 1982, pp. 225-27). As argued in Chap. 2, an explicit solution for the demand functions corresponding to this indirect utility function can be obtained by differentiating it with respect to prices and income and applying Roy's identity. Differentiating (4.8) with respect to prices $p_1, p_2, \ldots, p_n$, gives

$$\frac{\partial v}{\partial p_i} = - p_i^{-1} a_i b_i (m/p_i)^{b_i} \qquad (i = 1, 2, \ldots, n) \tag{4.9}$$

Similarly, differentiating (4.8) with respect to income m provides

$$\frac{\partial v}{\partial m} = \sum_j a_j b_j p_j^{-b_j} m^{b_j - 1} \tag{4.10}$$

Application of Roy's identity gives as the system of demand functions

$$q_i = \frac{a_i b_i m^{b_i} p_i^{-b_i - 1}}{\sum_j a_j b_j m^{b_j - 1} p_j^{-b_j}} = \frac{a_i b_i (m/p_i)^{1+b_i}}{\sum_j a_j b_j (m/p_j)^{b_j}} \qquad (i = 1, 2, \ldots, n) \tag{4.11}$$

It can be demonstrated that these demand functions are homogeneous of degree zero in income and all prices and that they satisfy the Engel aggregation and the Slutsky symmetry conditions (Yoshihara 1969, p. 264).

General properties of the demand system resulting from this indirect utility function are easily examined using elasticities. Taking the logarithm of (4.11) results in

$$\log q_i = \log a_i b_i + (1 + b_i)\log(m/p_i)$$
$$- \log \sum a_j b_j (m/p_j)^{b_j} \qquad (4.12)$$

for (i = 1, 2, ..., n). Own price, cross price, and income elasticities are then found by differentiating (4.12) and applying the familiar formulas. For the income elasticities the result is

$$\eta_i = (1 + b_i) - \sum_j b_j w_j \qquad (i = 1, 2, \ldots, n) \qquad (4.13a)$$

Observe that $\eta_i \gtreqless 1$ according to $b_i \gtreqless \Sigma_j b_j w_j$, and inferior goods are permitted. Furthermore, from (4.13a) we note that the differences between the income elasticities are constant and independent of the income level, that is, $\eta_i - \eta_j = b_i - b_j$.

For the direct or own price elasticities, insertion of the derivative of (4.12) with respect to price p_i into the traditional formula gives

$$e_{ii} = -(1 + b_i) + b_i w_i \qquad (i = 1, 2, \ldots, n) \qquad (4.13b)$$

Similarly, the cross price elasticities are obtained from

$$e_{ij} = b_j w_j \qquad (i, j = 1, 2, \ldots, n; i \neq j) \qquad (4.13c)$$

From (4.13c) observe that the cross price elasticities depend only on the commodity whose price is changing and not on the good whose quantity is responding. Finally, note that the complete set of demand parameters in the indirect addilog system can be estimated with 2n - 1 independent coefficients, the n b_i and the n - 1 a_i.

4.1.3 Flexible Functional Forms

This approach can be useful to test assumptions (such as additivity of preferences) implicit in the specifications of previously discussed systems (Diewert 1973; Christensen et al. 1975; Fortune 1979; Caves and Christensen 1980) because it expands the empirical content of the theory. The indirect translog function illustrates this approach.

Following Christensen et al. (1975), the quadratic approximation of the indirect translog utility function can be written

$$\ell n\ v = \sigma_0 + \sum_i \sigma_i \ell n(p_i/m) + (1/2)\sum_i \sum_j \beta_{ij} \ell n(p_i/m)\ell n(p_j/m) \qquad (4.14)$$

where σ_0, σ_i, and β_{ij} are parameters with $\beta_{ij} = \beta_{ji}$ $(i \neq j)$.

Application of Roy's identity to (4.14) yields the system of demand equations

$$\frac{p_i q_i}{m} = \frac{\sigma_i + \sum_j \beta_{ij}\ell n(p_j/m)}{\sum_j \sigma_j + \sum_j \sum_i \beta_{ij}\ell n(p_j/m)} \qquad (i = 1, 2, \ldots, n) \qquad (4.15)$$

These demand equations are homogeneous of degree zero. In order to estimate these parameters a normalization $\Sigma\, \sigma_i = -1$ is usually imposed. The budget constraint is that $\Sigma\, p_i q_i/m = 1$, meaning that only n - 1 of the equations are independent.

From (4.15) the income and price elasticities can be derived. The income elasticity of demand is given by

$$\eta_i = 1 + \frac{-\sum_j \beta_{ji}/w_i + \sum_i \sum_j \beta_{ij}}{1 + \sum_i \sum_j \beta_{ij}\ell n(p_j/m)} \qquad (4.16a)$$

Own price elasticities are

$$e_{ii} = \frac{-1 + \beta_{ii}/w_i - \sum_j \beta_{ji}}{1 + \sum_i \sum_j \beta_{ij}\ell n(p_j/m)} \qquad (4.16b)$$

and the cross price elasticities are

$$e_{ij} = \frac{\beta_{ij}/w_i - \sum_i \beta_{ij}}{1 + \sum_i \sum_j \beta_{ij}\ell n(p_j/m)} \qquad (4.16c)$$

A major limitation of this approach for estimating demand systems is the number of structural parameters required. Reference to (4.15) shows that the number of unrestricted and unknown structural parameters is (n - 1)(2n + 1). Thus, annual data series of usual length and more refined commodity groupings involve serious estimation problems (Berndt et al. 1977).

The generality achieved by the use of the flexible functional forms is not as full as initially argued and this generality and expansion of testable propositions is achieved at some cost. The number of parameters to be estimated is high. A more subtle cost is that of assumptions about the quality of the approximation. Tests and results of the estimation are conducted within the context of the approximation, not within the true system. Recently, qualifications associated with this observation have been synthesized and more completely understood; they involve local versus global properties of flexible functional forms, appropriate hypothesis testing methodology for approximate functions, and the closeness of the approximations achieved for familiar functional forms.

Caves and Christensen (1980) show that the proper choice of flexible functional form depends upon the nature of the utility function and consumer preferences over the entire range of possible or observed consumption bundles, prices and, incomes. They demonstrate the basis for choosing one flexible functional form instead of another, building on earlier work by and Theil and Gabrielson (1976) and Blackorby et al. (1977). If the approximation is local or other flexible functional forms can improve it, conclusions about the inconsistency of utility maximization (Wales 1977), structural hypotheses (Blackorby et al. 1977), or the nature of preferences (Theil and Gabrielson 1976) are special to the selection of the functional form and are arbitrary decisions.

For hypothesis testing, the preliminary choice of flexible form (Theil and Gabrielson 1976; Simmons and Weiserbs 1979) is crucial because statistical tests of demand systems propositions or the underlying preference structure depend upon this form and use of mechanically applied statistical tests will overstate the conclusions. Experimenting with flexible functional forms that might be reasonable, can create problems of overstatement through preliminary testing. The frailty of the conclusions from standard statistical models is apparent when this choice is combined with appropriate autoregressive or moving average assumption applied to the residuals. The flexible form to represent the system depends on the characterization used to accommodate the persistence of errors that are present when applying static models.

The one positive outcome of flexible functional forms is explained by Guilkey and Lovell (1980). Using Monte Carlo experiments, they show that the translog function, the form used for most empirical work, approximates most underlying structures relatively well over extended ranges. From a practical viewpoint, the translog may be safe to use; however, there are the added qualifications that the empirical results must carry.

4.2 DEMAND SYSTEMS DIRECTLY SPECIFIED

This section considers the Theil-Barten and Powell approaches to the specification and estimation of demand functions. Barten (1977) presents an alternative and more complete discussion of these demand systems obtained by direct specification.

4.2.1 Rotterdam Demand System

The Theil-Barten approach to the estimation of parameters of demand functions corresponding to (2.9a) is that they can be specified using prices and a measure of real income m^* (Barten, 1964, 1968, 1969; Theil 1967, 1971, 1975, 1976). Logarithmic differentials of demand functions developed under this specification can be written

$$d(\ell n\ q_i) = \sum_j e_{ij} d(\ell n\ p_j + \eta_i d(\ell n\ m^*)$$

$$(i = 1, 2, \ldots, n) \qquad (4.17)$$

where again e_{ij} is the cross price elasticity of the ith commodity with respect to the jth price and η_i is the income elasticity of the commodity i. Individual commodity demand functions as expressed in (4.17) are then weighted by their corresponding expenditure proportions w_i; that is, multiplying both sides of equation (4.17) by w_i gives

$$w_i d(\ell n\ q_i) = \sum_j \pi_{ij} d(\ell n\ p_j) + \mu_i d(\ell n\ m^*)$$

$$(i = 1, 2, \ldots, n) \qquad (4.18)$$

The price coefficient, $\pi_{ij} = (p_i p_j/m)(\partial q_i/\partial p_j)$, is the cross price elasticity e_{ij} weighted by the ith expenditure proportion, and the coefficient $\mu_i = p_i\ (\partial q_i/\partial m)$ is again the marginal budget share of the ith commodity.

Restrictions implied by the neoclassical formulation of the consumer optimization problem can be shown to hold for the parameters in the set of equations specified in (4.18) (Theil 1967, p. 330). Equations represented by (4.18), however, are formulated using nominal prices. The relative price version of the Rotterdam model is used here. For this purpose it will be instructive to write the price derivative $\partial q_i/\partial p_j$ in the form

$$\frac{\partial q_i}{\partial p_j} = \lambda u^{ij} - \frac{\lambda}{\partial \lambda/\partial m} \frac{\partial q_i}{\partial m} \frac{\partial q_j}{\partial m} \qquad (i, j = 1, 2, \ldots, n)$$

where u^{ij} is the (i, j)th element of the inverse of the Hessian matrix identified with the second order conditions of the consumer optimization problem (see Sec. 2.4). The price derivative $\partial q_i/\partial p_j$ is the total effect of a price change when real income is held constant (Theil 1967, pp. 575, 677). The logarithmic change in real income m* can be expressed as $d(\ell n\ m^*) = d(\ell n\ m) - \Sigma_k w_k d(\ell n\ p_k)$. With these results, (4.18) can be written in terms of relative prices,

$$w_i d(\ell n\ q_i) = \sum_j b_{ij}[d(\ell n \cdot p_j) - \sum \mu_k d(\ell n\ p_k)]$$

$$+ \mu_i[d(\ell n\ m) - \sum_k w_k d(\ell n\ p_k)]$$

$$(i = 1, 2, \ldots, n) \quad (4.19)$$

where $b_{ij} = \lambda p_i p_j u^{ij}/m$ is the coefficient of the relative price j (Theil 1967, pp. 575-78).

With the demand system so specified, the parameters μ_i and b_{ij} satisfy the conditions

$$\sum_i \mu_i = 1 \quad (4.20a)$$

$$b_{ij} = b_{ji} \quad (4.20b)$$

$$\sum_j b_{ij} = \phi\mu_i \quad (4.20c)$$

that is, the Engel aggregation, the symmetry relation, and the homogeneity condition, respectively. The term ϕ is called the income flexibility parameter or the reciprocal of Frisch's money flexibility; see (3.21). An additional restriction is obtained by summing over i in (4.20c) and using (4.20a) to show that the income flexibility parameter is equal to the sum of the price coefficients; they are negative, which implies that ϕ is negative.

Note that in practice (4.19) should be altered in two ways. First, since consumer expenditure data typically deal with finite changes, the system of demand functions is modified to accommodate discrete changes in the underlying variables. Applying a Taylor's series expansion to (4.19) and retaining only the first and second order terms yields

$$w^*_{it}\Delta(\ell n\ q_{it}) = \sum_j b_{ij}[\Delta(\ell n\ p_{jt}) - \sum_k \mu_k \Delta(\ell n\ p_{kt})]$$

$$+ \mu_i[\Delta(\ell n\ m_t) - \sum_k w^*_{kt}\Delta(\ell n\ p_{kt})] \quad (4.21)$$

for i = 1, 2, ..., n, where $w^*_{it} = (1/2)(w_{it} + w_{it-1})$ is the average of expenditure proportions between successive periods, Δ is a difference operator (i.e., $\Delta x_{it} = x_{it} - x_{it-1}$), and t denotes the current time period. Second, the term $[\Delta(\ell n\ m_t) - \sum w^*_{kt}\Delta(\ell n\ p_{kt})]$ can be replaced by $\Delta(\ell n\ q_t) = \sum w^*_{it}\Delta(\ell n\ q_{it})$, which is the sum over i of the left-hand variables of (4.21). This replacement involves an error of only the third degree in the logarithmic differentials. The advantage of this operation is that the approximated demand equations can be made to possess the adding-up property (Barten 1968).

With the second change, (4.21) is

$$w^*_{it}\Delta(\ell n\, q_{it}) = \sum_j b_{ij}[\Delta(\ell n\, p_{jt}) - \sum_k \mu_k \Delta(\ell n\, p_{kt})] + \mu_i \Delta(\ell n\, q_t) \qquad (4.22)$$

for i = 1, 2, ..., n. When the additivity condition is imposed, the constraint $\Sigma_j b_{ij} = \phi\mu_i$ can be replaced by $b_{ii} = \phi\mu_i$, and the constraint $\Sigma_i\Sigma_j b_{ij} = \phi$ by $\Sigma\, b_i = \phi$. The power of the additivity restrictions for estimability is apparent. The demand equation in (4.22) is simplified to

$$w^*_{it}\Delta(\ell n\, q_{it}) = \phi\mu_i[\Delta(\ell n\, p_{it}) - \sum_k \mu_k \Delta(\ell n\, p_{kt})] + \mu_i \Delta(\ell n\, q_t) \qquad (4.23)$$

for i = 1, 2, ..., n. In this form the demand functions contain only n parameters, n - 1 marginal budget shares, and ϕ. As a result of the additivity assumption, the complete set of price and income elasticities can be estimated on the basis of the n parameters.

For the Rotterdam model, the income elasticity is

$$\eta_i = \mu_i / w_i \qquad (i = 1, 2, \ldots, n) \qquad (4.24a)$$

With all μ_i positive, the income elasticities are positive. Furthermore, it is easily seen that $\eta_i \gtreqless 1$ according to the relationship $\mu_i \gtreqless w_i$. In particular, if $\mu_i > w_i$ then $\eta_i > 1$, and the commodity is a luxury item. Differentiation of (4.19) with respect to p_i and p_j and again applying the standard elasticity expressions yields

$$e_{ii} = (b_{ii} - b_{ii}\mu_i - \mu_i w_i)/w_i \qquad (4.24b)$$

$$e_{ij} = (b_{ii}\mu_j - w_j\mu_i)/w_i \qquad (4.24c)$$

These expressions can be simplified to

$$e_{ii} = \phi\eta_i - \eta_i w_i(1 + \phi\eta_i) \quad \text{and} \quad e_{ij} = -\eta_i w_j(1 + \phi\eta_i)$$

using the condition $b_{ii} = \phi\mu_i$. From the simplified expressions it is clear that $e_{ij} \gtreqless 0$ according to $|\eta_i w_j \phi\eta_j| \lesseqgtr |\eta_i w_j|$. For example, if $|\eta_i w_j| > |\eta_j w_j \phi\eta_i|$, then $e_{ij} < 0$ and the cross price elasticity reflects the income effect rather than the substitution effect of the price change.

Note explicitly that the Rotterdam demand system can be derived from the Klein and Rubin utility function (4.1) (Goldberger 1967; Yoshihara 1969). In particular, if $\gamma = 0$ in (4.1), then the special Cobb-Douglas utility function $u = \Sigma_{i=1}^{n} {}_i(\log q_i)$ applies. The expenditure and demand functions are, respectively, $p_i q_i = \mu_i m$ and $q_i = \mu_i(m/p_i)$ $(i = 1, 2, \ldots, n)$. This system of demand functions implies that all income elasticities = 1, all own price elasticities = -1, and all cross price elasticities = 0. Theil (1967, p. 203) answers this criticism by stating: "Since the starting point of the Rotterdam demand system was formulated in terms of first-order effects [infinitesimal changes], the implications of the demand equation should also be confined to first-order changes." Thus, the Rotterdam model under appropriate restrictions can be rationalized as following from a utility maximization process. At this point, these restrictions are highly qualifying.

4.2.2 Powell's System of Additive Preferences

Consider a complete system of n linear relations with the specification that

$$p_i q_i = \sum_j a_{ij} p_j + \mu_i m + c_i t \qquad (i = 1, 2, \ldots, n) \tag{4.25}$$

where $p_i q_i$ is per capita expenditure on the ith commodity, p_j is the price of the jth commodity, m is the total expenditure per capita, and t is a time related variable introduced to allow for shifts in consumer tastes (Powell 1966). For this system a_{ij}, μ_i, and c_i are parameters to be estimated. Differentiating (4.25) with respect to income and prices

$$\frac{\partial q_i}{\partial m} = \frac{\mu_i}{p_i} \qquad (i = 1, 2, \ldots, n) \tag{4.26}$$

$$\frac{\partial q_i}{\partial p_j} = \frac{a_{ij}}{p_i} - \delta_{ij}\frac{q_i}{p_i} \qquad (i, j = 1, 2, \ldots, n) \tag{4.27}$$

where δ_{ij} is the Kronecker delta; $\delta_{ij} = 1$ if $i = j$ and 0 otherwise. Solving for a_{ij} from (4.27) gives

$$a_{ij} = p_i \frac{\partial q_i}{\partial p_j} + \delta_{ij} q_i \tag{4.28a}$$

In particular, (4.28a) holds when the derivative $\partial q_i/\partial p_j$ is evaluated at the sample mean prices and quantities, say $\hat{p}_i$ and $\hat{q}_i$, respectively. Hence (4.28a) can be alternatively written

$$a_{ij} = \hat{p}_i \frac{\partial q_i}{\partial p_j} + \delta_{ij} \hat{q}_i \tag{4.28b}$$

The partial derivative $\partial q_i/\partial p_j$ can be expressed in terms of the substitution k_{ij} and the income effects $q_j(\partial q_i/\partial m)$,

$$\frac{\partial q_i}{\partial p_j} = k_{ij} - q_j \frac{\partial q_i}{\partial m} \tag{4.29}$$

using the notation from Chap. 2. Under the condition of directly additive preferences the term k_{ij} can be expressed as in (3.19):

$$k_{ij} = -\theta^* \frac{\partial q_i}{\partial m} \frac{\partial q_j}{\partial m} \qquad (i \neq j) \tag{4.30}$$

Substituting the value for k_{ij} from (4.30) into (4.29) and (4.28b) and using (4.26) yields

$$a_{ij} = \theta^* \mu_i \mu_j / \hat{p}_j - \mu_i \hat{q}_j \qquad (i \neq j) \tag{4.31}$$

Conditions for preserving the Engel aggregation are obtained by summing over i in (4.25), i.e.,

$$\sum_i p_i q_i = \sum_i \sum_j a_{ij} p_j + m \sum_i \mu_i + t \sum_i c_i$$

For the equality to hold the following conditions must hold:

$$\sum_i \sum_j a_{ij} p_j = 0 \tag{4.32a}$$

$$\sum_i \mu_i = 1 \tag{4.32b}$$

$$\sum_i c_i = 0 \qquad (4.32c)$$

Note specifically that (4.32a) implies that $\Sigma\, a_{ij} = 0$. Hence it follows that $a_{ii} = \Sigma_{i \neq j} a_{ij}$. These results, along with (4.31), can be used to show that

$$a_{ii} = -(\theta^* \mu_i \sum_{i \neq j} \mu_j / \hat{p}_i - \hat{q}_i \sum_{i \neq j} \mu_j)$$

$$= (\mu_i - 1)[(\theta^* \mu_i / \hat{p}_i) - \hat{q}_i] \qquad (4.33)$$

Substituting the values for a_{ii} and a_{ij} from (4.33) and (4.31) into (4.25) and rearranging the terms results in a useful interpretation:

$$p_i q_i = p_i \hat{q}_i + \theta^* \mu_i \sum_j \mu_j (p_j / \hat{p}_j - p_i / \hat{p}_i)$$

$$+ \mu_i (m - \sum_j p_j \hat{q}_j) + c_i t \qquad (i = 1, 2, \ldots, n) \qquad (4.34)$$

Equation (4.34) implies that the consumer first purchases minimum required quantities $\hat{q}_i$ $(i = 1, 2, \ldots, n)$ and then allocates remaining income $(m - \Sigma\, p_j \hat{q}_j)$ over all commodities in fixed proportions μ_i $(i = 1, 2, \ldots, n)$. The distribution of income is modified to reflect the substitution effects arising from price changes.

For this model the income and price elasticities are

$$\eta_i = \mu_i / w_i \qquad (i = 1, 2, \ldots, n) \qquad (4.35a)$$

$$e_{ij} = [(\theta^* \mu_i \mu_j - \mu_i \hat{p}_j \hat{q}_j) / (\hat{p}_i \hat{q}_i)] - \theta^* \delta_{ij} \mu_i / (\hat{p}_i \hat{q}_i) \qquad (4.35b)$$

for $i, j = 1, 2, \ldots, n$. The income elasticities follow directly from (4.26); the price elasticities are obtained by rewriting (4.27) in terms of elasticities and using (4.31) and (4.33).

It follows that the Engel aggregation is preserved globally but homogeneity and symmetry are only approximately satisfied. The system is homogeneous only for $t = 0$; the symmetry relation occurs only at points where $p_i / p_j = \hat{p}_i / \hat{p}_j$ (Powell 1966, pp. 663-4). Finally, the complete demand system (4.34) can be estimated on the basis of n parameters, the $(n - 1)$ μ_i and θ^*.

4.3 DEMAND FUNCTIONS INCONSISTENT WITH THEORY

A function often used for empirical analysis of consumer demand is

$$q_i = A_i m^{\eta_i} \prod_j p_j^{e_{ij}} \qquad (i = 1, 2, \ldots, n) \tag{4.36}$$

where η_i is the income elasticity of the ith commodity and e_{ij} is the cross price elasticity of the ith commodity with respect to the jth price. The value A_i is a scaling constant. In logarithmic form (4.36) is

$$\log q_i = \log A_i + \eta_i \log m + \sum_j e_{ij} \log p_j$$

$$(i = 1, 2, \ldots, n) \tag{4.37}$$

It is well known that these double log demand functions are inconsistent with standard utility theory assumptions. Except in special cases when the indifference curves are of an implausible form, the system of double logarithmic functions does not satisfy the integrability condition and thus cannot be deduced from maximization of a utility function (Wold and Jureen 1953, pp. 105-7).

A related and more serious problem for applied work is that the Engel aggregation condition is violated. This criterion may be of little consequence when only one equation is being estimated but in a complete system, violation of the Engel aggregation condition seriously affects the internal consistency of the results. If the Engel aggregation condition is imposed, all the income elasticities = 1 (Yoshihara 1969, p. 261).

Despite the above limitations, many research workers use the double logarithmic demand function because of superior fit, ease of estimation, and the ready interpretation of the estimated parameters. Since demand parameters are often estimated from market data, it has been argued that the log-log function in some sense approximates aggregated individual maximizing behavior. This is an unsubstantiated conjecture that means the theory cannot be directly tested empirically.

EXERCISES

1. Use the definitions from Chap. 2 to show that the demand functions (4.5) for the linear expenditure system satisfy the full set of restrictions imposed by the static theory, homogeneity of degree zero in prices and income, the Cournot and the Engel aggregations, and symmetry of the matrix of substitution terms.

2. Derive the expressions for the price and income elasticities for the linear expenditure system. How do the price elasticities change for the subsistence income as a proportion of total income changes?
3. Specify the extended linear expenditure system (4.6b) (Lluch 1973). Derive the corresponding demand functions and expressions for price and income elasticities.
4. Show that the demand functions (4.11) are homogeneous of degree zero in income and prices and satisfy the Engel aggregation and the Slutsky symmetry conditions.
5. Derive the expressions for the price and income elasticities, (4.16a), (4.16b), and (4.16c) for the indirect translog utility function.
6. Several demand functions can be derived from a quadratic additive utility function developed by Johansen (see Barten 1977, p. 38). The quadratic Johansen function is

$$u = \sum_i \frac{\beta_i}{\alpha_i}\left(\frac{q_i - \gamma_i\alpha_i}{\beta_i}\right) + (1/2)\sum_i\sum_j \beta_{ij}\frac{\zeta_i\zeta_j}{\delta_i\delta_j}\left(\frac{q_i - \varepsilon_i\delta_i}{\zeta_i}\right)\left(\frac{q_j - \varepsilon_j\delta_j}{\zeta_j}\right)$$

where $\alpha_i < 1$, $\beta_i > 0$, and $\gamma_i < q_i$.

(a) Show that the direct translog utility function

$$u = k + \Sigma\, \beta_i \ell n\, q_i + (1/2) \sum_i\sum_j \beta_{ij}\ell n\, q_i \ell n\, q_j$$

is a special case of the Johansen function.

(b) Show that the Klein-Rubin utility function is a special case of the Johansen function.

(c) Show that the direct addilog utility function $u = \Sigma_i\beta_i q_i^{\alpha_i}$ is a special case of the Johansen function.

(d) What conditions must hold for the direct translog utility function (a) to reduce to a linear logarithmic function?

(e) Repeat (d) for the Klein-Rubin utility function.

(f) How do the restricted utility functions in (d) and (e) relate to the utility function $u = \pi q_i^{\beta_i}$?

(g) Derive the demand functions in (a) and (c).

7. Several demand functions can also be derived from a quadratic additive indirect utility function (see Barten 1977). The function is

$$v = \sum_i \frac{\beta_i(\alpha_i - 1)}{\alpha_i} (Z_i - \rho_i)^{\alpha_i/(\alpha_i - 1)}$$

$$+ (1/2) \sum_i \sum_j \beta_{ij} \frac{\zeta_i \zeta_j}{\delta_i \delta_j} \left(\frac{Z_i - \varepsilon_i}{\zeta_i}\right)^{\delta_i} \left(\frac{Z_j - \varepsilon_j}{\zeta_j}\right)^{\delta_j}$$

where $Z_i = p_i/(m - m_0)$, with $m_0 = (\Sigma_k \gamma_k p_k^{\nu})^{1/\nu} < m$, $\alpha_i < 1$, $\beta_i > 0$, $\rho_i < Z_i$, and γ_i are constants.

(a) Show that the indirect translog utility function (4.14) is a special case of this quadratic utility function.

(b) Show that the indirect addilog model (4.8) is a special case of this quadratic utility function.

(c) What conditions must hold for the indirect translog utility function (a) to reduce to a linear logarithmic (Cobb-Douglas) function?

(d) Derive the demand functions associated with the utility functions in (a) and (b).

REFERENCES

Barten, A. P. 1964. Consumer demand functions under conditions of almost additive preference. Econometrica 32 (Jan.-Apr.):1-38.

———. 1968. Estimating demand equations. Econometrica 36 (Apr.): 213-51.

———. 1969. Maximum likelihood estimation of a complete system of demand equations. European Economic Review 1:7-73.

———. 1977. The systems of consumer demand functions approach: A review. Econometrica 45 (Jan.):23-51.

Berndt, E. R.; Darrough, M. N.; and Diewert, W. E. 1977. Flexible functional forms and expenditure distributions: An application to canadian consumer demand functions. Discussion Paper 77-10, Department of Economics, University of British Columbia.

Blackorby, C.; Primont, D.; and Russell, R. R. 1977. On testing separability restrictions with flexible functional forms. Journal of Econometrics 5 (Mar.):195-210.

Caves, D. W., and Christensen, L. R. 1980. Global properties of flexible functional forms. American Economic Review 70 (June):422-32.

Christensen, L. R.; Jorgenson, D. N.; and Lau, L. J. 1975. Transcendental logarithmic utility functions. American Economic Review 65 (Jan.): 37-54.

Diewert, W. E. 1971. An application of the Shepard duality theorem: A generalized Leontief production function. Journal of Political Economy 79 (May-June):481-507.

———. 1973. Separability and a generalized Cobb-Douglas cost, production and utility functions. Technical Report 86, IMSS, Stanford University (Jan.):1-127.

Fortune, J. N. 1979. The translog utility function, quotas, tariffs and consumers. Canadian Journal of Economics 12 (Nov.):735-43.

Frisch, R. A. 1959. A complete scheme for computing all direct and cross demand elasticities in a model with many sectors. Econometrica 27 (Apr.):177-96.

Goldberger, A. S. 1967. Functional form and utility: A review of consumer demand theory. Social Systems Research Institute, University of Wisconsin: Systems Formulation, Methodology, and Policy Workshop Paper 6703.

Guilkey, D., and Lovell, C. A. K. 1980. On the flexibility of the translog approximation. International Economic Review 21 (Feb.):137-47.

Houthakker, H. S. 1960. Additive preferences. Econometrica 28 (Apr.): 244-57.

Klein, L. R., and Rubin, H. 1947-48. A constant utility index of the cost of living. Review of Economic Studies 15:84-7.

Lluch, C. 1973. The extended linear expenditure system. European Economic Review 15 (Apr.):21-32.

Murty, K. N. 1982. Theoretical restrictions on the parameters of indirect addilog demand equations--a comment. Econometrica 59 (Jan.):225-27.

Parks, R. W. 1969. Systems of demand equations: An empirical comparison of alternative functional forms. Econometrica 37 (Oct.):629-50.

Powell, A. A. 1966. A complete system of consumer demand equations for the australian economy fitted by a model of additive preferences. Econometrica 34 (July):661-75.

Simmons, P., and Weiserbs, W. 1979. Translog flexible functional forms and associated demand systems. American Economic Review 69 (Dec.):892-901.

Stone, R. 1954. Linear expenditure systems and demand analysis: An application to the pattern of British demand. Economic Journal 64 (Sept.):511-27.

Theil, H. 1967. Economics and Information Theory. Amsterdam: North Holland.

Theil, H., and Gabrielson, A. 1976. A critique of the translog consumption function. Report 7635, Center for Mathematical Studies in Business and Economics, University of Chicago.

Wales, T. J. 1977. On the flexibility of flexible functional forms: An empirical approach. Journal of Econometrics 5 (Mar.):183-94.

Wold, H., and Jureen, L. 1953. Demand Analysis. New York: John Wiley.

Yoshihara, K. 1969. Demand functions: An application to the Japanese expenditure pattern. Econometrica 37 (Apr.):257-74.

5 • Dynamic Demand Systems

The demand systems discussed in Chap. 4 are static because the consumer is assumed to adjust instantly to a new equilibrium when income or prices change. In reality this assumption is overly restrictive, since it ignores adjustments that occur due to habit formation and purchases of durable goods. Consequently, static models may yield results indicating that consumers are not behaving optimally when in reality the model ignores the many adjustments that occur. To overcome some of the more obvious of these deficiencies, attempts have been made to incorporate explicitly dynamic structures into demand systems specifications.

This chapter reviews the specifications and implications for selected dynamic demand systems, including the state adjustment model of Houthakker and Taylor (1970), a dynamic version of the linear expenditure system developed by Phlips (1972, 1974), and the intertemporal specification provided by Lluch (1974). In general, these systems are selected to represent dynamic models because of their comparative popularity and acceptance, their being natural extensions of the models in Chap. 4, and their representativeness of the recent work in dynamic modeling.

5.1 APPROACHES

Dynamic demand systems employ three approaches to the modeling of consumer behavior over time. The present section discusses these approaches, identifies examples of analyses that typify them, and presents the theoretical structure that has evolved to evaluate them.

The first approach includes several ad hoc specifications representing different degrees of sophistication. The simplest of these adds trend variables to the demand equations derived from the static theory. The objective, as in the Powell model, is to reflect changes in tastes and other socioeconomic factors through the trend term but an underlying theoretical justification for introducing variables in this manner is lacking. Closely related to this specification is one that introduces a trend term for the parameters of demand models (Stone et al. 1964). Results obtained are limited with respect to structural interpretation; that is, while adding such terms may improve at least short-run predictive performance of the estimated demand systems, the interpretation of the results is not constrained by an overall behavioral hypothesis. The state adjustment model of Houthakker and Taylor (1970) assumes that quantities purchased depend on existing stocks--either physical stocks of goods or psychological stocks of habits. Although this specificaltion explicitly considers the influence of past consumption behavior on current consumption patterns, it still does not introduce these factors through an overall, integrated utility maximizing framework. An underlying theoretical structure for rationalizing the introduction of habit formation into the model is still lacking.

The second approach to the problem of explaining persistence in consumption patterns follows from the use of a dynamic utility function. The utility function is made dynamic by directly incorporating changing tastes. The quadratic model of Houthakker and Taylor (1970) and the dynamic linear expenditure system of Phlips (1972, 1974) represent this approach. These models are called <u>myopic</u>, since the current expenditure allocation is assumed to be influenced by past consumption, but the effects of current expenditure allocation on future preferences are ignored. Although the utility function is dynamic, the sequential consumption decision rule implied by the methods used to estimate the parameters is not optimal.

The third approach integrates both past and future considerations into a more coherent treatment of the consumer choice problem. The allocation problem is cast into a control theory format, with the consumer attempting to maximize a discounted utility function subject to wealth and stocks constraints. The models developed by Phlips (1974), Lluch (1974), and Klijn (1977) exemplify these more realistic attempts to characterize this sequential consumption decision problem. A major limitation of these formulations is the arbitrary way that the consumers' incomplete information about the future is modeled.

5.2 STATE ADJUSTMENT MODEL

The basic structural equation (Houthakker and Taylor 1970) is

$$q_i = \theta_i + \alpha_i s_i + \kappa_i m + \nu_i p_i \tag{5.1}$$

where q_i is the rate of demand at time t; m is the rate of income at time t; p_i is the relative price at time t; s_i is the stock of the commodity at time t (may be viewed either as a physical stock in the case of durable goods or a psychological stock of habits in the case of habit forming goods); and θ, α, κ, and ν are the underlying structural parameters. According to the interpretation of the model, $\alpha > 0$ for habit forming goods and $\alpha < 0$ for durable goods. Assume further that

$$\dot{s}_i = q_i - \delta_i s_i \tag{5.2}$$

where $\dot{s}_i$ denotes the rate of change in the stock of commodity i (ds_i/dt), and δ_i is a constant depreciation rate normally taken as positive.

Equations (5.1) and (5.2) constitute the complete structure for the state adjustment model. Equation (5.1) implies that the quantity demanded is determined by the quantity in stock, price, and income, while (5.2) relates the rate of change in stock to the rate of purchase and the depreciation rate.

For empirical implementation this basic model is modified in several respects. First, note that (5.1) contains an unobservable variable, s_i, that can be eliminated by solving (5.1) for s_i and using (5.2) to obtain

$$\dot{s}_i = q_i - (\delta_i/\alpha_i)(q_i - \theta_i - \kappa_i m - \nu_i p_i) \tag{5.3}$$

It is possible to differentiate (5.1) with respect to time and use (5.3) to obtain

$$\dot{q}_i = \theta_i \delta_i + (\alpha_i - \delta_i) q_i$$

$$+ \kappa_i \dot{m} + \kappa_i \delta_i m + \nu_i \dot{p}_i + \nu_i \delta_i p_i \tag{5.4}$$

In this form the model includes only variables that are, at least in principle, observable.

Second, a discrete time version of (5.4) is required and can be generated by using differences and letting $s_{it} = (s_{it} + s_{it-1})/2$ in (5.1). Introducing these approximations and rearranging the terms provides

$$q_t = \frac{\theta\delta}{1 - (1/2)(\alpha - \delta)} \frac{1 + (1/2)(\alpha - \delta)}{1 - (1/2)(\alpha - \delta)} q_{t-1}$$

$$+ \frac{\kappa[1 + (1/2)\delta]}{1 - (1/2)(\alpha - \delta)} \Delta m_t + \frac{\kappa - \delta}{1 - (1/2)(\alpha - \delta)} m_{t-1}$$

$$+ \frac{\nu[1 + (1/2)\delta]}{1 - (1/2)(\alpha - \delta)} \Delta p_t + \frac{\nu\delta}{1 - (1/2)(\alpha - \delta)} p_{t-1} \tag{5.5a}$$

where for convenience the i subscript has been omitted.

Alternatively, (5.5a) can be rewritten

$$q_t = A_0 + A_1 q_{t-1} + A_2 \Delta m_t + A_3 m_{t-1} + A_4 \Delta p_t + A_5 p_{t-1} \quad (5.5b)$$

with the commodity subscript i again omitted. The structural parameters are determined from (5.5b) using the algebraic correspondences

$$\theta = \frac{2A_0[A_2 - (1/2)A_3]}{A_3(A_1 + 1)} \quad (5.6a)$$

$$\alpha = \frac{2(A_1 - 1)}{A_1 + 1} + \frac{A_3}{A_2 - (1/2)A_3} \quad (5.6b)$$

$$\kappa = \frac{2[A_2 - (1/2)A_3]}{A_1 + 1} \quad (5.6c)$$

$$\nu = \frac{2[A_4 - (1/2)A_5]}{A_1 + 1} \quad (5.6d)$$

$$\delta = \frac{A_3}{A_2 - (1/2)A_3} = \frac{A_5}{A_4 - (1/2)A_5} \quad (5.6e)$$

Note that the method results in two estimates for δ_i; this is apparent from (5.6e). Unfortunately, the estimators for δ_i are not necessarily the same. To overcome this problem (5.5b) is estimated subject to the constraint

$$A_2 A_5 = A_3 A_4 \quad (5.7)$$

assuring a unique estimator for δ_i.

The short-run derivatives of consumption with respect to income and price are given by κ and ν, respectively, since it is assumed that stocks do not have a chance to adjust in the short run.

Long-run derivatives are obtained by assuming that in the limit (5.2) takes the form

$$\dot{s}_i = q_i - \delta_i s_i = 0 \quad (5.8)$$

implying that the stock adjustment has reached an equilibrium state, with the quantity acquired just equal to the amount depreciated. Substitution of (5.8) into (5.1) gives

$$q_i = \theta_i + (\alpha_i/\delta_i)q_i + \kappa_i m + \nu_i p_i \tag{5.9}$$

or simplifying,

$$q_i = \frac{\theta_i \delta_i}{\delta_i - \alpha_i} + \frac{\kappa_i \delta_i}{\delta_i - \alpha_i} m + \frac{\nu_i \delta_i}{\delta_i - \alpha_i} p_i \tag{5.10}$$

Assuming that $\delta_i \neq \alpha_i$, the long-run derivatives of consumption with respect to income and price are given by coefficients of m and p, respectively, in (5.10). Note that the relationship between the short-and long-run price derivatives is the same as between the short- and long-run income derivatives, with $\delta_i/(\delta_i - \alpha_i)$ the constant factor.

The results from applications of this model must be put into perspective, because the model is not derived from a utility maximization framework and the demand equations are estimated separately rather than simultaneously, as they are in a complete system. Thus, there is no reason to assume that hypotheses tests conducted in the context of this model have theoretical implications. While it may be practical, the model has very important limitations as an empirical construct to evaluate or use the theory.

5.3 LINEAR EXPENDITURE SYSTEM: A DYNAMIC VERSION

Recall that the static linear expenditure system (LES) is derived from a Klein-Rubin utility function, (4.1),

$$u = \mu' \log(q - \gamma) \tag{5.11a}$$

where $\mu = [\mu_i]'$ and $\gamma = [\gamma_i]'$ are parameters to be estimated with $0 < \mu_i < 1$, $\iota'\mu = 1$, and $(q - \gamma) > 0$. Assume that the elements of the parameter vector γ are related to certain state variables, say $s = [s_i]'$, according to the linear function

$$\gamma = \theta + \bar{\alpha}s \tag{5.12}$$

where $\theta = [\theta_i]'$ and $\alpha = [\alpha_i]'$ are constants that may take positive or negative values. Following the already employed notational convention, $\bar{\alpha}$ denotes an n x n diagonal matrix with nonzero elements given by the vector α. Assume further that

$$\dot{s} = q - \bar{\delta}s \tag{5.13}$$

where $\dot{s} = [\dot{s}_i]'$ denotes an n-element vector of the rate of change in stock around time t and $\delta = [\delta_i]'$ is a constant depreciation rate, normally taken as positive.

Redefining the utility function (5.11a) on the basis of a substitution for γ from (5.12) yields

$$u = \mu' \log(q - \theta - \bar{\alpha}s) \tag{5.11b}$$

Maximizing the utility function (5.11b) subject to the budget constraint $p'q = m$ results in first order conditions

$$[\bar{q} - (\theta + \bar{\alpha}s)]^{-1}\mu - \lambda p = 0 \tag{5.14}$$

$$p'q - m = 0 \tag{5.15}$$

To obtain the demand functions for the dynamic LES, first solve (5.14) for μ:

$$\mu = \lambda[\bar{q} - (\theta + \bar{\alpha}s)]p = \lambda\bar{p}[q - (\theta + \bar{\alpha}s)] \tag{5.16}$$

On premultiplying (5.14) by the sum vector ι', making use of $p'q = m$, and rearranging the terms, it follows that

$$\lambda = (\iota'\mu)[m - p'(\theta + \bar{\alpha}s)]^{-1} \tag{5.17}$$

Inserting (5.17) into (5.16) and solving for q gives demand functions

$$q = \theta + \bar{\alpha}s + (\iota'\mu)^{-1}\bar{p}^{-1}\mu[m - p'(\theta + \bar{\alpha}s)]$$

$$= \theta + \bar{\alpha}s + \mu/(\lambda\bar{p}) \tag{5.18a}$$

where it will be assumed that $\mu > 0$, $\iota'\mu \neq 1$, and $q - (\theta + \bar{\alpha}s) > 0$. For reference the ith equation in the system of demand equations shown in (5.18a) is

$$q_i = [\mu_i/(p_i\Sigma\mu_i)][m - \sum_j p_j(\theta_j + \alpha_i s_j)] + \theta_i + \alpha_i s_i$$

$$= \theta_i + \alpha_i s_i + \mu_i/\lambda p_i \qquad (i = 1, 2, \ldots, n) \tag{5.18b}$$

The functions in (5.18b) are considered short-run demand equations. Corresponding long-run demand equations are now derived. Assume that in the adjustment (5.13) takes the stationary form

$$\dot{s}_i = q_i - \delta_i s_i = 0 \qquad (i = 1, 2, \ldots, n)$$

or more simply, $q_i = \delta_i s_i$. Replacing s_i by q_i/δ_i in (5.18b), multiplying (5.18b) by p_i, making use of $\Sigma\, p_i q_i = m$, and rearranging the terms results in the expression for the system of long-run demand equations

$$q_i^* = \frac{\delta_i\mu_i/(\delta_i - \alpha_i)}{p_i \sum_j \delta_j\mu_j/(\delta_j - \alpha_j)}\left[m - \sum_j p_j \frac{(\delta_j\theta_j)}{\delta_j - \alpha_j}\right] + \frac{\delta_i\theta_i}{\delta_i - \alpha_i} \tag{5.19}$$

or more simply,

$$q_i^* = \gamma_i^* + (\mu_i^*/p_i)(m - \sum_j p_i\gamma_j^*) \tag{5.20}$$

where

$$\gamma_i^* = \frac{\delta_i\theta_i}{\delta_i - \alpha_i} \quad \text{and} \quad \mu_i^* = \frac{\delta_i\mu_i/(\delta_i - \alpha_i)}{\Sigma_j\delta_j\mu_j/(\delta_j - \alpha_j)}$$

Note that γ_i^* is the long-run counterpart of the short-run parameter θ_i. Moreover, $\gamma_i^* > \theta_i$ when $\alpha_i > 0$, that is, commodity i is habit forming; $\gamma_i^* < \theta_i$ when $\alpha_i < 0$, that is, commodity i is durable; and μ_i^* is the long-run marginal budget share satisfying the condition $\Sigma_i\mu_i^* = 1$.

From (5.18b) and (5.20) the short-run and long-run demand elasticities can be derived. The short-run derivative of consumption with respect to income is

$$\frac{\partial q_i}{\partial m} = \mu_i/[(\sum_j \mu_j)p_i] \tag{5.21}$$

Hence the short-run income elasticity is

$$\eta_i = \mu_i/[\sum_j \mu_j)w_i] \tag{5.22}$$

where w_i is again the ith expenditure proportion. The short-run derivative of consumption with respect to price is

$$\frac{\partial q_i}{\partial p_i} = \{-q_i + (\theta_i + \alpha_i s_i) - \mu_i/[(\sum_j \mu_j)(\theta_j + \alpha_j s_j)]\}/p_i \tag{5.23}$$

To obtain the short-run price elasticity, solve (5.18b) for $\theta_i + \alpha_i s_i$ to obtain

$$\theta_i + \alpha_i s_i = q_i - \frac{\mu_i}{p_i(\Sigma\,\mu_i)}[m - \sum_i p_i(\theta_i + \alpha_i s_i)] = \frac{\mu_i}{\lambda p_i} = \gamma_i \tag{5.24}$$

Substituting (5.24) into (5.23), using the usual elasticity formula, and rearranging the terms provides an expression for the short-run own price elasticity for the commodity that is the familiar form

$$e_{ii} = -1 + [1 - (\mu_i/\Sigma\, \mu_j)](\gamma_i/q_i) \tag{5.25}$$

The cross price elasticities can be similarly developed and are expressed

$$e_{ij} = -(\mu_i/\Sigma\, \mu_j)[p_j\gamma_j/(p_iq_i)] \qquad (i \neq j) \tag{5.26}$$

Expressions for the long-run income and price elasticities are similarly derived by differentiating (5.20) and using the usual elasticity formula. Note that (5.22), (5.25), and (5.26) have exactly the same structure as those obtained for the static linear expenditure system; however, the estimated parameter values are different because of addition of the dynamic adjustment mechanism.

For empirical work, (5.18a) is modified in two respects: (1) The unobservable state variables s are eliminated and (2) the model is approximated by one involving a discrete time interval (Phlips 1974, p. 190). After making these adjustments, the equations in the approximated demand system are

$$q_{it} = \frac{2\delta_i\theta_i}{2 - \alpha_i + \delta_i} + \frac{2 + \alpha_i - \delta_i}{2 - \alpha_i + \delta_i} q_{it-1} + \frac{\mu_i(\delta_i + 2)}{2 - \alpha_i + \delta_i} \frac{1}{\lambda_t p_{it}} + \frac{\mu_i(\delta_i - 2)}{2 - \alpha_i + \delta_i} \frac{1}{\lambda_{t-1} p_{it-1}} \tag{5.27a}$$

$$= k_{i0} + k_{i1}q_{it-1} + k_{i2}\frac{1}{\lambda_t p_{it}} + k_{i3}\frac{1}{\lambda_{t-1}p_{it-1}} \tag{5.27b}$$

where the values for the newly defined parameters k_{i0}, k_{i1}, k_{i2}, and k_{i3} are indicated by comparing (5.27a) and (5.27b). Solving for the structural coefficients in terms of the newly defined composite parameters yields

$$\delta_i = 2(k_{i2} + k_{i3})/(k_{i2} - k_{i3}) \tag{5.28}$$

$$\mu_i = (k_{i2} - k_{i3})/(1 + k_{i1}) \tag{5.29}$$

$$\alpha_i = 2(k_{i2} + k_{i3})/(k_{i2} - k_{i3}) - 2(1 - k_{i1})/(1 + k_{i1}) \tag{5.30}$$

$$\theta_i = k_{i0}(k_{i2} - k_{i3})/[(1 + k_{i1})(k_{i2} + k_{i3})] \tag{5.31}$$

The structural coefficients can be clearly calculated from the estimated regression coefficients for (5.27b); that is, the complete set of demand parameters in the dynamic linear expenditure model can be estimated with 4n coefficients. It can be shown that the demand equations in the dynamic linear expenditure model are homogeneous of degree zero in income and all prices and satisfy the Engel aggregation and Slutsky symmetry conditions (Phlips 1974, p. 183).

5.4 INTERTEMPORAL DEMAND SYSTEMS

The approach discussed here is based on Klijn's (1977) modification of Lluch's (1974) original formulation. Lluch's original model had an erroneous wealth constraint that affected some, but not all, of his results.
In an intertemporal framework the consumer choice problem is to find that time path of consumption, q(t) $(0 < t < \infty)$ such that

$$\int_0^{\infty} e^{-\iota t} u[q(t), s(t)]dt \tag{5.32}$$

is maximized, subject to

$$w + \int_0^{\infty} e^{-\rho t} m(t)dt = p' \int_0^{\infty} e^{-\rho t} q(t)dt$$

$$\dot{s}(t) = q(t) - \bar{\delta} s(t), \quad s(0) = s$$

given $[\rho, \iota, m(t), p, \bar{\delta}]$ and where

- q(t) = an n x 1 vector of consumption values at time t
- s(t) = an n x 1 vector of psychological stock of habits at time t
- w(t) = wealth [w(0) = w]
- ρ = discount rate
- p(t) = an n x 1 vector of commodity prices at time t
- m(t) = consumer income at time t
- ι = constant rate of time preference
- $\bar{\delta}$ = n x n diagonal matrix of constant depreciation or "memory loss" rates

According to (5.32) the consumer attempts to maximize a discounted utility function subject to two constraints. The first is the lifetime budget constraint while $\dot{s}(t)$ is the vector valued function describing the change in the state variables. The instantaneous utility function u(·) is expressed as a function of consumption rates and stocks. The control problem with an integral constraint is known as the <u>isoperimetric</u> problem (Intriligator 1971, pp. 317-18).

Phlips (1974) assumes that the consumer follows a strategy of consistent planning with respect to future prices, income, and preferences. Strotz (1955-56) says that the consumer only selects a consumption plan without regard for future consequences. This approach differs from that of Lluch (1974) and Klijn (1977), who assume that the consumer only considers the first period in the time horizon as real time and the remaining periods as planning time. For each time period the consumer faces a different type of choice problem described by (5.32). This approach is more plausible for nondurable commodities, since replanning can be considered an essentially zero cost activity.

If Lluch's approach is taken, the Hamiltonian corresponding to the problem given in (5.32) is

$$H = e^{-lt}u[q(t), s(t)] - \xi e^{-\rho t}[m(t) - p'q(t)]$$

$$+ \psi'(t)[q(t) - \bar{\delta}s(t)] \quad (5.33)$$

where $\psi(t)$ is an n x 1 vector of auxiliary variables associated with the vector function $\dot{s}(t)$ and ξ is the auxiliary variable associated with the lifetime budget constraint.

For the path $q(t)(0 \leq t < \infty)$ to be an optimum, the set of necessary conditions is

$$e^{-lt}\frac{\partial u}{\partial q}(t) + \psi(t) = \xi e^{-\rho t}p \quad \text{for all } t \quad (0 \leq t < \infty) \quad (5.34a)$$

$$w + L(m) = p'L(q) \quad (5.34b)$$

$$\dot{s} = q(t) - \bar{\delta}s(t), \qquad s(0) = s \quad (5.34c)$$

$$\dot{\psi}(t) = \bar{\delta}\psi(t) - e^{-lt}(\partial u/\partial s)(t) \quad (5.34d)$$

where the notation $L(x) = \int_0^\infty e^{-\rho t}x(t)dt$ denotes present values with ρ the discount rate. For a discussion of the maximum principle of control theory see Arrow and Kurz (1970) and Intriligator (1971). Klijn (1977) points out that these necessary conditions do not uniquely determine the optimal control, contrary to Lluch's (1974) claim.

The set of first order conditions can be given an economic interpretation. For optimal behavior, (5.34a) states that the discounted marginal utility, the consumption component, $e^{-lt}(\partial u/\partial q)(t)$, plus the component derived from net additions to the stock of habits, $\psi(t)$ per unit of expenditure must be the same for all commodities. By dividing both sides of (5.34a) by price p, (5.34b) is the lifetime budget constraint facing the consumer. The left-hand side consists of initial wealth and L(m) the discounted rate of future labor income. Equation (5.34b) states that this must be equal to the present value of consumption expenditures p'L(q). The notation L(x) represents the present value of x and (5.34c) is the constraint describing the change in habits with respect to time. Finally, (5.34d) represents the time rate of change in the implicit utility valuations of the stock of habits $\psi(t)$ and is analogous to the concept of shadow prices or opportunity costs in linear programming.

By differentiating (5.34a) and using (5.34c) and (5.34d), a system of differential equations of demand under habit formation can be obtained. The system is

$$\frac{\partial^2 u(t)}{\partial q^2}\dot{q}(t) = \frac{\partial u(t)}{\partial s} + (\iota + \bar{\delta})\frac{\partial u(t)}{\partial q} - \frac{\partial^2 u(t)}{\partial q \partial s}[q(t) - \bar{\delta}s(t)]$$

$$- (\rho + \bar{\delta})\lambda^{e(\iota-\rho)t}p \qquad (5.35)$$

where $\lambda(t) = \xi e^{-\rho t}$ and $\lambda(0) = \lambda$. From (5.35) the necessary conditions can be expressed as

$$\dot{s}(t) = q(t) - \bar{\delta}s(t), \qquad s(0) = s \qquad (5.36a)$$

$$\dot{q}(t) = g[q(t), s(t), \lambda, t] \qquad (5.36b)$$

$$w + L(m) = p'L(q) \qquad (5.36c)$$

The time path of $[q(t), s(t)]$ can be obtained from (5.36a, 5.36b, and 5.36c).

For an instantaneous Klein-Rubin utility function of the form

$$u[q(t), s(t)] = \sum_{i=1}^{n} \mu_i \log x_i(t) \qquad (5.37)$$

where the subsistence quantity is postulated to be a linear function of habits, that is,

$$x_i(t) = q_i(t) - \alpha_i s(t) - \theta_i \qquad (5.38)$$

the necessary conditions can be shown (Lluch 1974, pp. 788-93) to yield a demand system given by

$$p_i x_i = \tilde{\mu}_i \Sigma p_i x_i \qquad (5.39)$$

where $\tilde{\mu}_i = \mu_i(1 - \xi_i)(1 - \Sigma\mu_i\xi_i)^{-1}$ and $\xi_i = \alpha_i(\rho + \delta)^{-1}$. This system characterizes demand behavior at the beginning of an optimal consumption plan under the Klein-Rubin utility function modified to allow for habit formation (Lluch 1974).

Recently Dixon and Lluch (1977) have modified this intertemporal approach to cover the case of durables. Their

TABLE 5.1 A summary of demand systems characteristics

Demand System	Utility Function	Functional Form	Constraints: Engel	Constraints: Symmetry	Constraints: Homogeneity	Elasticity: Income (η_i)	Elasticity: Price (e_{ii})	Number of Parameters Estimated
Linear expenditure	$u = \mu'\log(q-\gamma)$	$\bar{p}q = \bar{p}\gamma+(m-p\gamma)\mu$	Holds	Holds	Holds	μ_i/w_i	$-1+(1-\mu_i)\frac{\gamma_i}{q_i}$	2n
Indirect addilog	$u^* = \sum_i a_i(m/p_i)^{b_i}$	$q_i = \frac{a_ib_i(m/p_i)^{1+b_i}}{\sum_j a_jb_j(m/p_j)^{b_j}}$	Holds	Holds	Holds	$(1+b_i)-\sum_j b_jw_j$	$-(1+b_i)+b_iw_i$	2n
Indirect translog	$\ln u^* = \sigma_0+\sum_i\sigma_i\ln(p_i/m)$ $+1/2\sum_i\sum_j\beta_{ij}\ln(p_i/m)\ln(p_j/m)$	$\frac{p_iq_i}{m} = \frac{\sigma_i+\sum_j\beta_{ij}\ln(p_j/m)}{\sum_j\sigma_j+\sum_j\sum_i\beta_{ij}\ln(p_j/m)}$	Holds	Holds	Holds	$1+\frac{-\sum_j\beta_{ji}/w_i+\sum_i\sum_j\beta_{ij}}{1+\sum_i\sum_j\beta_{ij}\ln(p_j/m)}$	$\frac{-1+\beta_{ii}/w_i-\sum_j\beta_{ji}}{1+\sum_i\sum_j\beta_{ij}\ln(p_j/m)}$	(n-1)(2n+1)[a]
Rotterdam	. . .	$w^*_{it}\Delta(\ln q_{it}) = \phi\mu_i(\Delta(\ln p_{it})$ $-\sum_k\mu_k\Delta(\ln p_{\cdot t}))+\mu_i\Delta(\ln q_t)$	Holds	Holds	Holds	μ_i/w_i	$\phi\eta_i-\eta_iw_i(1+\phi\eta_i)$	n+1
Powell	. . .	$p_iq_i = \sum_j a_{ij}p_j+\mu_im+c_it$	Holds	Holds[b]	Holds[b]	μ_i/w_i	$(\chi\mu_i\mu_i-\mu_i\hat{p}_i\hat{q}_i)/\hat{p}_i\hat{q}_i$ $-\chi\delta_{ij}\mu_i/\hat{p}_i\hat{q}_i$	n+1
Double logarithmic	. . .	$q_i = A_im\eta_i\Pi p_j^{e_{ij}}$	. . .	. . .	. . .	η_i	e_{ii}	n^2+n
State adjustment	. . .	$q_i = \theta_i+\alpha_is+\kappa_im+\nu_ip$	. . .	. . .	. . .	(SR) $\kappa_i\frac{m}{q_i}$ (LR) $\frac{\kappa_i\delta_i}{\delta_i-\alpha_i}\frac{m}{q_i}$	(SR) $\nu_i\frac{p_i}{q_i}$ (LR) $\frac{\nu_i\delta_i}{\delta_i-\alpha_i}\cdot\frac{p_i}{q_i}$	5n
Linear expenditure (dynamic)	$u = \mu'\log(q-\theta-\bar{\alpha}s)$	$q = (\theta+\bar{\alpha}s)$ $+(\iota'\mu)^{-1}\bar{p}^{-1}$ $\mu(m-p'(\theta+\bar{\alpha}))$	Holds	Holds	Holds	(SR) $\mu_i/(\Sigma\mu_i)w_i$ (LR) μ_i^*/w_i	(SR) $\phi\eta_i-\eta_iw_i(1+\phi\eta_i)$ (LR) $-1+(1-\mu_i^*)\frac{\gamma_i^*}{q_i}$	4n

[a]Unrestricted.

[b]Homogeneity and symmetry are approximately satisfied.

modifications include replacing the psychological stock of habits constraint under (5.32) with a durable goods constraint. The time rate of change for planned holdings of durables is assumed to decay exponentially. Although a treatment of durables in demand systems is certainly needed, there have been difficulties in obtaining meaningful empirical estimates of these specifications (Fisher et al. 1979; McAleer and Gorman 1979).

5.5 A SYNTHESIS

Results for the demand systems discussed here and in Chap. 4 are summarized in Table 5.1, which gives the utility function assumed (where appropriate), the functional form for the equations in the demand system, an evaluation of whether the constraints imposed by the theory are satisfied, expressions for the price and income elasticities, the number of parameters to be estimated. It provides an easy reference for evaluating alternative, commonly used empirical demand systems. Each approach has advantages, but the important point is that each has certain theoretical and empirical implications that should be reflected in interpreting applied results.

EXERCISES

1. The state adjustment and dynamic linear expenditure models have expression denoting the time rate of change in the stock (of habits), $\dot{s}_i = q_i - \delta_i s_i$. Rewrite this equation as $q_i = \delta_i s_i + \dot{s}_i$ and interpret the two components of consumption in economic terms.
2. Derive the price and income elasticities for the state adjustment model.
3. How do habits affect the price and income elasticities in the state adjustment model? Obtain expressions for $\partial e_{ii}/\partial s_i$ and $\partial \eta_i/\partial s_i$.
4. Repeat Exs. 2 and 3 for the dynamic linear expenditure system.
5. Are the state adjustment and dynamic linear expenditure systems homogeneous of degree zero in income and all prices? What does it mean for a dynamic demand function to be homogeneous of degree zero in all prices and income; that is, how does one treat the lagged variables included in the dynamic specifications? In your answer consider short-run conditioned expressions and long-run or steady state versions of the models.
6. For the intertemporal demand system, explain Phlips's approach. What does it mean for a consumer to select a consumption plan to follow without regard for future

consequences? When would this be and not be a good approximation of consumer behavior?

7. Describe Lluch and Klijn's approach. What does it mean for a consumer to consider only the first period in the time horizon as real time and the remaining periods as planning time?
8. How do the models for Exs. 6 and 7 differ? In a choice theoretic framework explain how you would model the two approaches, assuming an adjustment cost term in the utility function.
9. What are the incentives for deferred consumption in these models? Analyze the treatment of saving in the three dynamic models.
10. Consider the following additive quadratic utility function:

$$u = a'q + b's + (1/2)q'Aq + q'Bs + (1/2)s'Cs$$

where a and b are constant vectors; A, B, and C are constant diagonal matrices; and q and s are as previously defined.

(a) Maximize u subject to the budget constraint and derive the estimating equations for the dynamic quadratic model.
(b) Using the results in (a), obtain expressions for the structural coefficients a, A, B, and D.
(c) Derive the short and long-run effects of changes in prices and income.
(d) What are the stability conditions for the dynamic linear expenditure system and the dynamic quadratic model? Explain the implications on long-run price and income effects if stability conditions are not satisfied.

REFERENCES

Arrow, K., and Kurz, M. 1969. Optimal consumer allocation over an infinite horizon. Journal of Economic Theory 1 (June):68-91.

Dixon, P. B., and Lluch, C. 1977. Durable goods in the extended linear expenditure system. Review of Economic Studies 44 (June):381-84.

Fisher, G.; McAleer, M.; and Whistler, D. 1979. A note on problems of estimating the linear expenditure system and its related forms. Discussion Paper No. 355, Institute for Economic Research, Queen's University, Kingston, Ontario, Canada.

Houthakker, H. S., and Taylor, L. D. 1970. Consumer Demand in the United States, 2d ed. Cambridge, Mass.: Harvard University Press.

Intriligator, M. D. 1971. Mathematical Optimization and

Economic Theory. Englewood Cliffs, N.J.: Prentice-Hall.

Klijn, N. 1977. Expenditure, savings and habit formation: A comment. International Economic Review 18 (Oct.):771-78.

Lluch, C. 1974. Expenditure, savings and habit formation. International Economic Review 15 (Oct.):786-97.

McAleer, M., and Gorman, I. E. 1979. Durable goods in the extended linear expenditure system: An empirical appraisal. Discussion Paper No. 333, Institute for Economic Research, Queen's University, Kingston, Ontario, Canada.

Phlips, L. 1972. A dynamic version of the linear expenditure model. Review of Economics and Statistics 64 (Nov.):450-58.

———. 1974. Applied Consumption Analysis. Amsterdam: North-Holland.

Stone, R.; Brown, A.; and Row, D. A. 1964. Demand analysis and projections for Britain 1900-1970: A study in method. In Europe's Future Consumption, ed. J. Sandie, pp. 200-25. Amsterdam: North Holland.

Strotz, R. H. 1955-56. Myopia and inconsistency in dynamic utility maximization. Review of Economic Studies 23:165-80.

6 • Nonlinear Estimation

The systems of demand equations presented in Chaps. 4 and 5 are estimable on the basis of sample time series data. While this proposition is true in principle, the actual estimation process for these equation systems presents important difficulties because the demand systems, particularly with autocorrelation and habit formation (Chap. 8), are nonlinear in the parameters. As a consequence, least squares and maximum likelihood methods cannot be directly applied to yield expressions for the estimators that are linear functions of the observed random variables. Instead, parameter values implied by nonlinear first order conditions for minimizing the sum of squared residuals or maximizing the value of the likelihood function must be numerically approximated. Serious problems are associated with the choice of approximation methods and their application when errors are not identically and independently distributed and parameters are restricted.

This chapter presents a survey of approaches to nonlinear estimation, reviews existing results of comparative performances of computational algorithms, and assesses their applicability to nonlinear estimation problems for systems of demand equations. This final objective is the most important. Useful surveys of nonlinear estimation methods already exist, although for different purposes (Malinvaud 1970b; Goldfeld and Quandt 1972; Bard 1974; Gallant 1975; Judge et al. 1980). Evaluations of available computational approaches are highly specialized (Bard 1970; Himmelblau 1972; Murry 1972; Parkinson and Hutchinson 1972). The emphasis here is on the problem of adapting these general results to demand systems estimation problems, both from a conceptual and from a computational viewpoint.

Specification of the nonlinear optimization problem in general form is presented and selected approaches for obtaining parameter estimates and approximating their variance covariance matrices are briefly discussed. Computational and convergence results are evaluated in the next section, followed by a short discussion of numerical differentiation. Finally, two sections on applications to demand systems are included, which consider (1) the problem specified with independently and identically distributed disturbances for the component equations and (2) more complex disturbance generating processes, the imposition of parameter restrictions, and tests of hypotheses for selected demand systems.

6.1 NONLINEAR ESTIMATION

The statement and analysis of nonlinear estimation problems has been facilitated by a linear pseudomodel (Malinvaud 1970b). This concept suggests a number of useful parallels to linear models and linear estimators that are familiar in econometric literature. The pseudolinear model allows us to take advantage of the intuition that has evolved from widespread use of least squares and maximum likelihood estimators for linear statistical models.

6.1.1 Problem and Pseudolinear Model

The multivariate linear regression model can be represented

$$y = X\beta + \varepsilon \tag{6.1}$$

where y is a T x 1 vector of observable random variables, X is a matrix of T observations on K conditioning variables, β is a conformably defined parameter vector, and ε is a vector of non-observable disturbance terms that are assumed identically and independently distributed with mean zero and variance $\sigma^2 I$. The least squares estimator for parameter vector β is

$$\hat{\beta} = (X'X)^{-1}X'y \tag{6.2}$$

The residual estimation for σ^2 is

$$\hat{\sigma}^2 = \hat{\varepsilon}'\hat{\varepsilon}/(T - K) \tag{6.3}$$

where $\hat{\varepsilon} = y - X\hat{\beta}$. The estimators $\hat{\beta}$ and σ^2 are unbiased and consistent. The variance of β, $\text{Var}(\hat{\beta}) = \sigma^2(X'X)^{-1}$, is the smallest among the linear unbiased estimators for β (Schmidt 1976).

The model for the nonlinear estimation problem in y and X is

$$y = f(X, \beta) + \varepsilon \tag{6.4}$$

where f is an arbitrary real valued function defined by the elements of the parameter vector β. There is no reason for vector

β in (6.4) to be of dimension K as was assumed in (6.1). However, for now it will be presumed so without loss of generality.

A Taylor's series approximation of the nonlinear term $f(X, \beta)$ in (6.4) is

$$f(X, \beta) \doteq f(X, \beta_0) + (\partial f/\partial \beta)\big|_{\beta_0}(\beta - \beta_0) \tag{6.5}$$

at the assumed value for β, β_0. Observe that the remainder defined by the higher order derivatives evaluated at β_0 has been omitted. If this expansion is sufficiently local, the associated approximated value for $f(X, \beta)$ can be claimed arbitrarily close to the true value of the function. The new term introduced in expression (6.5) is the partial derivative of the vector valued function $f(X, \beta)$ with respect to β evaluated at β_0 or $(\partial f/\partial \beta)|_{\beta_0}$. Since $f(X, \beta)$ is a vector valued function, the derivative will have K terms for each sample value. Let the matrix of these values be $X(\beta_0)$; thus, $X(\beta_0)$ is a T x K matrix.

Using (6.5) and (6.1), the nonlinear model can be rewritten

$$y_0 = X(\beta_0)\beta + \varepsilon \tag{6.6}$$

where y_0 is an approximation of y, that is,

$$y_0 = y - f(X, \beta_0) + X(\beta_0)\beta_0 \tag{6.7}$$

Expression (6.6) is called the <u>linear pseudomodel</u>. Clearly, it will yield estimators for β by application of standard least squares methods if the rank of $X(\beta_0)$ is K. These estimators are a function of the value β_0, for β, employed in (6.5). The least squares estimator for β from (6.6) is $\hat{\beta}_0$ and, corresponding to (6.2), can be written

$$\hat{\beta}_0 = [X(\beta_0)'X(\beta_0)]^{-1}[X(\beta_0)'y_0] \tag{6.8}$$

Similarly, it has variance covariance matrix

$$\mathrm{Var}(\hat{\beta}_0) = \sigma^2[X(\beta_0)'X(\beta_0)]^{-1} \tag{6.9}$$

The residual estimator, $\hat{\sigma}_0^2$ for σ_0^2, is

$$\hat{\sigma}_0^2 = \hat{\varepsilon}_0'\hat{\varepsilon}_0/(T - K) \tag{6.10}$$

where $\hat{\varepsilon}_0 = y - \hat{y}_0 = y - X(\beta_0)\hat{\beta}_0$.

The analogy to ordinary least squares estimation in the linear model should now be apparent. If a method of selecting successive values of β_0 can be determined that converges to a minimum for $\hat{\sigma}_0^2$, then the estimators $\hat{\beta}_0$, $\mathrm{Var}(\hat{\beta}_0)$, and $\hat{\sigma}_0^2$ will approximate the maximum likelihood and least squares estimators for the nonlinear model (6.4) (Malinvaud 1970b, Lutkepohl 1980).

This framework for representing the nonlinear estimation problem can be conveniently generalized to the cases of nonspherical disturbances and linear restrictions on the parameter vector β. Most important, when we have iterated to an optimal estimator for β (the final $\hat{\beta}_0$), the results in equations (6.8), (6.9), and (6.10) provide workable expressions for use in prediction and hypotheses testing.

6.1.2 Nonlinear Estimators and Nonspherical Disturbances

The results in Sec. 6.1.1 can be directly generalized to the case of nonspherical disturbances by analogy to least squares and maximum likelihood estimation using the linear pseudomodel. The estimator developed is a member of the class of feasible generalized least squares estimators; that is, it follows from a two step process where the residuals are first estimated and then employed to estimate the parameters of the variance covariance matrix. The corresponding estimated variance covariance matrix is in turn used to obtain the feasible generalized least squares estimation for β. An alternative approach is to solve simultaneously for the parameters of the variance covariance matrix and the vector β. In practice and for complex covariance structures this approach is not attractive because the nonlinear estimation problems in β alone commonly stretch the capacity of available computer algorithms.

The nonspherical disturbance vector ε is assumed to have expectation zero and variance covariance matrix

$$E(\varepsilon\varepsilon') = \sigma^2\Omega \tag{6.11}$$

with Ω positive definite. The model to be estimated is thus the same as in (6.4) but with the covariance matrix for the disturbances given by (6.11). Sound prior reasoning must underlie the parametric structure for Ω. In nonlinear estimation, exploratory specifications for Ω can be quite expensive and the procedure is bad statistical practice. For demand systems estimation, the rationalization of the structure for Ω is typically provided by observed persistence in consumption behavior.

The two step feasible generalized least squares estimator is obtained using the residuals

$$\hat{\varepsilon}_0 = y - \hat{y}_0 \tag{6.12}$$

corresponding to the final iteration for the estimation problem without the assumption of nonspherical disturbances. Based on the assumed structure for Ω, the estimator $\hat{\varepsilon}_0$ is processed to estimate the parameters $\hat{\Omega}(\hat{\beta}_0)$ defining Ω. The second step is to calculate a new estimator for β:

$$\tilde{\beta}_0 = [X(\hat{\beta}_0)'\hat{\Omega}^{-1}(\hat{\beta}_0)X(\hat{\beta}_0)]^{-1}[X(\hat{\beta}_0)'\hat{\Omega}^{-1}(\hat{\beta}_0)y_0] \quad (6.13)$$

This estimator is designed to minimize

$$\tilde{\sigma}_0^2 = \hat{\varepsilon}_0'\hat{\Omega}^{-1}(\hat{\beta}_0)\hat{\varepsilon}_0/(T - K) \quad (6.14)$$

the generalized least squares estimator for the error sum of squares. The variance covariance matrix for this final round estimator is

$$\mathrm{Var}(\tilde{\beta}_0) = \sigma_0^2[X(\hat{\beta}_0)'\Omega^{-1}(\hat{\beta}_0)X(\hat{\beta}_0)]^{-1} \quad (6.15)$$

This estimation process can be reinitialized using the new estimator for the residuals leading to a new estimator for Ω, say $\Omega(\hat{\beta}_0)$. Then $X(\tilde{\beta}_0)$ can be defined to correspond to $X(\hat{\beta}_0)$. In general, however, there is no reason to iterate the two stage estimation because the large sample properties that can be claimed for $\tilde{\beta}_0$ and $\tilde{\sigma}_0^2$ hold after the first application of the two step or feasible generalized least squares process. For small samples the results may justify such iterations; however, no general propositions available now unambiguously affirm this supposition.

6.1.3 Linear Restrictions and Nonlinear Estimation

The linear restrictions on the structural parameters β are assumed to be

$$R\beta = r \quad (6.16)$$

where R is a $(J < K) \times K$ matrix and r is a $J \times 1$ column vector of constants, each of which, of course, can be and frequently is zero. If the restrictions are nonlinear, they can be linearized using methods identical to those suggested for construction of the linear pseudomodel in Sec. 6.1.1. They would then be linear pseudorestrictions and interpreted as the linear pseudomodel.

The restricted least squares estimator for the parameters from (6.1) under the exact linear restrictions (6.16) is

$$\hat{\beta}_R = \hat{\beta} + (X'X)^{-1}R'[R(X'X)^{-1}R']^{-1}(r - R\hat{\beta}) \quad (6.17)$$

The covariance matrix for this estimator $\hat{\beta}_R$ is shown to be (Theil 1971)

$$\mathrm{Var}(\hat{\beta}_R) = \mathrm{Var}(\hat{\beta}) - \mathrm{Var}(\hat{\beta})R'[R\ \mathrm{Var}(\hat{\beta})R']^{-1}R\ \mathrm{Var}(\hat{\beta}) \tag{6.18}$$

The estimator $\hat{\beta}_R$ is unbiased and efficient if the restrictions are unbiased. These results can be extended to encompass bias in the restrictions (6.16), but such extensions and associated developments on biased estimation are outside the purview of this discussion (Judge et al. 1980).

The analogy to the results in Sec. 6.1.1 should now be evident. The model is (6.4) with the addition of restrictions expressed in (6.16). Again, the Taylor's series of (6.4) can be used to obtain the linear pseudomodel (6.6) and, if necessary, the linear pseudorestrictions. To streamline the notation, the restrictions are assumed to be linear. Following essentially the same methods as in Sec. 6.1.1, the restricted least squares nonlinear estimator for β is

$$\tilde{\beta}_{0R} = \hat{\beta}_0 + [X(\hat{\beta}_0)'X(\hat{\beta}_0)]^{-1}R'\{R[X(\hat{\beta}_0)'X(\hat{\beta}_0)]^{-1}R'\}^{-1}[r - R\hat{\beta}_0] \tag{6.19}$$

with $\mathrm{Var}(\tilde{\beta}_{0R})$ defined to correspond to (6.18). It is assumed that the values for β_0 used to initiate the process are selected to satisfy the restrictions (6.16). In general, this occurs for each iteration to the final estimator $\tilde{\beta}_{0R}$; that is, the successive estimators for β would satisfy the linear or linear pseudorestrictions, since the restrictions matrix would be applied and updated at each stage in the iterative process.

These conclusions for linear restrictions on the β are easily extended for the case of nonspherical disturbances. Since the extension is merely one of applying the notation of Sec. 6.1.2 to the present problem, it is left to the interested reader (see Ex. 3 at the end of the chapter).

6.1.4 Equation Systems

The results from 6.1.1 and the linear pseudomodel are easily generalized for equation systems. To simplify matters, it is initially assumed that these equation systems are only linked by a contemporaneous correlation of the disturbances, as in the case of the seemingly unrelated regressions model (Schmidt 1976). The right-hand variables are all assumed to be predetermined or nonstochastic. If this were not the case, appropriate instrumental variables would have to be developed, probably as functions of the predetermined variables in the system.

Let the equation system be represented as

$$Y = F(X, B) + u \tag{6.20}$$

where Y is a T x G matrix of T observations on the G dependent variables; F(X, B) is a T x G matrix; and B is a matrix, say K x

G, of parameters for the G equations. For the systems examined here and for most in econometrics, F(X, B) is specified so that the nonlinearities occur only within the equations; that is,

$$F(X, B) = [f_1(X_1, \beta_1), f_2(X_2, \beta_2), \ldots, f_G(X_G, \beta_G)] \qquad (6.21)$$

The variance covariance matrix is assumed to be composed of row vectors that are identically and independently distributed with mean 0 and contemporaneous variance covariance matrix Σ. Thus, the estimation of the set of G equations as a system will improve asymptotic efficiency by introducing the information on Σ. The reasoning here is parallel to that for seemingly unrelated regressions and the method proposed for estimating the elements of B is a straightforward extension of this approach.

The linear pseudomodel for each equation in the system can be written

$$y_{0i} = X(\beta_{0i})\beta_i + \varepsilon_i \qquad (i = 1, 2, \ldots, G) \qquad (6.22)$$

Stacking the equations, the system is

$$\begin{bmatrix} y_{01} \\ y_{02} \\ \vdots \\ y_{0G} \end{bmatrix} = \begin{bmatrix} X_1(\beta_{01}) & 0 & 0 \ldots 0 & \\ 0 & X_2(\beta_{02}) & 0 \ldots 0 & \\ \vdots & & & \\ 0 & \ldots & 0 & X_G(\beta_G) \end{bmatrix} \begin{bmatrix} \beta_1 \\ \beta_2 \\ \vdots \\ \beta_G \end{bmatrix} + \begin{bmatrix} \varepsilon_1 \\ \varepsilon_2 \\ \vdots \\ \varepsilon_G \end{bmatrix} \qquad (6.23)$$

The variance covariance matrix for the system expressed in this form is $\Omega = \Sigma \otimes I$. The methods of Sec. 6.1.2 are applied to estimate the parameters $(\beta_1', \beta_2', \ldots, \beta_G')$. Estimation in this case occurs first, equation by equation; that is, the estimators

$$\tilde{\beta}_i = [X_i(\hat{\beta}_{0i})'X_i(\hat{\beta}_{0i})]^{-1}X_i(\hat{\beta}_{0i})y_{0i}$$

are first obtained for each of the i equations employing the methods in Sec. 6.1.1. Then the residuals are calculated using these estimators and applied to estimate the elements of Σ:

$$\hat{\sigma}_{0ij} = \hat{\varepsilon}_{0i}'\hat{\varepsilon}_{0j}/(T - K) \qquad (i, j = 1, 2, \ldots, G) \qquad (6.24)$$

The estimators (6.24) are used to form $\hat{\Sigma}$ and the final round of the two stage, feasible generalized least squares process is complete. The method here is identical to that discussed in Sec. 6.1.2 except for generalizing the notation to reflect the systems representation.

A restricted least squares solution to this model is also possible and is required for the demand systems problem. The restrictions can include within and across equation relationships among the parameters. However, the results from Sec. 6.2.3 apply, with the notation appropriately generalized. More complex autocorrelation hypotheses for the matrix, as employed for the results in Chap. 8, are possible and can be accommodated by using the residuals $\hat{\varepsilon}_{0i}$ to estimate the parameters of the associated structure for Ω (see Sec. 6.3.3).

6.1.5 Hypotheses Testing

The hypotheses testing results are abbreviated and only the tests used to evaluate the parameters of the demand system models are reviewed. Interested readers are referred to Gallant (1975) for a more complete discussion of the subject. The present analysis considers results for tests of linear hypotheses (6.16) on the structural parameters β. Then the likelihood ratio test is developed. This test is ultimately employed to examine the more complex demand systems formulations that convolute persistence hypotheses on the structure and disturbances (Chap. 8). In both cases, the results are obtained using the generalized least squares formulation of the nonlinear model discussed in Sec. 6.1.2 because of the focus on error processes in examining the demand systems estimates.

Other testing procedures that are asymptotically equivalent to the likelihood ratio method, include the Wold test and the Lagrange-multiplier test (Judge et al. 1980). The choice of which test statistic to use in a given situation is difficult; all are asymptotically equivalent but they may differ in small samples. Since the likelihood ratio procedure is more widely known, we employ it to test various hypotheses in the empirical sections of this book.

The likelihood function for the nonlinear problem is

$$L(\beta, \Omega|X) = [(2\Pi)^{T/2}|\Omega|^{1/2}]^{-1} \exp[(-1/2)\theta'\Omega^{-1}\theta)] \qquad (6.25)$$

where $\theta = y - f(X, \beta)$. It can be shown for $\Omega = I$ (or a suitably transformed model with nonspherical disturbances) that the nonlinear estimators (6.8) and (6.10) approximate the maximum likelihood estimators. They are efficient, having an asymptotic variance coincident with the Rao-Cramer lower bound (Malinvaud 1970b; Gallant 1977).

Because the estimators (6.8) and (6.10)--and if necessary for the transformed generalized least squares model--are maximum likelihood, they are asymptotically normally distributed. Standard t and F statistics can be employed with the parameter estimates $\hat{\beta}_0$ or $\tilde{\beta}_0$ and their estimated covariance matrices, (6.9) and (6.15), respectively. That is, the standard results on hypotheses testing in the linear model carry over directly, albeit asymptotically (Theil 1971) to this nonlinear context.

The likelihood ratio is formed by using the values for the likelihood functions for restricted and unrestricted models. In the case of the restrictions $R\beta = r$, it is

$$\ell = -2[\ell n\ L(\hat{\beta}_0,\ \hat{\sigma}_0^2|X) - \ell n\ L(\hat{\beta}_{0R},\ \hat{\sigma}_{0R}^2|X)] \tag{6.26}$$

For the persistence hypotheses tests, the likelihood ratio for the spherical versus nonspherical disturbances is

$$\ell = -2\ \ell n\ L(\tilde{\beta}_0,\ \hat{\Omega}(\hat{\beta}_0)|X) - \ell n\ L(\tilde{\beta}_{0R},\ \hat{\sigma}_{0R}^2 I|X) \tag{6.27}$$

In either case, (Gallant and Holly 1978) show that asymptotically the statistic ℓ has a χ^2 distribution with J or G degrees of freedom, where for (6.27) G is the number of parameters required to identify the variance covariance matrix Ω up to a scalar multiple.

6.2 COMPUTATION OF PARAMETER ESTIMATES

This section provides an overview of approaches used to estimate parameters of nonlinear regression models, focusing on the principles that make the various estimation procedures work. Extensive reviews of these methods and surveys of computation routines are available elsewhere. First, the linear pseudomodel results from the previous section are made operational; that is, the mechanics for this framework, along with an arbitrary nonlinear estimation routine, can produce the parameter estimates for the systems of demand equations.

6.2.1 Application of the Linear Pseudomodel

Applied researchers and students involved in demand systems applications may find that available nonlinear computer programs are not well supported. It is likely that the programs will give the parameter estimates but not their estimated variance covariance matrix. In such circumstances, the pseudomodel provides a useful way to use the existing software to obtain a full set of estimators for the demand system model.

To illustrate, consider the specification of the pseudomodel from Sec. 6.1.1. Extensions of the model to feasible restricted least squares and systems problems have already been explained, so this simpler model can be used with no sacrifice of generality. The procedure involves a sequence of steps:

1. Use the available computer algorithm to obtain an approximation of the optimum value for the vector β. Call this estimator $\bar{\beta}_0$.

2. Using $\bar{\beta}_0$, compute the values for the matrix $X(\bar{\beta}_0)$, the derivatives $\partial f(X,\ \beta)/\partial\beta|_{\bar{\beta}_0}$, and $y_0 = y - f(X,\ \bar{\beta}_0) + X(\bar{\beta}_0)\bar{\beta}_0$ for the sample observations. For some nonlinear problems this may be computationally and algebraically difficult. In models with less complex nonlinear expressions, evaluating the derivatives

of the function f(X, β) with respect to the β_i can be handled directly.

3. Apply these results in a standard least squares program to compute $\hat{\beta}_0$ and $\hat{\sigma}_0^2$. As shown in Sec. 6.1, these least squares estimators approximate the maximum likelihood estimators for the nonlinear model.

If a numerical differentiation routine is available (see Sec. 6.2.2.2), this process can be directly applied. As step 2 indicates, the numerical value of the derivative of the function is needed, evaluated at the values for the conditioning variables and conditional on a particular set of parameter estimates.

6.2.2 Solution Approaches

Most of the methods of solving nonlinear estimation problems require the evaluation of the derivatives of the term f(X, β). These include the ordinary gradient method and what will be called modifications of the gradient method. More capital intensive approaches, termed search techniques, have been used. They involve comparisons of the function to be optimized at points selected according to more flexible search strategies.

6.2.2.1 Gradient Methods.

Gradient methods use the derivatives of the function to be maximized to indicate the direction the search should take. To illustrate, consider two points or iterations in the optimization process, β_{j+1} and β_j. Assume that they are related by the expression

$$\beta_{j+1} = \beta_j + \delta_j \Delta_j \tag{6.28}$$

where δ_j is a scalar and Δ_j is a matrix indicating the direction of movement. The direction matrix Δ_j is selected as a weighted function of the matrix of partial derivatives of the function being optimized. Let this function be denoted g(X, β) so that the direction matrix is

$$\Delta_j = W_j (\partial g | \partial \beta) |_{\beta_j} \tag{6.29}$$

where W_j is a weighting matrix.

With W_j known *a priori*, (6.28) becomes

$$\beta_{j+1} = \beta_j + \delta_j W_j (\partial g | \partial \beta) |_{\beta_j} \tag{6.30}$$

that is known up to the scaling factor δ_j. The various versions of the gradient method reflect alternative choices for δ_j and

W_j, which are made according to a rationalization that the approach to the optimum should be as fast as possible given a predetermined search criterion.

The steepest ascent method presumes that $W_j = I$ and provides for the determination of δ_j so that it maximizes the increment in the value $g(X, \beta)$ as given by a second order Taylor's series approximation. The expansion is the same as that for $f(X, \beta)$ in (6.5) except that the second order term is retained. Specifically, the approximation evaluated at β_j is

$$g(X, \beta) = g(X, \beta_j) + (\beta - \beta_j)'(\partial g|\partial\beta)|_{\beta_j} + (\beta - \beta_j)'(\partial^2 g|\partial\beta^2)|_{\beta_j}(\beta - \beta_j) \qquad (6.31)$$

where $(\partial^2 g/\partial\beta^2)|_{\beta_j}$ is the matrix of second partials of $g(X, \beta)$ evaluated at β_j. According to the definitions in Chap. 2, $(\partial^2 g/\partial\beta^2)$ is the Hessian matrix for $g(X, \beta)$.

For the steepest ascent method, the value of β at iteration $(j + 1)$ is selected by rewriting (6.31) for the value of $g(\cdot)$ as β_{j+1},

$$g(X, \beta_{j+1}) = g(X, \beta_j) + (\beta_{j+1} - \beta_j)'(\partial g|\partial\beta)|_{\beta_j} + (\beta_{j+1} - \beta_j)'(\partial^2 g|\partial\beta)|_{\beta_j}(\beta_{j+1} - \beta_j) \qquad (6.32)$$

In this form, (6.29) is an approximation for the difference between $g(X, \beta_{j+1})$ and $g(X, \beta_j)$.

The method of steepest ascent maximizes $g(X, \beta_{j+1}) - g(X, \beta_j)$ as given by (6.32) subject to the restriction (6.28) with Δ_j as in (6.29) and $W_j = I$. Substituting (6.28) into (6.32) and maximizing the difference mentioned above with respect to δ_j (Goldfeld and Quandt 1972) gives

$$\delta_j = -[(\partial g|\partial\beta)'|_{\beta_j}(\partial^2 g|\partial\beta^2)|_{\beta_j}(\partial g|\partial\beta)|_{\beta_j}]^{-1} \cdot [(\partial g|\partial\beta)'|_{\beta_j}(\partial g|\partial\beta)|_{\beta_j}] \qquad (6.33)$$

The scaling is entirely in terms of the derivatives for $g(X, \beta)$. The process yields a maximum if and only if the first term of the right-hand of (6.31) is negative and is assured if the Hessian is negative definite. The method is limited because it may identify a local maximum of the function, for badly behaved

$g(X, \beta)$ it may cause an unnecessarily large number of iterations, and because it does not accumulate information for the new iteration based on errors of past iterations.

The Newton-Raphson method maximizes (6.32) directly with respect to the unknown parameter vector β_{j+1}. This yields

$$\beta_{j+1} = \beta_j - (\partial^2 g | \partial\beta^2)^{-1}|_{\beta_j} (\partial g | \partial\beta)|_{\beta_j} \tag{6.34}$$

The weighting matrix is selected as the inverse of the Hessian for $g(X, \beta)$. In simple applications of this method δ_j is taken as one. Obviously, combinations of these two methods are possible if the step direction is taken to maximize the approximation with respect to β_{j+1} and the scale is chosen to maximize the difference between the two function points.

The Gauss method recognizes the nature of the function $g(X, \beta)$ in the case of least squares and for the generalized least squares problem results in

$$W_j = [X(\beta_j)'\Omega^{-1}X(\beta_j)]^{-1} \tag{6.35}$$

This expression uses the design matrix for the pseudomodel as a basis for making the choice of weights to be applied to the directional derivations. Thus, β_{j+1} is chosen by using a least squares solution for β_{j+1} from the pseudomodel based on β_j. The next step in the iteration is the value β_j plus some portion of the new estimate for β conditioned on β_j; that is,

$$\beta_{j+1} = \beta_j + \delta_j\hat{\beta}_j(\beta_j) \tag{6.36}$$

Several modifications of this approach are possible; the most widely known are by Marquardt (1963) and Brown and Dennis (1971). The Marquardt method uses a ridge-like estimator for determining (β_j); that is,

$$W_j = [(X(\beta_j)'\Omega]^{-1}X(\beta_j) + \lambda_j I]^{-1} \tag{6.37}$$

A similar interpretation, augmenting the design matrix, is employed for the Brown and Dennis approach.

Other iteration methods are available; these are indicative of the possibilities and are chosen to illustrate the gradient methods because of their different approaches. The Gauss methods use a concept of the linear pseudomodel; the steepest ascent method maximizes the second order approximation with respect to the scaling factor for $W_j = I$; and the Newton-Raphson method maximizes the second order approximation with respect to β_{j+1} to find a weighting matrix W_j, but for a given scaling factor. Of those not mentioned, the Davidson-Fletcher-Powell quadratic hill climbing method and the method of scoring are the most widely used. Goldfeld and Quandt (1972) and Lutkepohl (1980) develop these and compare them with the methods discussed here.

6.2.2.2 Numerical Differentiation. Approximating derivatives numerically is not difficult in principle. First derivatives are calculated as the slope of a secant over a specified interval. If f(·) is a function of two variables, x and y, then

$$\frac{\partial f(x, y)}{\partial x} = \Bigg|_{\substack{x = a \\ y = b}} = \frac{f(a + \Delta x, b) - f(a - \Delta x, b)}{2\Delta x} \tag{6.38}$$

Second derivatives are computed as changes in first derivatives over some interval:

$$\frac{\partial^2 f(x, y)}{\partial x^2} = \Bigg|_{\substack{x = a \\ y = b}} = \frac{f(a+2\Delta x, b) - 2f(a, b) + f(a-2\Delta x, b)}{(2\Delta x)^2} \tag{6.39}$$

$$\frac{\partial^2 f(x, y)}{\partial x \partial y} = \Bigg|_{\substack{x = a \\ y = b}} = [f(a+\Delta x, b+\Delta y) - f(a-\Delta x, b+\Delta y) - f(a+\Delta x, b-\Delta y) + f(a-\Delta x, b-\Delta y)]/(4\Delta x\Delta Y) \tag{6.40}$$

The question is, what the increments Δx and Δy should be set to. Goldfeld et al. (1966) suggest that it is adequate to set the increment in the kth direction at the (j + 1)th iteration equal to

$$\max[|f(\beta_{j+1})|\varepsilon_1, |\beta_{j+1,k} - \beta_{j,k}|\varepsilon_2, (|\beta_{j+1,k}|\varepsilon_3)\varepsilon_4] \tag{6.41}$$

where $\beta_{j+1,k}$ is the value of the kth parameter at the (j + 1)th iteration and ε_1, ε_2, ε_3, and ε_4 are preassigned small constants. This rule sets the increment in the kth direction equal to a fraction of the change in the value of the variable since the last iteration unless the absolute value of the variable, the values of the variables, or the values of the function, become large. Bard (1974) presents two other alternatives to this rule.

The inaccuracy of the derivative approximation comes from two sources: the rounding error arising when two closely spaced values of β are subtracted from each other, and the truncation error associated with (6.38) that is accurate only in the limit as the increment goes to zero. To minimize the maximum total error, the increment in the kth direction should be set to $[4\varepsilon|f(\beta_{j+1})h^{kk}_{j+1}]^{1/2}$, where $\varepsilon = 2^{-b}$, b is the number of binary digits carried by the computer in use, and $h^{kk}_{j=1}$ is the kth diagonal element of H_{j+1}.

Alternatively, to minimize the mean square error we choose an increment in the kth direction equal to $[2\sqrt{2}\varepsilon|f(\beta_{j+1})/h^{kk}_{j+1}]^{1/2}$. Whatever formulas are used, should be employed with caution. Upper and lower bounds on the increments should be used. These formulas apply specifically to one-sided difference approximations as opposed to the symmetric, central difference scheme presented in (6.38)-(6.40) and represent conservative values for the increments. Thus the numerical procedure for calculating derivatives, though computationally complex and involving judgments affecting errors, is directly applicable in this demand systems context.

6.2.2.3 Search Procedures. Search procedures typically start by specifying a grid in the values of the parameters to be estimated. The coordinates in this grid are then searched according to a specific criterion. This can be an attractive approach when natural a priori restrictions on the parameter values are suggested by the theory.

The most obvious search method is to enumerate all the grid points and compare the solutions. For problems where extensive prior information exists, this procedure is reasonable (Schmidt 1974). More complex search techniques are also possible, ranging from those in which the gradient is evaluated at selected points to those that feature random search (Schrack and Borowski 1972). The choice of a grid search technique depends on the problem to be solved.

6.3 APPLICATIONS FOR DEMAND SYSTEMS

The demand systems described in Chaps. 4, 5, and 8 are estimated using several nonlinear algorithms. The algorithms chosen are a function of convergence, flexibility, computer routines available and empirical analysis carried on over a long period of time at several different institutions. Nevertheless, the general exposition of the nonlinear estimation problem in Secs. 6.1 and 6.2 is sufficiently general to encompass the basics of each of the algorithms applied.

6.3.1 Carlevaro-Sadoulet

This nonlinear algorithm is contained as a subroutine in a computer program especially designed for estimating demand systems (Carlevaro and Sadoulet 1973). It is used to estimate the parameters for the linear expenditure system (LES) and indirect addilog (ADILOG) systems discussed in Chaps. 4 and 7.

This program employs variants of the Newton-Raphson and Gauss methods to obtain solutions for the nonlinear least squares problems implied by the two demand systems. Recall from (6.34) that in the Newton-Raphson procedure the weights used to move the parameter vector from one iteration to the next are given by the inverse of the matrix of second order partials of the nonlinear function. Thus, the weights are optimal vis-a-vis the Taylor's series approximation. The scaling of the movement is also a parameter in the computer program, selected arbitrarily or by the researcher. The least squares minimizing estimators approximate the maximum likelihood estimators with arguments paralleling those in Sec. 6.1.

Approximations described in Carlevaro and Sadoulet (1973) are employed to assist in evaluating the derivatives required for Newton-Raphson type procedures. Carlevaro and Sadoulet show that the variance estimators obtained asymptotically attain the Rao-Cramer lower bound and thus are asymptotically efficient. The system disturbance terms are handled using generalized least squares similar to the approach indicated in Sec. 6.1.3.

6.3.2 Wegge

The LES system with and without habit formation (see Chap. 8) is estimated using a program developed by Wegge (1968, 1969) that generates full information, quasi-maximum likelihood estimates of the parameters of the LES. The estimators are obtained by minimizing the determinant of the matrix of sum of squares and cross products of the reduced form disturbances for the system.

The method of solution for the Wegge algorithm is similar to that of Newton-Raphson. The advantage is that the iteration formula in Wegge's program almost never requires the analytical computation of first or second order partial derivatives as do many of the other gradient methods. In place of the partial derivatives, suitable computationally advantageous approximations are chosen.

In order to understand how the program is applied, the user must supply two simple subroutines. The LES is first written in the form $AX_t = u_t$, where A is the matrix of parameters to be estimated, X_t is the matrix of endogenous and exogenous variables at time t, and u_t is the vector of disturbance terms. For the first subroutine the user must specify the matrix of coefficients A together with all the restrictions on the parameters. (For the LES these include all the cross equation restrictions implied by the model.) Second, the derivatives of each row of A with respect to each parameter in the system must be programmed. Both subroutines require a minimum of FORTRAN programming.

First order autocorrelation of the disturbances can be introduced directly by multiplying the equations in the system by the common autocorrelation parameter ρ, lagging one time period, and subtracting the resulting equation from the original expression. Thus, the autocorrelation parameter can be estimated simultaneously with those for the structure. Because the autocorrelation coefficient is bounded in the unit interval, this process is simple.

The disturbance terms sum to zero because of the additivity condition, so the contemporaneous variance covariance matrix is singular. This singularity problem is overcome by arbitrarily deleting an equation after the first order autoregressive error scheme is accounted for by the first order transformation process. The program is then applied to the remaining (n - 1) equations in the system.

Wegge's program, like most nonlinear packages, requires the user to supply initial values of the parameters that can be obtained from preliminary ordinary least squares estimates or judgments based on a priori reasoning. In order to obtain the parameter estimates, the adjustment factor in the iteration formula is set equal to 0.1 unless otherwise specified by the programmer.

If the derivatives of the likelihood function are all less than 0.00001 and the variance covariance matrix between the estimated parameters is positive definite, then the program terminates; a relative minimum of the determinant formed by the matrix of sums of squares and cross products of the reduced form residuals has been found.

6.3.3 Hall and Hall

The Time Series Processor (TSP) computer program (Hall and Hall 1979) is also used to estimate the nonlinear demand systems in Chap. 8. The full information maximum likelihood method portion of the TSP package has three options to obtain the parameter estimates: the Gauss, Grad, and Davidson-Fletcher-Powell methods. These are the gradient techniques that have already been discussed plus the Grad method described in Berndt et al. (1974).

Recall that the Gauss method involves linearizing a model by taking a Taylor's expansion in its variables and then applying least squares to the reduced form. Hall and Hall (1979, p. 47) recommend this method for models that have linear variables; however, for nonlinear models this procedure gives an incorrect approximation of the standard errors of the estimates. In order to overcome this deficiency, Hall and Hall recommend using one additional iteration of the Grad method after reaching convergence with the Gauss procedure. This combined approach gives consistent estimates of the standard errors of the parameters and is used to obtain estimates of the LES model in Chap. 8.

With respect to operational procedures, the TSP package can be easily applied to obtain estimates of the LES. The first step is to express the demand system in algebraic form, explicitly including all the nonlinear parameter restrictions. The TSP package understands and operates on these algebraic formulas. The autocorrelation and singularity conditions are handled as in Wegge's program--by a first order transformation of the model's variables and the deletion of one equation.

For the first iteration, arbitrary initial values for the parameters may be used. The program allows the user to specify the method for the step-size search in iterating to improved values for the parameters. The iterations terminate; that is, convergence is achieved if the directional values are all less than some prescribed tolerance level or if the maximum of the ratio of the directional values and the values of the parameters is less than the same specified tolerance.

6.3.4 Other Methods

More specialized methods are used to estimate the Rotterdam and dynamic systems. In most cases these are variants of the gradient method but with derivatives approximated and iterations selected in a somewhat arbitrary manner. This approach is not without precedent. From Sec. 6.2.1, such computer time-intensive methods can be used advantageously when software is limited. In general, the nonlinear estimation problems can be solved using least squares programs if the derivatives of $g(X, \beta)$ can be computed simply or can be approximated.

6.4 CONCLUSION

The results demonstrate processes to solve the nonlinear estimation problems encountered in demand systems estimation. The discussion intentionally concentrates on the construction of such iterative estimation methods from a general viewpoint, because the programs that are used to estimate the demand systems from the Canadian data are not generally available. Thus, it is more important to know the structure of the solution approaches than to know a particular method.

EXERCISES

1. Consider the linear expenditure system in Chap. 4, (4.6b). For an arbitrary equation in the system:
   (a) Obtain the derivatives of the systematic part (right-hand-side) with respect to the parameters μ_i and γ_i. Form the matrix of terms corresponding to $X(\beta_0)$, where β_0 are assumed values of μ_i and γ_j.
   (b) Write the expression for the pseudolinear model from the results obtained in (a).
   (c) Using the data listed in the appendix, use an OLS computer package to obtain estimates of β from the pseudolinear model.

(d) What is the estimated variance covariance matrix for $\hat{\beta}$ found in (c)?

2. Repeat Ex. 1 for the indirect addilog system given in logarithmic form by (4.12).
3. The above two questions use the pseudolinear model to obtain nonlinear estimates of the parameters for a single equation model. Extend the approach in Ex. 1 to estimate the static linear expenditure system.
4. Use the stacking methods outlined in Sec. 6.1.4 to represent the linear expenditure system in reduced form. Specify the across equation parameter restrictions. Are they linear? Can they be linearized using the approach employed for the function f(X, β) in this chapter?

REFERENCES

Bard, Y. 1970. Comparison of gradient methods for the solution of nonlinear parameter estimation problems. SIAM Journal of Numerical Analysis 7 (Jan.):157-86.

———. 1974. Nonlinear Parameter Estimation. New York: Academic Press.

Berndt, E. K.; Hall, B. H.; Hall, R. E.; and Hausman, J. A. 1974. Estimation and inference in nonlinear structural models. Annals of Economic and Social Measurement 4 (Oct.):653-65.

Brown, K. M., and Dennis, J. E. 1971. A new algorithm for nonlinear least squares curve fitting. In Mathematical Software, ed. J. R. Rice. New York: Academic Press.

Carlevaro, F., and Sadoulet, E. 1973. Trois programmes d'estimation d'une classe generale de fonctions de consummution additives. Centre d'Econometric, Universite' de Gene've.

Gallant, A. R. 1975a. Nonlinear regression. American Statistician 25 (May):73-81.

———. 1975b. Testing a subject of the parameters of a nonlinear regression model. Journal of the American Statistical Association 70 (Dec.):927-32.

———. 1977. Testing a nonlinear regression specification: A non-regular case. Journal of the American Statistical Association 72 (Sept.):523-30.

Gallant, A. R., and Holly, A. 1980. Statistical inference in an implicit, nonlinear, simultaneous equation model in the context of maximum likelihood estimation. Econometrica 48 (Apr.):697-720.

Goldfeld, S. M., and Quandt, R. E. 1972. Nonlinear Methods in Econometrics. Amsterdam: North Holland.

Goldfeld, S. M.; Quandt, R. E.; and Trotter, H. F. 1966. Maximization by quadratic hill-climbing. Econometrica 34:541-51.

Hall, B. H., and Hall, R. E. 1979. Time Series Procession,

Version 3.3. Users Manual. Stanford, Calif.

Himmelblau, D. M. 1972. A uniform evaluation of constrained optimization techniques. In Numerical Methods for Nonlinear Optimization, ed. F. A. Lootsma. London: Academic Press.

Judge, G. G.; Griffiths, W. E.; Hill, R. C.; and Lee, T. C. 1980. The Theory and Practice of Econometrics. New York: John Wiley.

Lutkepohl, H. 1980. Nonlinear statistical models: Estimation, computational methods and inference. In The Theory and Practice of Econometrics, ed. G. G. Judge et al., pp. 719-77. New York: John Wiley.

Malinvaud, E. 1970a. Statistical Methods of Econometrics. Amsterdam: North Holland.

———. 1970b. The consistency of nonlinear regressions. The Annals of Mathematical Statistics 41 (June):956-69.

Marquardt, D. W. 1963. An algorithm for least squares estimation of nonlinear parameters. Journal of the Society of Industrial and Applied Mathematics 11 (June):431-41.

Murry, W. 1972. Failure, the causes and cures. In Numerical Methods of Unconstrained Optimization, ed. W. Murry, pp. 107-22. London: Academic Press.

Parkinson, J. M., and Hutchinson, D. 1972. An investigation into the efficiency of variants on the simplex method. In Numerical Methods for Nonlinear Optimization, ed. F. A. Lootsma, pp. 115-35. London: Academic Press.

Schmidt, P. 1976. Econometrics. New York: Marcel Dekker.

———. 1974. A modification of the almon distributed lag. Journal of the American Statistical Association 69 (Sept.):679-81.

Schrack, G., and Borowski, N. 1972. An experimental comparison of three random searches. In Numerical Methods for Nonlinear Optimization, ed. F. A. Lootsma, pp. 137-47. London: Academic Press.

Theil, H. 1971. Principles of Econometrics. New York: John Wiley.

Wegge, L. L. 1968. Full information quasi-maximum likelihood estimators. University of California, Davis. Mimeo.

———. 1969. A family of functional iterations and the solution of maximum likelihood estimating equations. Econometrica 37 (Jan.):122-30.

7 • Application with Canadian Data

The demand systems methods applied to the time series data for Canada are restated here in the form used for estimation with the error assumptions specified, permitting specialization of the results on nonlinear estimation from Chap. 6. Sample data and dynamic demand systems methods are presented with estimates for static and dynamic versions of the linear expenditure system, indirect addilog, Rotterdam, and state adjustment models. These results are compared and evaluated in relation to those obtained in other empirical investigations and conclusions and implications from the application are developed.

7.1 ESTIMATION METHODS

Chapters 4 and 5 include demand systems in addition to those reported here. Development of estimation methods in this chapter is limited to special problems associated with those systems actually applied to the Canadian data.

7.1.1 Linear Expenditure and Indirect Addilog Systems

For empirical implementation, the tth observation on the linear expenditure and indirect addilog demand systems are written

$$p_{it}q_{it} = p_{it}\gamma_i + \mu_i(m_t - \sum_j p_{jt}\gamma_j) + \varepsilon_{it} \tag{7.1}$$

$$p_{it}q_{it} = a_i b_i m_t (m_t/p_{it})^{b_i} \left[\sum_j a_j b_j (m_t/p_t)^{b_j - 1}\right] + \varepsilon_{it} \tag{7.2}$$

where the variables p_{it}, q_{it}, and m_t are previously defined and

ε_{it} is a structural disturbance term. Using vector notation, it is assumed that

$$E(\varepsilon_t) = 0 \quad \text{and} \quad E(\varepsilon_t \varepsilon_t') = \delta_{tt}' \Omega$$

with δ_{tt}' again the Kronecker product; that is, the error vectors ε_t have means 0, are temporarily uncorrelated, and have a contemporaneous variance covariance matrix Ω.

Because of the adding-up criterion, the variance covariance matrix is singular. Summing ε_{it} over i gives the restriction $\Sigma_i \varepsilon_{it} = 0$, and it follows that $\iota'\Omega = 0'$ (Berndt and Savin 1975). In estimating the parameters for (7.1) and (7.2), the singularity of the matrix Ω must be recognized. When there is no autocorrelation, this problem is handled by arbitrarily deleting the nth equation in the system (Berndt and Savin 1975). The resulting system of n - 1 equations has a positive definite contemporaneous variance covariance matrix of full rank (Parks 1971; Carlevaro and Sadoulet 1973). The nth expenditure equation and the full covariance estimator are then obtained by applying the Engel aggregation condition. Alternatively, the full system of n equations can be estimated using a generalized inverse for the singular covariance matrix (Theil 1971; Powell 1974).

Deletion of the nth expenditure equation is employed here based on the availability of a specialized program for obtaining maximum likelihood estimates of the parameters. Specifically, a nonlinear computer program is used to obtain maximum likelihood estimates for the linear expenditure and the indirect addilog systems (Carlevaro and Sadoulet 1973). This program uses a modified gradient method for numerically solving the maximum likelihood estimation problem (see Chap. 6).

7.1.2 Rotterdam Model

The Rotterdam model must be modified in several respects to estimate the parameters. First, note from (4.23) that disturbance terms must be added; a structure for these disturbance terms can be introduced in the model as follows:

$$w_{it}^* \Delta q_{it} = \phi\, \mu_i [\Delta p_{it} - \sum_k \mu_k \Delta p_{kt}] + \mu_i \Delta q_t + \varepsilon_{it} \tag{7.3}$$

where it is assumed that

$$E(\varepsilon_t) = 0 \quad \text{and} \quad E(\varepsilon_t \varepsilon_t') = \delta_{tt}' \Omega = \delta_{tt}' [(1/\phi)B - \mu\mu']$$

and Δ is the difference operator for the variables in logarithms x_{it}; that is, $\Delta_{it} = \ell n\, x_{it} - \ell n\, x_{it-1}$. Once again the error vectors ε_t have zero means, are temporally uncorrelated, and have a contemporaneous variance covariance matrix Ω. In the case of direct addivity where $b_{ij} = 0$ $(i \neq j)$ and $b_{ii} = \phi\mu_i$, the covariance matrix takes the special form $\Omega = \sigma^2(M - \mu\mu')$, where M is an n x n diagonal matrix whose diagonal is the vector μ. Second, (7.3) is not linear in the parameters to be estimated, a problem solved by taking a Taylor series expansion and using a linear version of (7.3). Taking the expansion and omitting second and higher order terms results in

$$w^*_{it}\Delta q_{it} - \mu^0_i\Delta q_{it} = b_{ii}\Delta\mu^0_{it} - \mu^0_i \sum_k b_{kk}\Delta\mu^0_{it} + \varepsilon_{it} \qquad (7.4)$$

where μ^0_i represents initial value of μ_i, $\Delta\mu^0_{it} = \Delta p_{it} + \Delta\lambda^0_t$ is the log change in the marginal utility of income, $\Delta\lambda^0_t = 1/\phi^0\ \Delta q_t - \Sigma_k\ \mu^0_k\ \Delta p_{kt}$ is the log change in λ due to logarithmic income and price changes, and ϕ^0 is an initial value for ϕ.

In matrix notation the system represented by equation (7.4) can be written

$$Y_t = Z_tB - \mu^0Z'_tB + \varepsilon_t = (1 - \mu^0\iota')ZB + \varepsilon_t = X_tB + \varepsilon_t \qquad (7.5a)$$

The full system for the set of T observations is

$$Y = XB + \varepsilon \qquad (7.5b)$$

where Y, X, B, and ε are matrices and vectors of appropriate dimension. To obtain estimates for the elements of vector B, we account for and eliminate the problem of singularity of the covariance matrix Ω by using the generalized least squares estimator $b = (X'HX)^{-1}X'HY$, where H is an nT x nT diagonal matrix defined by $H = I - M_0^{-1}$. If $b_{ii} = \phi\mu_i$ and $\Sigma_i\ b_{ii} = \phi$, estimates for ϕ and μ are defined as $\phi = \iota'b$ and $\mu = (1/\phi)b$.

7.1.3 Linear Expenditure System: A Dynamic Version

The dynamic linear expenditure system is estimated by embedding the equations similar to those for the indirect addilog and Rotterdam systems in a stochastic framework:

$$q_{it} = k_{i0} + k_{i1}q_{it-1} + k_{i2}\frac{1}{\lambda_t p_{it}} + k_{i3}\frac{1}{\lambda_{t-1}p_{it-1}} + \varepsilon_{it} \qquad (7.6)$$

where it is assumed that the error term ε_{it} satisfies the usual conditions required for application of ordinary least squares. Equation (7.6) is estimated using an iterative procedure (method

2) suggested by Houthakker and Taylor (1970, p. 202) that begins by selecting initial values for λ_t and applying ordinary least squares to estimate the remaining parameters. Then, from the estimates of the coefficients just obtained, a new set of values for λ_t is obtained by making the calculation (Phlips 1974, p. 192):

$$\lambda_t = \frac{\Sigma\, k_{i2}}{m_t\, \Sigma\, p_{it} k_{i0} - \Sigma\, p_{it} k_{i1} q_{it-1} - (1/\lambda_{t-1})\, \Sigma\, k_{i3} p_{it}/p_{it-1}} \qquad (7.7)$$

These λ_t values are again substituted into (7.6) and a new set of least squares estimates of the coefficients is computed. The process is continued until the budget constraint is approximately satisfied for each time period. For example, the iteration might be stopped at

$$(m_t - \Sigma\, p_{it}\tilde{\bar{q}}_{it})/m_t \leq 0.001$$

where $\tilde{\bar{q}}_{it}$ is the predicted value of q_{it} from the iterative least squares estimation procedure.

7.1.4 State Adjustment Model

For the state adjustment model, the estimating equations take the form

$$q_t = A_0 + A_1 q_{t-1} + A_2 \Delta m_t + A_3 m_{t-1} + A_4 \Delta p_t + A_5 p_{t-1} + \varepsilon_t \qquad (7.8)$$

where it continues to be assumed that the error vector ε_t satisfies the conditions just mentioned. Since (7.8) is overidentified (see 5.6e), the coefficients are estimated under the restriction $A_2 A_5 = A_3 A_4$. A nonlinear least squares procedure based on the use of the linear pseudomodel developed in Chap. 6 is used to find parameter estimates for (7.8).

7.2 DATA AND COMMODITY GROUPINGS

Annual time series data on personal consumption expenditures and prices are used to estimate the demand systems parameters. The sample period covers 1947-1972. Personal consumption expenditures data for major groups of commodities and services are based on official estimates of Statistics Canada (1976) and are contained in Appendix Tables 1, 2, 4, and 5. These annual estimates of personal consumption are available continuously from 1926 and provide detailed information about the composition of consumer spending. The other data required, implicit price indexes (1971 = 100) for the commodities and services groups, are available from the same source and are derived by dividing expenditure in current dollars by expenditure in constant dollars. They are called implicit deflators, since the composition of the commodity groups and thus the weights for the price index change over time. Population data used to express consumption expenditures on a per capita basis for midyear (June 1) are also available from Statistics Canada (1976) and are provided in Appendix Table 3.

7.2.1 Special Transformations

Several special transformations are required to organize the basic time series data for application of the five demand systems models. For the linear expenditure and the indirect addilog systems, the expenditure data $p_{it}q_{it}$ are per capita current dollar personal expenditures on the ith commodity. The price series p_{it} are implicit and indexed at 1971 = 100. Income m is measured using the per capita total personal expenditure in current dollars.

For the Rotterdam model, the following transformation is used to develop the quantities for the dependent variables $w^*_{it}\Delta q_{it}$. First, logarithms of the total quantities are calculated from the expenditure data from the identity $\ell n\ q_{it} = \ell n\ (p_{it}q_{it}) - \ell n\ p_{it}$. Next, the logarithm in midyear population is subtracted from the logarithm of quantity previously derived to obtain the per capita quantity demand for each year. First differences are calculated, and the values for the dependent variables are derived by multiplying the average expenditure proportions by the corresponding first differences. The income or total expenditures variable for the Rotterdam model is $\Sigma_k w^*_{kt}\Delta q_{kt} = \Delta q_{it}$. When the values for the dependent variables are summed, per capita income defined in this context is obtained.

In the state adjustment model, the quantity data q_{it} are per capita constant (1971) dollar expenditures. The price series are relative prices obtained by dividing expenditure in current dollars by expenditure in constant dollars for each of the commodity groups, and by deflating resulting price indexes by the implicit price index for total personal expenditure on all consumer goods and services. The income variable m_t is the total personal expenditure in constant dollars per capita. For the dynamic linear expenditure system, the quantity data q_{it} are the per capita personal expenditures in constant dollars. The price series p_{it} are implicit and income m_t is total expenditure in current per capita dollars.

7.2.2 Commodity Groups

Parameters of the demand systems are estimated for four (Appendix Tables 1 and 2) and nine (Appendix Tables 4 and 5) groups of commodities and services. In both cases groups are mutually exclusive and account for total expenditures of consumers. The more complete application of demand systems methods is for the four commodity group organization of data.

The grouping of goods and services follows principles of classification used by Statistics Canada. The four groups to be studied are durable goods (D) and semidurable goods (SD), and non-durable goods (ND) and services (S). The letters in parentheses denote durability classification and are used to relate the four and nine commodity groupings. The following list is for the nine commodity groups. The aggregation to four commodity groups is defined by the letters found in parentheses. For example, food is a separate group in the nine commodity grouping but becomes part of nondurable goods for the four commodity grouping.

- Food (ND)
- Alcoholic beverages and tobacco products (ND)
- Clothing and footwear
  - men's and boy's clothing (SD)
  - women's and children's clothing (SD)
  - footwear and repair (SD)
- Gross rent, fuel, and power
  - gross imputed rent (S)
  - gross rent paid (S)
  - other lodging (S)
  - electricity (ND)
  - gas (ND)
  - other fuels (ND)
- Furniture, furnishing, household equipment, and operation
  - furniture, carpets, and other floor coverings (D)
  - household appliances (D)
  - semidurable household furnishings (ND)
  - laundry and dry cleaning (S)
  - domestic services (S)
  - other household services (S)
- Medical care and health services
  - drugs and sundries (ND)
- Transportation and communication
  - new and used (net automobiles) (D)
  - repairs and parts (D)
  - gasoline, oil, and grease (ND)
  - other auto-related services (S)
  - purchased transportation (S)
  - communications (S)
- Recreation, entertainment, education, and cultural services
  - recreation, sporting, and camping equipment (D)
  - books, newspapers, and magazines (SD)

recreational services (S)
education and cultural services (S)

Personal goods and services
jewelry, watches, and repairs (SD)
toilet articles, cosmetics (SD)
personal care (S)
expenditure on restaurants and hotels (S)
operating expenses of nonprofit organizations (S)

With only two exceptions, grouping of commodities and services is the same as that of Statistics Canada (1976). The exceptions are: (1) Under "Medical care and health services" the components of medical care, hospital care, and other medical care expenses are deleted because of discontinuities in the data from 1961 on. Because expenditures for nonprofit hospitals for 1962-1971 moved from the private to the government sector and to various provincially administered medical care plans, personal expenditures for medical services have progressively shifted to government accounts. (2) Also, "Net expenditure abroad" has been deleted because it is calculated residually to balance tourist revenue; since it is a minor part of any of the expenditure groups used in the analysis, it should not alter results.

7.3 EMPIRICAL RESULTS

The major empirical results are for the demand systems models using four commodity groups. They are reported first for static systems and then for dynamic systems. The discussion in each case reviews and compares the basic parameter estimates with an evaluation of the associated elasticity estimates.

7.3.1 Static Systems: Basic Parameter Estimates

Estimates of parameters for the three static systems are presented in Table 7.1. For the Rotterdam model, all values for the estimated coefficients are more than twice the corresponding estimates of standard errors. The parameter estimates are also consistent with the qualitative restrictions implied by behavioral assumptions and model structure. All estimated price coefficients b_{ii} are negative, indicating an inverse relationship between consumption levels and price. Estimated marginal budget shares μ_i are positive. The estimated income flexibility coefficient ϕ is -0.7715, implying that the marginal utility of income decreases by 1.30 percent in response to a 1 percent increase in income. This value is similar to the 1.55 reported by Powell (1965). Furthermore, this value lies between Frisch's money flexibility of -2 for the median part of the population and -0.7 for the wealthier part of the population (1959, p. 189).

Parameter estimates for the linear expenditure system show that the marginal budget shares are positive and statistically

TABLE 7.1 Basic parameter estimates for static demand systems

Commodity Group	Rotterdam Model: Price coefficient b_{ii}	Rotterdam Model: Marginal budget share μ_i	LES: Minimum required quantity γ	LES: Marginal budget share μ_i	Indirect Addilog System: $a_i b_i$	Indirect Addilog System: b_i	Indirect Addilog System: Marginal budget share[b]
Durables	-.1799	.2331	10.32	.1844	.0999	-.1539	.1934
	(.0571)[a]	(.0323)	(4.21)	(.0151)	(.0073)	(.1334)	
Semidurables	-.0931	.1207	167.12	.0836	.1878	-.9665	.0853
	(.0370)	(.0226)	(2.70)	(.0052)	(.0065)	(.1793)	
Nondurables	-.1764	.2287	333.60	.2373	.3956	-.8280	.2524
	(.0448)	(.0306)	(6.59)	(.0122)	(.0166)	(.1572)	
Services	-.3221	.4175	46.88	.4947	.3167	-.3083	.4689
	(.0993)	(.0486)	(24.23)	(.0293)	(.0279)	(.2870)	
Income flexibility	-.7715						
	(.2162)						

[a]Standard errors are in parentheses.
[b]Calculated as the income elasticity multiplied by the expenditure share.

TABLE 7.2 Comparison of elasticities estimated from parameters for static demand systems

Commodity Group	Expen-diture share	Income Elasticity: Rotterdam	Income Elasticity: LES	Income Elasticity: Indirect addilog	Direct Price Elasticity, Uncompensated: Rotterdam	Uncompensated: LES	Uncompensated: Indirect addilog	Direct Price Elasticity, Compensated: Rotterdam	Compensated: LES	Compensated: Indirect addilog
Durables	0.1375	1.69	1.34	1.40	-1.23	-0.96	-0.86	-1.00	-0.77	-0.67
Semidurables	0.1435	0.84	0.58	0.59	-0.69	-0.44	-0.17	-0.57	-0.36	-0.08
Nondurables	0.3446	0.66	0.68	0.73	-0.62	-0.59	-0.45	-0.39	-0.35	-0.20
Services	0.3744	1.11	1.32	1.25	-0.91	-0.96	-0.80	-0.50	-0.47	-0.33

significantly different from 0. The estimates γ_i represent minimal consumption levels for the various commodities and are positive, ranging from 333.60 for nondurable goods to 10.32 for durable goods. The basic parameter estimates for the indirect addilog system appear as reliably estimated as those for the other systems in Table 7.1. All the estimates of b_i are negative and lie within the interval (-1, 0), while all the estimated a_ib_i are positive. Little can be concluded for the indirect addilog model from these observations, since the underlying system yields no qualitative restrictions on a_i and b_i (Akin and Stewart 1979).

When comparing estimates for the three systems, it is reassuring that variations in marginal budget shares are not substantial. Specifically, the results for the three models suggest budget shares for durables, semidurables, nondurables, and services near 0.20, 0.10, 0.25, and 0.45, respectively. The stability of these parameters across systems specifications and estimation methods contributes to the robustness of conclusions based on these results.

7.3.2 Static Systems: Elasticities

Income elasticities, direct price elasticities (compensated and uncompensated), and expenditure shares for the Rotterdam, linear expenditure, and indirect addilog systems are presented in Table 7.2. The main features of the results can be summarized as follows:

- All income elasticities are positive, ranging from 1.69 for durable goods (Rotterdam model) to 0.58 for semidurables (linear expenditure system). Commodity groups are superior, a result consistent with the level of aggregation.
- Durable goods and services have estimated income elasticities that are greater than one, suggesting that some commodities within the groups are luxuries. Alternatively, semidurable and nondurable commodity groups have estimated income elasticities that are less than one. This implies that the commodities they are composed of are largely necessities.
- Differences between the income elasticity estimates of the three systems are sizable in some cases. Generally, the estimates from the linear expenditure and indirect addilog systems are closer. The Rotterdam model produces notably higher income elasticity estimates for durable and semidurable goods and lower estimates for services.
- Direct uncompensated price elasticity estimates for the three demand systems are negative. The compensated price elasticity estimates are substantially lower than the uncompensated estimates.
- For durable goods the range in uncompensated price elasticity estimates is from -1.23 for the Rotterdam model to -0.86 for the indirect addilog model. For services, a similar

comparison shows a high value of -0.96 for the linear expenditure system and a low value of -0.80 for the indirect addilog model.

- For semidurable goods, the uncompensated price elasticities are more variable, ranging from -0.17 for the indirect addilog system to -0.69 for the Rotterdam system.

Other than results for semidurables, the price elasticity estimates from the three systems are similar. Except for services in the linear expenditure system, price elasticities from the Rotterdam model are the highest. The lowest price elasticity estimates are obtained for the indirect addilog system.

7.3.3 Dynamic Systems: Basic Parameter Estimates

Estimates of parameters for the state adjustment model are reported in Table 7.3. Most of the parameter estimates are statistically significant at the 5 percent level. A priori restrictions on these parameter estimates for the structural model are minimal. All A_1 estimates (the parameters on lagged consumption q_{t-1}) are positive and within the unit interval. Since (5.5b) is the reduced form for the structure, values for A_1 outside the unit interval would indicate stability problems. The parameter estimates on Δp_t (A_4) are negative, with the sign determined by the price coefficient in the structural model (5.1). Parameter estimates on the income terms A_2 and A_3 are positive, so both income levels and increments to income are positively related to consumption for the four aggregated commodity groups.

Results for parameters of the dynamic linear expenditure system are shown in Table 7.4. All regression coefficients are significantly different from 0 at the 5 percent level. All estimated coefficients have correct signs according to a priori reasoning. In general, these results are quite favorable when compared with the theory and previous estimates based on United States data (Phlips 1974).

TABLE 7.3 Estimates of basic parameters for state adjustment model

Commodity Group	A_0	A_1	A_2	A_3	A_4	A_5
Durables	10.58	.4843	.3355	.0879	-223.63	-58.59
		(.1286)[a]	(.0401)	(.0268)	(93.75)	
Semidurables	16.46	.8448	.1676	.0164	-93.65	-9.16
		(.0729)	(.0169)	(.0062)	(52.29)	
Nondurables	245.85	.6244	.1590	.0919	-292.30	-168.95
		(.1771)	(.0364)	(.0428)	(151.23)	
Services	35.43	.7550	.2423	.1174	-138.03	-66.87
		(.2782)	(.1003)	(.1072)	(436.73)	

[a]Standard errors are in parentheses.

TABLE 7.4 Estimates of basic parameters for dynamic linear expenditure model

Commodity Group	k_{i0}	k_{i1}	k_{i2}	k_{i3}
Durables	15.98	.4332	156.32	-114.72
		(.0469)[a]	(7.11)	(9.24)
Semidurables	15.38	.8618	68.77	-61.91
		(.0568)	(5.45)	(6.76)
Nondurables	146.63	.5353	88.85	-33.30
		(.0842)	(9.04)	(16.00)
Services	12.51	.6978	121.35	-47.74
		(.0300)	(13.00)	(14.62)

[a]Standard errors are in parentheses.

7.3.4 Dynamic Systems: Structural Parameters and Elasticities

Estimates of the structural parameters for the state adjustment model are reported in Table 7.5. Observations based on these results follow:

- Durable and semidurable goods are subject to inventory adjustment ($\alpha_i < 0$), while purchases of nondurables and services show habit formation ($\alpha_i > 0$). In each case the results seem plausible.
- All depreciation rates δ_i are positive and are plausible in magnitude except possibly for semidurable goods. The higher estimated depreciation rates for the nondurables and services commodity groups and the positive values for α_i reflect a lack of strong persistence of habit.
- For each commodity group, the short-run income coefficient κ_i is positive and the short-run price coefficient ν_i is negative.
- For durable and semidurable goods the short-run income elasticity exceeds the long-run income elasticity. The converse is true for the short-run and long-run income elasticities for the nondurables and services. This result is consistent with the Houthakker and Taylor (1970) rationalizations for inventory adjustment and habit formation.

TABLE 7.5 Structural coefficients and elasticities for state adjustment model

Commodity Group	θ	α	κ	ν	δ	Elasticities: Income	Elasticities: Price
Durables	47.28	-.393	.3928	-261.85	.301	SR 3.30	-1.31
						LR 1.43	-0.57
Semidurables	173.44	-.065	.1728	-96.56	.103	SR 1.19	-0.35
						LR 0.73	-0.21
Nondurables	372.36	.350	.1392	-255.88	.813	SR 0.42	-0.43
						LR 0.74	-0.76
Services	63.14	.360	.2092	-119.17	.690	SR 0.52	-0.13
						LR 1.19	-0.31

• The direct price elasticities of demand have the anticipated negative signs. Price elasticities for durable goods are higher than for the other three groups.

Estimated structural parameters for the dynamic linear expenditure system are shown in Table 7.6 and reveal that:

• All depreciation rates δ_i are positive. They range from 0.10 for semidurables to 0.91 for nondurables. The rate of 0.30 for durables implies that these goods are depreciated more than 90 percent by the end of seven years.

• Two commodity groups, durables and semidurables, have negative stock coefficients α_i, and are subject to habit formation. For nondurables and services, however, the larger depreciation rates and the positive stock coefficients indicate, as do results for the state adjustment model, a rather fast rate for habits to wear off.

• All estimated short-run marginal budget shares μ_i are positive, indicating a decreasing marginal utility for each commodity.

• In every case θ_i, an autonomous or necessary consumption level, is positive, with larger values for semidurables and nondurables than for durables and services commodity groups.

• The adjustment coefficients ρ_i^* are between 0 and 1 in every case, indicating the appropriateness of partial adjustment hypotheses for the state variables.

• Estimated short- and long-run income elasticities are all positive. For durables and semidurables, the short-run income elasticities (3.13 and 1.11, respectively) are larger than the long-run income elasticities (1.09 and 0.71, respectively). The results are consistent with expectations. The situation for nondurables and services is reversed, indicating habit formation.

• All price elasticities are negative, and the compensated ones are smaller. The short-run uncompensated price elasticity estimates for durables (-1.44), semidurables (-0.671), and services (-0.49) are larger than those obtained from the state adjustment model.

• During the estimation process and in the final iteration, the marginal utility of money λ declined continuously with time. Since real income increased over the time period, this result corroborates the apparent reasonable estimates for the other structural parameters for the model.

As a basis for some additional observations on the elasticity estimates from the dynamic demand systems, the results in Tables 7.5 and 7.6 can be compared with those in Table 7.2. These comparisons show that:

• The income elasticity for durable goods in static systems is about 1.4, which is between the short- and long-run estimates in the dynamic models: 1.4 to 3.3 for the state

TABLE 7.6 Structural coefficients and elasticities for dynamic linear expenditure model

Commodity Group	δ_i	μ_i	α_i	θ_i	ρ_i^{*a}	γ_i^*	μ_i^*	Income Elasticity		Direct Price Elasticity: Uncom-pensated	Direct Price Elasticity: Compen-sated
Durables	.30696	189.12	-.4840	72.65	.79096	28.19	.15095	SR	3.13	-1.44	-1.01
								LR	1.09	-0.89	-0.74
Semidurables	.10498	70.19	-.04347	157.36	.14846	111.29	.10289	SR	1.11	-0.67	-0.51
								LR	0.71	-0.63	-0.53
Nondurables	.90953	79.56	.30435	210.04	.60518	315.67	.24590	SR	0.53	-0.41	-0.23
								LR	0.71	-0.62	-0.37
Services	.87049	99.59	.51464	16.93	.3559	41.41	.50106	SR	0.60	-0.49	-0.27
								LR	1.33	-0.97	-0.47

[a] $\rho_i^* = \delta_i - \alpha_i$.

TABLE 7.7 Comparison of price and income elasticities estimated for different static models

Commodity Group	Expen-diture share	Income Elasticity: Rotterdam	Income Elasticity: LES	Income Elasticity: Double Log	Direct Price Elasticity, Uncompensated: Rotterdam	Uncompensated: LES	Uncompensated: Double Log	Compensated: Rotterdam	Compensated: LES	Compensated: Double Log
Food	0.1845	0.55	0.39	0.86	-0.42	-0.30	-0.20	-0.32	-0.23	-0.04
Tobacco, alcohol	0.0691	0.80	0.79	0.37	-0.54	-0.52	-0.63	-0.49	-0.47	-0.60
Clothing	0.0904	0.74	0.63	0.69	-0.52	-0.43	-0.42	-0.45	-0.37	-0.35
Gross rent, fuel, power	0.1838	1.04	1.30	0.65	-0.74	-0.86	-0.91	-0.54	-0.62	-0.79
Furniture, furnishings, household equipment, operations	0.1072	1.05	0.68	0.97	-0.72	-0.47	-0.48	-0.60	-0.39	-0.37
Drugs, sundries	0.0137	1.20	1.28	1.44	-0.78	-0.81	-1.02	-0.77	-0.79	-1.00
Transportation, communication	0.1425	1.55	1.25	2.38	-1.00	-0.82	-1.88	-0.78	-0.64	-1.54
Recreation, entertain-ment, educational, cultural services	0.0744	170	2.18	1.62	-1.09	-1.30	-0.38	-0.96	-1.14	-0.26
Personal goods, services	0.1344	1.76	1.07	0.63	-0.55	-0.71	-0.10	-0.44	-0.57	-0.01

adjustment model and 1.1 to 3.1 for the dynamic linear expenditure system.

- Except for the income elasticity estimates from the Rotterdam model, all short- and long-run income elasticities for semidurables are higher for the dynamic than for the static systems.
- For nondurables, estimates of income elasticities from the two types of models are about the same. Since this group includes necessities, the result is anticipated.
- For services, income elasticity estimates from the static models are similar to the long-run estimates from the dynamic models.
- Values of estimated short- and long-run uncompensated price elasticities bracket values from the static models.

In summary, the results demonstrate that the adjustment, habit, and inventory features of the dynamic models more than in the static models have plausibly captured the behavior of consumers. The flexibility of these models provided variations in the parameter estimates and elasticities, between the long- and short-run, that were in agreement with simple hypotheses formed from the compositions of the four commodity groups.

Additional estimates allowing for serial correlation (Berndt and Savin (1975) in the errors for the static systems are also computed. Generally, the model with autocorrelated errors produces more variable structural parameter estimates but results in elasticities similar to the ones obtained for the static systems, suggesting that persistence in consumption patterns and inventory effects of durable goods purchases are best accommodated by allowing for them in the systematic portion of demand models rather than in the assumed time related structure for the error terms.

7.4 EVALUATION

In addition to the comparisons just made, it is useful to evaluate the demand systems estimates in relation to those obtained from another commodity grouping and from other studies and to examine the forecasting potential of the models. In Sec. 7.2.2 the alternative representation of nine commodity groups is more disaggregated. The available estimates of prices and income elasticities provide a basis to evaluate the applied implications of different data bases, estimation methods, demand systems, and commodity groups. Forecasts within and outside the sample period are made using the two dynamic models applied because their structural parameter estimates and elasticities compare favorably with those from the static systems.

7.4.1 Nine Commodity Groups

Price and income elasticity estimates obtained by applying two static demand systems and a double log model to the Canadian data, disaggregated to nine commodity groups, are contained in

Table 7.7. The same exercise was attempted for the indirect addilog and dynamic demand systems but the solutions were erratic or the algorithms used to estimate the parameters failed to converge, suggesting problems with multicollinearity or with the capacity of the computer programs employed for the larger models. The double log estimates obtained without forcing the income elasticities to one are included only to provide a contrast to the more theoretically consistent Rotterdam and linear expenditure systems. Results from the double log model are more erratic and less plausible than those from the other two demand systems, so comparative comments are confined to the Rotterdam and linear expenditure systems.

In Table 7.7, the pattern of the estimated income elasticities shows that, like the four commodity groups, all income elasticities are positive. For the Rotterdam and linear expenditure systems, commodity groups with an income elasticity less than unity are food, tobacco, and alcoholic beverages; clothing; and personal goods and services. Thus, consumption of these goods tended to remain more stable for differing income levels. In particular, the results for food are worth noting, since Engel's law concerning the decreasing share of expenditures on food with income increases is confirmed. Income elasticity estimates for housing and furniture are close to one, so these commodity groups may be considered moderate luxuries. The highest estimated income elasticities are obtained for transportation and recreation, implying that as income rises, demand for these commodities should increase. For transportation, this result is markedly different from that for the United States. For the commodity groups, transportation and recreation are highly influenced by durable goods purchases, a type of consumption behavior not especially well modeled by the static assumptions underlying the elasticity estimates presented in Table 7.7.

Several differences are observed in comparing the Rotterdam model income elasticities with the linear expenditure system elasticities. For example, income elasticities for food, clothing, furniture, and transportation are slightly lower for the linear expenditure system than for the Rotterdam model. Income elasticities for tobacco and alcoholic beverages, drugs, and sundries are almost identical in the models, in contrast to the results from the four commodity case that showed the Rotterdam estimates uniformly higher, with the exception of services.

Examination of the direct uncompensated price elasticity estimates in Table 7.7 shows that all are negative as the theory suggests. With three exceptions, the estimates have magnitudes that indicate an inelastic price response. The exception for the linear expenditure system corresponds to the recreation and entertainment commodity group where the necessary consumption level γ is estimated as negative. For the Rotterdam model, the estimated uncompensated price elasticities are 1.00 for transportation and communication and 1.09 for recreation and entertainment. The larger differences between the uncompensated price elasticity estimates for the Rotterdam and linear expenditure models are for furniture, furnishings, household equipment and operations, and personal goods and services.

The estimates from the nine commodity groups support the results and associated observations drawn from application of the static models to the four commodity groups. Even at lower levels of disaggregation, these static models do not produce results that are as satisfactory for commodity groups of durable goods as do the dynamic models. For example, in furniture, furnishing, household equipment and operation, and transportation groups the income and price elasticities show comparatively large differences between the Rotterdam and linear expenditure system estimates and durable goods estimates obtained when the dynamic models are applied to the four commodity groups. Although the overlap in commodity groups is not complete, the stability of the estimates between the dynamic systems and their discrepancies between the static models suggest an improvement from the more flexible partial adjustment structures.

7.4.2 Estimates from Other Studies

Comparisons of estimates for the four and nine commodity cases with those from other studies must be made with some caution, since the latter involve different models, data bases, estimation methods, and commodity groups. These results can be evaluated in relation to their applied implications. Results of income and price elasticities from several studies using Canadian and U.S. data have been assembled in Table 7.8. The table includes the source, information about the country, the time period used for estimation, the demand system employed, the commodity groups, and the elasticity estimates. Other studies using Canadian data include those by Carlevaro (1971); Schweitzer (1971); Oksanen and Spencer (1972); and Goldberger and Gameltsos (1977).

The comparisons afforded by the information in Tables 7.2, 7.5, 7.6, 7.7, and 7.8 are numerous, including the observation that our income elasticity estimates for food are similar to those in other studies. Food is income inelastic with a coefficient in the range of 0.31 to 0.64. In the four commodity group models, food is in the class of nondurables. Our estimates of income elasticities for this nondurable commodity group show the short- and long-run income elasticities range from about 0.4 to 0.7, the latter being the long-run estimate. This compares to an income estimate of 0.68 obtained for a nondurables and semidurables class by Berndt et al. (1970).

For clothing, our income elasticity estimates are consistent with those of Powell (1965), Wales (1971), and McIntosh (1974) for Canada. However, they are lower than those obtained by Hassan et al. (1974), Weiserbs (Phlips 1974), and Lluch and Williams (1975) for the United States. The semidurables in the four commodity group models have somewhat higher income

TABLE 7.8 Comparison of price and income elasticity estimates with other studies

Study	Time Period/ Country	Demand System[a]	Commodity Group	Elasticity Price	Elasticity Income
Powell (1965)	1949-63/ Canada	additive preference	food	-0.46	0.58
			tob./alcoh.	-0.54	0.79
			clothing	-0.52	0.74
			housing	-0.38	0.51
			hshld. exp.	-1.28	2.13
			transportation	-1.37	2.32
			personal/medical	0.05	-0.07
			miscellaneous	-0.67	0.97
Wales (1971)	1947-68/ Canada	LES	food	-0.27[b]	0.31[b]
				(-0.39)[c]	(0.86)[c]
			clothing	-0.24	0.33
				(-0.31)	(0.95)
			shelter	-0.81	1.14
				(-0.20)	(0.42)
			miscellaneous	-1.02	1.67
				(-0.71)	(1.52)
McIntosh (1974)	1949-68/ Canada	LES	food	-0.26	0.45
			clothing	-0.22	0.51
			housing	-0.67	1.30
			trans./commun.	-0.59	1.41
			rec./ed., enter.	-0.58	1.19
			health	0.35	-0.69
			miscellaneous	-0.70	1.39
Berndt, Darrough, Diewert (1977)	1952-71/ Canada	TLOG	durables	-1.18	1.59
			non/semidurables	-0.68	0.35
			services	-0.42	1.61
Hassan, Johnson, Finley (1974)	1929-69/ U.S.A.	Rotterdam	durables	-0.86	2.43
			food	-0.33	0.64
			clothing, shoes	-0.44	1.13
			gasoline, oil	0.28	0.79
			other nondurabs.	-0.47	1.15
			housing	-0.20	0.46
			hshld. exp.	-0.33	0.89
			transportation	-0.36	1.04
			other services	-0.32	0.71
Weiserbs (Phlips 1974)	1929-70/ U.S.A.	LES-D	autos, parts	-2.13[d]	7.57[d]
				(-1.35)[e]	(1.65)[e]
			furn., hshld. equipment	-0.89	2.35
				(-0.90)	(0.92)
			other durables	-0.48	1.27
				(-1.50)	(1.88)
			food, bev.	-0.30	0.53
				(-0.53)	(0.58)
			clothing, shoes	-0.47	1.11
				(-0.97)	(1.04)
			gasoline, oil	-0.15	0.36
				(-1.17)	(1.76)
			other nondurabs.	-0.33	0.76
				(-0.92)	(1.21)
			housing	-0.12	0.24
				(-1.43)	(3.49)
			hshld. exp.	-0.24	0.58
				(-1.38)	(2.23)
			transportation	-0.31	0.80
				(-0.87)	(1.03)
			other services	-0.27	0.56
				(0.85)	(-0.99)
Lluch, Williams (1975)	1930-72/ U.S.A.	LES	food	-0.28	0.41
			clothing	-0.48	0.90
			housing	-0.61	1.13
			durables	-0.83	1.61
			other	-0.74	1.13

[a]LES denotes linear expenditure system, LES-D indicates linear expenditure system-dynamic, TLOG denotes translog reciprocal indirect utility function.

[b]Linear expenditure system "static".

[c]Linear expenditure system "habit formation".

[d]Short-run estimates.

[e]Long-run estimates.

elasticities than those reported for clothing. This is true even for the state adjustment and dynamic linear expenditure models that suggest a range of 0.7 to 1.2 for short-and long-run income elasticities for semidurables.

The estimates for shelter and transportation from the present analysis are in general agreement with those in Table 7.8. Our results and those in Table 7.8 show a systematic difference between the United States and Canada in the income elasticity for transportation. It may be due to subsidies in the United States and the excise tax in Canada having the effect of decreasing and increasing the price of consuming this commodity, respectively. On a more general level, the durable goods group estimates in Table 7.8 and our estimates for this commodity group indicate a similar income elasticity. Again, the flexibility of the dynamic models is suggested by the fact that the income elasticity estimates for durables in Tables 7.5 and 7.6 are within the range of most of those reported in Table 7.8.

Price elasticity estimates seem to be roughly similar for food, clothing, and durable goods, for estimates obtained from the linear expenditure system and the indirect addilog models. For durable goods, elasticities estimated from the static models lie between those for durable goods from the two dynamic models. For shelter, price elasticities differ from those in Table 7.8 but the difference appears to be due more to the variable results from other studies than to a systematic effect in the Canadian data or models employed.

Two other comparative studies of alternative demand systems have been made from U.S. data for the period covered by the present analysis. In this application, like the one undertaken by Klevmarken (1979), the additive models, linear expenditure systems in various forms, performed comparably to the nonadditive Rotterdam model. This information contradicts Deaton (1974) and suggests that at higher levels of aggregation the additivity assumption may be overly restrictive. The analysis in Chap. 8 helps to examine these results for assumed serial correlation of residuals. The appropriateness of this hypothesis for the static systems is suggested by the superior performance of the dynamic models that introduce a systematic explanation for persistence in consumption behavior.

7.4.3 Forecasting Performance

Forecasts from the two dynamic models are plotted along with the observed values for the dependent variables in Figs. 7.1 and 7.2. In viewing Figs. 7.1 and 7.2, it should be recognized that the data for estimating the models are for 1947-1972. The outside sample data used (1973, 1974) are revised series from Statistics Canada (1975) and are substantially different for services. These revised values are used without adjustment to simulate the model. Forecasts or simulations are calculated using actual initial values of the lagged endogenous variables. Simulated values for the lagged endogenous variables

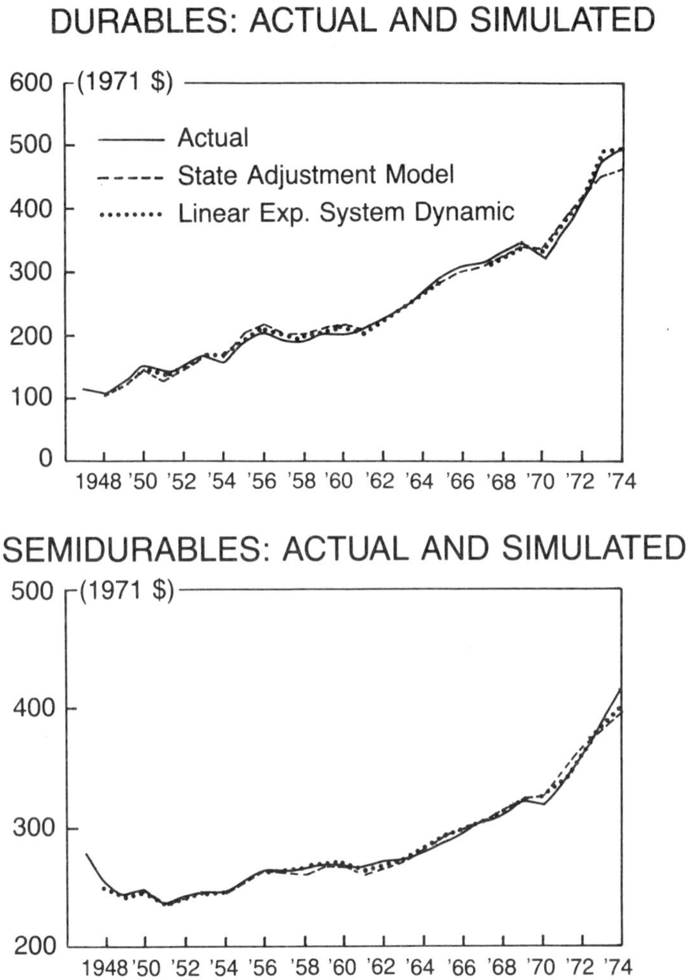

FIG. 7.1. Performance of dynamic demand systems; durables and semidurables, 1947-1974.

are used after the first period and no calibration is undertaken to ensure better fits.

Results of the simulations are encouraging because most of the turning points are properly reflected and there are few major discrepancies in the levels of the actual and simulated expenditures. These observations from Figs. 7.1 and 7.2 are substantiated in Table 7.9, containing the root mean square errors (absolute and percentage) for the models in and outside the sample period. Generally, these results suggest the same

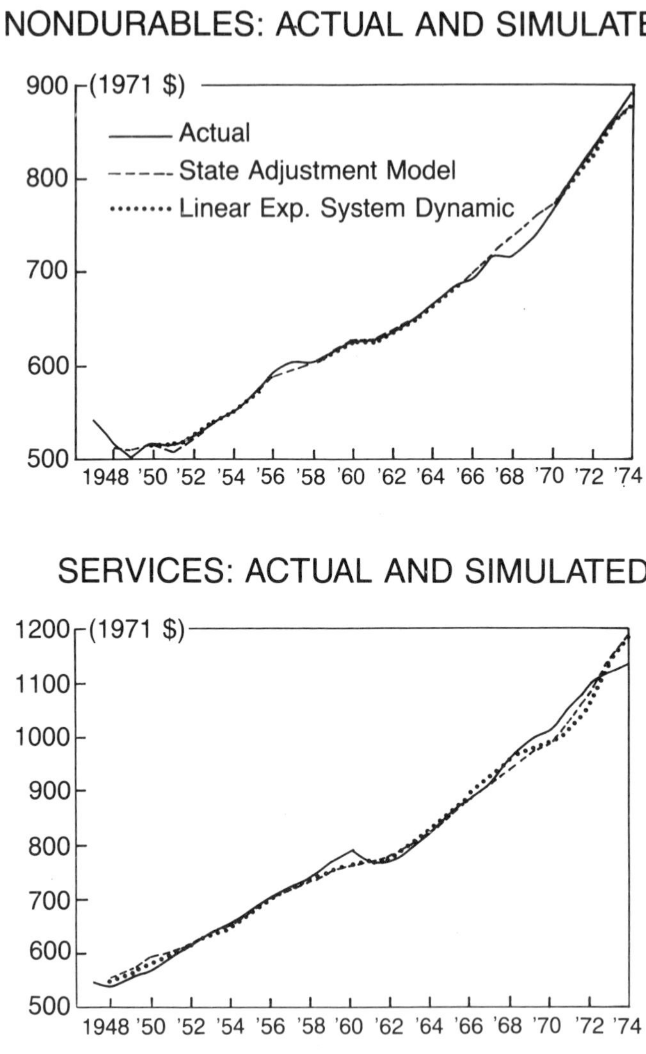

FIG. 7.2. Performance of dynamic demand systems; nondurables and services, 1947-1974.

conclusion: the dynamic linear expenditure system produces the better fit; errors are largest for services, smallest for nondurable goods outside the sample period, and largest for durables within the sample period.

7.5 CONCLUSION

Estimates of structural parameters and price and income elasticities reported and evaluated for several models and

TABLE 7.9 Evaluative statistics for simulation of dynamic models

Commodity Group	State Adjustment Model				LES-Dynamic			
	RMS (error)		RMS (% error)		RMS (error)		RMS (% error)	
	47-72	73-74	47-72	73-74	47-72	73-74	47-72	73-74
Durables	8.56[a]	28.60[b]	4.24	5.86	6.50	10.14	2.93	2.13
Semidurables	3.87	10.03	1.25	4.34	2.87	12.01	1.03	2.88
Nondurables	7.00	11.07	1.03	1.24	7.31	13.11	1.05	1.46
Services	15.21	42.41	1.89	3.72	14.98	42.62	1.67	3.73

[a]Inside the sample period.
[b]Outside the sample period and with unincorporated revisions of the services series.

applied to two sets of commodity groups reflect a substantial similarity, even between static and dynamic models. Differences that occur between our estimates and those from other studies are apparently due to unsystematic variation in results from other studies rather than from any obvious factor associated with the data bases or underlying models. These observations apply to both the nine and four commodity group results.

The static models, except for the double log, produce estimates that have similar implications and are comparable with those summarized from other studies, if these other results are not erratic. For food, clothing, and transportation, all the results from the comparative studies are similar to the nine commodity group estimates in Sec. 7.2.2. Discrepancies in other studies are as much a function of differences in commodity group classifications as they are differences in models or data bases. For the four commodity groups, our results are comparable and provide representative values for those from other studies. In some limited instances the income and price elasticities from prior work seem implausible, but the four and nine commodity group results can all be rationalized for relative values and signs.

Of the two dynamic models, the linear expenditure system performed better in simulations within and outside of our sample. This is consistent with results obtained by Klevmarken (1979) and this improved performance is probably due to a more flexible adjustment mechanism. For comparable commodity groups, elasticity estimates from our dynamic models are near those reported in Lluch and Williams (1975) and Berndt et al. (1977). Elasticity estimates using more refined commodity groups usually fall between the long- and short-run estimates for the corresponding, more aggregated commodity groups used with the two dynamic systems. The elasticity estimates seem more consistent and satisfactory for the durables and nondurables than for semidurables and services, possibly because of the homogeneity within classes. Plausible adjustment implications and relationships of estimated long-run price effects to those for the static models provide an empirical impetus for extending the demand systems models to accommodate more persistence in consumption patterns.

EXERCISES

1. Use the parameters from Table 7.1 and the expressions for the elasticities in terms of these structural parameters from Chap. 4 to verify the price elasticity estimates provided in Table 7.2. Use the data in the Appendix if necessary.
2. How are the uncompensated and compensated price elasticity estimates interpreted? Deduce the value adjustment used in the case of each of these models for the estimates reported in Table 7.2.
3. Compute the cross price elasticities from the structural parameter estimates in Table 7.1. What do the cross price elasticities suggest about restrictive assumptions that underlie the systems specifications?
4. Use the structural coefficient estimates in Table 7.6 to verify the elasticity calculations in that table. Refer to Chap. 5 for the appropriate formulas.
5. Calculate the cross price elasticities from the parameter estimates in Table 7.6. Compare these results with those obtained in Ex. 3.
6. Use the commodity classifications described in the text to compare and evaluate the consistency of the results for the four and nine commodity groupings; from Tables 7.2 and 7.7.

REFERENCES

Akin, J. S., and Stewart, J. F. 1979. Theoretical restrictions on the parameters of indirect addilog demand equations. Econometrica 47 (May):779-80.

Berndt, E. R., and Savin, N. E. 1975. Estimation and hypothesis testing in singular equation systems with autoregressive disturbances. Econometrica 43 (Sept.-Nov.):937-57.

Berndt, E. R.; Darrough, M. N.; and Diewert, W. E. 1970. Flexible functional forms and expenditure distributions: An application to canadian consumer demand functions. Discussion Paper 77-10, Department of Economics, University of British Columbia.

Carlevaro, F. 1971. Specifications and estimation of partially aggregated consumption functions. Canadian Journal of Economics 4 (Nov.):441-70.

Carlevaro, F., and Sadoulet, E. 1973. Trois programmes d'estimation d'une classe generale de fonctions de consummution additives. Centre d'Econometric, Universite' de Gene've.

Deaton, A. S. 1974. A reconsideration of the empirical implications of additive preferences. Economic Journal 84 (June):338-48.

Frisch, R. A. 1959. A complete scheme for computing all direct and cross demand elasticities in a model with many sectors. Econometrica 27 (Apr.):177-96.

Goldberger, A. S., and Gameltsos, T. 1977. A cross country consumption of consumer expenditure patterns. European Economic Review 1 (Spring):357-400.

Hassan, Z. A.; Johnson S. R.; and Finley, R. M. 1974. Further evidence on the structure of consumer demand in the United States: An application of the separability hypothesis. Southern Economic Journal 41 (Oct.):244-57.

Houthakker, H. S., and Taylor, L. D. 1970. Consumer Demand in the United States, 2nd ed. Cambridge, Mass.: Harvard Univ. Press.

Klevmarken, N. A. 1979. A comparative study of complete systems of demand functions. Journal of Econometrics 10 (Apr.):165-91.

Lluch, C., and Williams, R. 1975. Consumer demand systems and aggregate consumption in the U.S.A.: An application of the extended linear expenditure system. Canadian Journal of Economics 8 (Feb.):49-66.

McIntosh, C. E. 1974. Canadian food expenditures in 1980. Canadian Journal of Agricultural Economics 22 (Nov.):45-51.

Oksanen, E. H., and Spencer, B. T. 1972. Testing an aggregate consumption model for Canada. Canadian Journal of Economics 5 (Feb.):96-109.

Parks, R. W. 1971. Maximum likelihood estimation of the linear expenditure system. Journal of the American Statistical Association 66 (Dec.):900-903.

Phlips, L. 1974. Applied Consumption Analysis. Amsterdam: North Holland.

Powell, A. A. 1965. Post-war consumption in Canada: A first look at aggregates. Canadian Journal of Political Science 31 (Nov.):559-65.

———. 1974. Empirical Analytics of Demand Systems. Lexington, Mass.: D. C. Heath.

Schweitzer, T. T. 1971. Personal consumer expenditures in Canada, 1926-1975, (Parts 1, 2, 3). Staff Study No. 26, Economic Council of Canada, Ottawa.

Statistics Canada. 1975. Estimated Population of Canada by Province. Catalogue No. 91-201.

———. 1976. National Income and Expenditure Accounts, vol. 1, Catalogue 13-531, Ottawa.

Theil, H. 1971. Principles of Econometrics. New York: John Wiley.

Wales, T. J. 1971. A generalized linear expenditure model of the demand for non-durable goods in Canada. Canadian Journal of Economics 4 (Nov.):471-84.

8 • Habit Formation and Autocorrelation

Economists traditionally estimate demand systems parameters from time series data with the assumption that the only difference between time frames is the alternative sets of prices and incomes to which consumers respond. If this is correct, then application of demand systems based on the assumption that consumers maximize an instantaneous utility function subject to a budget constraint can provide an appropriate representation of the choice problem. In Chap. 2 these assumptions, along with regularity conditions on the utility function, yield as a maintained hypothesis the static "constant taste" demand specification. However, dynamic formulations reviewed in Chap. 5 imply that economists are more frequently challenged about the appropriateness of the static maintained hypothesis.

Specifications that allow for the changed circumstances of consumers are more realistic and suggest generalized demand systems formulations with the static models as nested or restricted cases. Statistical procedures can be used to test the appropriateness of these more flexible formulations; that is, more flexible models can be tested with the data to determine if what will be called the changing taste version of the system is more likely to have generated the observed series.

Nonnested tests presented by Cox (1961), Pesaran (1974), and Pesaran and Deaton (1978) can be used to evaluate different habit schemes if one model is not a restricted version of the other. For example, the difference between a time trend model and a partial adjustment model is that the former includes the trend term t but the latter includes lagged consumption, q_{it-1}. Choice between the two models cannot be made using the classical likelihood ratio procedure; it requires nonnested procedures or a Bayesian posterior odds procedure (see Gaver and Geisel 1974).

Pollak (1978) has given four reasons why, in an analysis of household behavior, tastes can be considered endogenous: (1)

habit formation where taste changes are related to past consumer decisions; (2) interdependent preferences, that is, preferences that are related to the consumption patterns of others; (3) advertising that explicitly attempts to influence and/or modify consumer tastes; and (4) prices or "snob appeal," whereby individuals prefer higher priced goods because they think they are better.

Stigler and Becker (1977) state that all economic analyses should avoid taste formation and change. They use the household production specification to circumvent problems raised in treating changes in tastes explicitly in static specifications. This viewpoint is challenged by Pollak (1978).

The primary focus here is on alternative methods to incorporate taste changes into demand systems specifications. Dynamic demand systems discussed previously as extensions of the static models emerge in this context but with a more general motivation. The first section presents an overview of customary ways of introducing habit formation hypotheses, including a discussion of the meaning of habit formation. What economists refer to as habits or persistence in consumption patterns may be due to a number of factors in addition to changing tastes.

The second section examines linear and proportionate habit formation in the linear expenditure system, and the demand system used as a basis for empirical results is reported later in the chapter. Expressions for price and income elasticities are investigated for parametric changes in the habit formation structures and a framework for analyzing the empirical results for the different versions of the LES is developed.

Stochastic specifications that can accommodate persistence effects in consumption behavior are reviewed in Sec. 8.3. By assuming no autocorrelation, a first order autoregressive scheme, or more general autoregressive moving average error processes, very different estimates of the effects of changes in prices, income, and habits are often obtained. Comparisons of the estimated relationships incorporating these processes on the disturbances can be made across constant taste and endogenous taste demand systems formulations.

The fourth section presents empirical results of two habit formation specifications (proportional and linear) in the linear expenditure system with two different stochastic assumptions (disturbances independently distributed and disturbances following a first order vector autoregressive process). A discussion of the structural implications and significance of treating endogenous tastes with alternative disturbance hypotheses in demand analyses follows.

8.1 HABIT FORMATION

Preferences may change as a result of the consumer's developing habits (Pollak 1970). When this occurs, economists refer to a consumer who becomes attached to a certain product, for example tobacco, a particular brand of soda pop, or a specific vacation location. Then the past consumption level of the particular product will be higher in the future more than it would have been in the absence of the affinity for the commodity. For demand systems specifications and results this means that the consumer may be less sensitive to price and income changes when habits have developed.

One of the common methods of treating changing tastes in demand relations (see Chap. 5) is either to add an exogenous time trend or to assume that the parameters of the demand systems models are time dependent. In the latter case the parameters are assumed to vary linearly with time and past consumption levels. Related characterizations are of course possible. Under rather restrictive conditions, the state adjustment model can be derived from a utility maximization process. El-Safty (1976) shows that it is a special case of a more generalized "learning by doing" model. These ad hoc approaches are popular primarily for their simplicity and it is sometimes difficult to improve upon them (Stone 1954; Pollak and Wales 1969).

An extensive treatment of habit formation is developed by Houthakker and Taylor (1970), the state adjustment model described in Chap. 5. According to this specification, the quantity demanded of the ith commodity is hypothesized to be a function of physical stock (in the case of durable goods) or a psychological stock of habits (in the case of habit forming goods), prices, and income. The rate of change in the stock is related to the rate of purchase and the depreciation rate.

Habit effects are introduced and tested in the translog demand system by Manser (1976) and in the linear expenditure system by Pollak and Wales (1969), Phlips (1974), El-Safty (1976), Hammond (1976), and Pollak (1976, 1978). Lluch and Williams (1975), MacKinnon (1976), and Green et al. (1978) provide estimates of the linear expenditure system with autoregressive errors. More recently, Howe et al. (1979) and Green et al. (1980) have estimated the LES by considering simultaneously effects of autocorrelation and habits. Habit formation hypotheses have been introduced into intertemporal demand systems by Lluch (1974) and Klijn (1977).

The habit formation schemes considered here are consistent with those in Chap. 5 for dynamic demand systems. Habits are examined within the linear expenditure system. The general expression used for introducing habits or persistence is

$$\gamma_{it} = \gamma_i^* + \beta_i q_{it-1}$$

That is, the required level of consumption for commodity i in period t is equal to a constant $_i$ plus a parameter $_i$, usually positive, times the consumption level in the previous period q_{it-1}.

Substituting (8.1) into the static LES model from Chap. 4

$$p_{it}q_{it} = p_{it}\gamma_{it} + \mu_i(m_t - \sum_j p_{tj}\gamma_{jt}) \qquad (i = 1, 2, \ldots, n) \qquad (8.2)$$

yields the generalized linear expenditure system

$$p_{it}q_{it} = [(1 - \mu_i)\gamma_i^*]p_{it} - \sum_{j\neq i}(\mu_i\gamma_j^*)p_{jt} + [(1 - \mu_i)\beta_i]p_{it}q_{it-1}$$

$$- \sum_{j\neq i}(\mu_i\beta_j)p_{jt}q_{jt-1} + \mu_i m_t \qquad (i = 1, 2, \ldots, n) \qquad (8.3)$$

with time subscripts added to distinguish the observations for different periods. The linear habit formation structure in (8.1) reduces to a proportional relation when $\gamma_i^* = 0$; that is,

$$\gamma_{it} = \beta_i q_{it-1} \qquad (8.4)$$

The linear expenditure function given in equation (8.3) simplifies by the omission of the first two terms involving γ_i^* on the right-hand side.

8.2 HABIT FORMATION SPECIFICATION

Discussion of the habit formation specifications in Sec. 8.1 speculates that their incorporation into the LES leaves consumption less responsive to price and income changes. While this proposition is generally true, it is useful to explore the consequences of the habit formation specification in some detail in order to provide background for interpreting the empirical estimates presented later. They highlight the distinctions that must be made in analyzing parametric shifts in the habit formation structure, intertemporal relationships, and specification errors as they affect estimated consumption responses to price and income changes.

Parametric shifts in the habit formation structure are conveniently generated by expressing the expenditure function (8.3) as a demand equation; that is, dividing (8.3) by price p_{it} we obtain

$$q_{it} = \beta_0' + \beta_1' q_{it-1} + \beta_2'(1/p_{it}) \qquad (i = 1, 2, \ldots, n) \qquad (8.5)$$

where $\beta_0' = [(1 - \mu_i)\gamma_i^*]$, $\beta_1' = [(1 - \mu_i)\beta_i]$, and $\beta_2' = [-\Sigma_{j\neq i}(\mu_i\gamma_j^*)p_{jt} - \Sigma_{j\neq i}(\mu_i\beta_j)p_{jt}q_{jt-1} + m_t\mu_i]$. Recall that the habit parameters are β_i and γ_i^* $(i = 1, 2, \ldots, n)$. Parametric results for the habit formation specification are thus obtained by examining consumption responses for changes in these parameters in the <u>varying parameters model</u> (8.5).

Before determining these consumption responses in terms of the price and income elasticities, examine the graph of (8.5) in

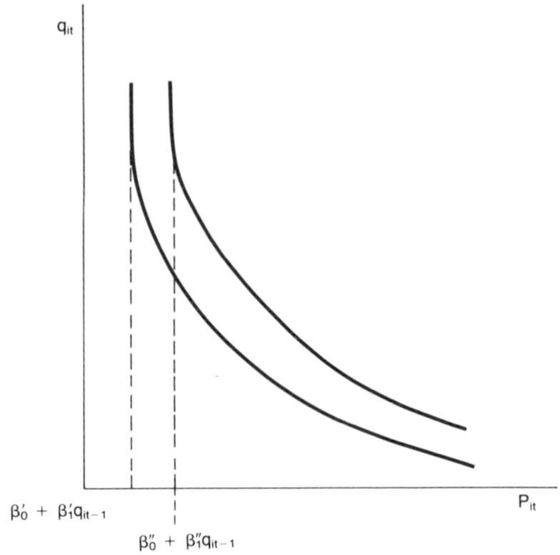

FIG. 8.1. Effects of changes in habits on the demand function from the linear expenditure system.

Fig. 8.1. Since β_i appears only in the composite parameter for q_{it-1}, $\beta_1' = [(1 - \mu_i)\beta_i]$, the effect of a change in β_i is simply to shift the constant. This follows because q_{it-1} is held constant by our ceteris paribus assumption. If $\beta_i > 0$, an increase in q_{it-1} shifts the demand function in Fig. 8.1 to the right as indicated by the intercept shift to $\beta_0'' + \beta_1'' q_{it-1}$. That is, an increase in habits increases the quantity demanded for the commodity q_{it} at a specific price if other factors are assumed unchanged.

Given the habit formation specification, the parametric effects of β_i and γ_i^* on the income and price elasticities can be easily deduced. From Chap. 5, the own price elasticity for the linear expenditure system is $e_{ii} = -1 + (1 - \mu_i)(\gamma_i/q_{it})$. Substituting the linear habit formation specification (8.1) and appropriately redefining q_{it} as in (8.3), the derivatives of e_{ii} with respect to β_i and γ_i^* can be obtained:

$$\frac{\partial e_{ii}}{\partial \gamma_i^*} = \frac{\partial e_{ii}}{\partial \gamma_{it}} = (1 - \mu_i)\left[\frac{q_{it} - \gamma_{it}(1 - \mu_i)}{q_{it}^2}\right] > 0 \tag{8.6}$$

$$\frac{\partial e_{ii}}{\partial \beta_i} = \frac{\partial e_{ii}}{\partial \gamma_{it}} \frac{\partial \gamma_{it}}{\partial \beta_i} = \frac{\partial e_{ii}}{\partial \gamma_{it}} \left[\sum_{j=1}^{\infty} [\beta_i(1 - \mu_i)]^{j-1} q_{it-j} \right] > 0 \qquad (8.7)$$

An increase in γ_i^* in the habit formation structure has the same impact as an increase in γ_i for the standard LES model if we ignore across equation effects. This is reasonable, since both γ_i^* and γ_i are additions to the required amounts of the commodity and $\gamma_i = \gamma_i^*$ for $\beta_i = 0$. The change in the elasticity for changes in β_i is larger than that for γ_i^* in (8.7), since q_{it-1} in (8.3) is in turn a function of β_i. The expression for $\partial\gamma_{it}/\partial\beta_i$ is an infinite sum, with the weights given by a geometrically declining function of β_i and μ_i. The habit hypothesis (8.1) implies stronger restrictions on current consumption behavior, based on past consumption levels, than is at first apparent. Increases in both γ_i^* and β_i reduce the supernumerary income and thus the potential for responding to price changes, and the result is that consumer response to price is less elastic.

For income elasticity the expression for LES (again from Chap. 5) is $\eta_i = \mu_i/w_i$, where w_i is the expenditure proportion. The derivatives of this expression with respect to β_i and γ_i^* are

$$\frac{\partial \eta_i}{\partial \beta_i} = - \frac{m\mu_i(1 - \mu_i)}{(p_i q_{it})^2} \left[\sum_{j=1}^{\infty} [\beta_i(1 - \mu_i)]^{j-1} q_{it-j} \right] < 0 \qquad (8.8)$$

$$\frac{\partial \eta_i}{\partial \gamma_i^*} = - \frac{m\mu_i(1 - \mu_i)}{(p_i q_{it})^2} < 0 \qquad (8.9)$$

Since LES specification admits only superior goods, it follows that increases in both parameters of the habit specification reduce the magnitude of the income elasticity. Consumption responses become less income elastic.

Intertemporal consumption responses to habit formation can be viewed in two ways. First is the impact on the short- and long-run elasticities, as explained in Chap. 5. Expressions for the elasticities are observed to be the same except for the dynamic adjustment mechanism, which involves habit parameters here. Second, period to period relationships between consumption levels can be studied with the aid of the derivatives of the elasticity expressions with respect to q_{it-1}.

For the price elasticity,

$$\frac{\partial e_{ii}}{\partial q_{it-1}} = \frac{(1 - \mu_i \beta_i)[q_{it} - (1 - \mu_i)\gamma_{it}]}{q_{it}^{2}} \tag{8.10}$$

For habits, an increase in the commodity consumption level in the previous period implies that the current period own price elasticity will be more inelastic for usual values of the variables and parameters in the right-hand side of (8.10). Clearly, this line of argument can be carried further by differentiating (8.10) with respect to β_i and γ_i^*, the habit structure parameters.

The derivative of the income elasticity is

$$\frac{\partial \eta_i}{\partial q_{it-1}} = - \frac{m\mu_i[(1 - \mu_i)\beta_i]}{(p_i q_{it})^2} \tag{8.11}$$

With habits, an increase in consumption from the previous period q_{it-1} causes the income elasticity to become more inelastic. This expression can also be investigated for changes in β_i and γ_i^*, and the result would depend upon the impact of changing previous period consumption levels for different habit parameter values.

All the above results have been obtained by assuming that the habit specification is appropriate and the parameters are known. For applications of habit models and comparisons of estimates from habit and non-habit models an additional complication is introduced that involves the impact of the potential misspecification errors associated with estimation of two types of models from the same data set. For example, if the LES with habits is the true model then parameter estimates for the LES without habit formation have a specification bias. The magnitude of this bias is a function of the values of the auxiliary regression coefficients relating the included and omitted variables (Goldberger 1964). In short, the only case in which a clear comparison of estimated values can be made is one in which the omitted variable is orthogonal to the remainder of the data set, hardly likely for the terms involving q_{it-1} in (8.3).

For the systems of equations estimation problem, across equations restrictions are another complication. The existence of these restrictions makes it difficult to deduce the impact of specification errors on the estimated values of parameters for static and dynamic systems. When evaluating the parameter estimates in Sec. 8.4, remember that the estimated relationships or parameters potentially include these specification error effects. Hence, the parametric results presented here represent tendencies that we will examine in the estimated parameters. The fact that persistence or habits are also incorporated using the autocorrelation hypotheses makes the comparisons of results based upon conclusions from the parametric analysis more difficult. For this reason, the focus of Sec. 8.4 is the choice of the appropriate model more than detailed comparisons of parameter estimates from the various LES specifications.

8.3 STOCHASTIC SPECIFICATIONS

For application of the LES model, the error term ε_{it} is added to (8.3). Due to complications in estimation, especially when the specifications include lagged endogenous regressors, the disturbances are usually assumed to be time independent. With this assumption and using vector notation, since the error structure is for the equation system, we have $E(\varepsilon_t) = 0$ and $E(\varepsilon_t \varepsilon_{t'}) = \delta_{tt'}\Omega$, where E is the expectation operator and $\delta_{tt'}$ the Kronecker product; that is, the error term has expectation 0, is temporally uncorrelated, and has a contemporaneous variance covariance matrix Ω.

Hendry (1974) has argued that an autoregressive vector process should be part of the maintained hypothesis for systems estimation; that is, an autocorrelation hypothesis should be integrated into the structural specification of a model. If autocorrelation is assumed in the present context, then

$$\varepsilon_t = R\varepsilon_{t-1} + v_t \quad \text{for } t = 2, 3, \ldots, T \tag{8.12}$$

where R is a n x n parameter matrix and v_2, v_3, ..., v_T are independently, identically distributed normal random vectors with means 0 and contemporaneous covariance matrix Σ. More complicated autoregressive moving average stochastic specifications than the first order autoregressive process can be introduced, and can be handled using time series specifications (Box and Jenkins 1970). With the autoregressive assumption in (8.5) and linear habit formulation version of the LES given by (8.1), the maintained hypothesis has been augmented to accommodate persistence in consumption patterns either structurally or through a process on the disturbances.

Since the sum of individual expenditures equals the total, it follows that the contemporaneous covariance matrix is singular. Barten (1969) shows that maximum likelihood parameter estimates can still be obtained by arbitrarily deleting an equation and that these estimates are invariant to the deleted equation. However, this result does not hold for autocorrelated disturbances according to Berndt and Savin (1975), who show that the adding-up property for expenditures implies certain restrictions on the autoregressive parameter matrix R. For R diagonal (that is with no assumed autocorrelation across equations), these results indicate that the autocorrelation coefficients must be the same for each equation. With this stochastic assumption, a program developed by Hall and Hall (1979) and discussed in Berndt et al. (1974) is used to obtain full information maximum likelihood estimators of the parameters of the linear expenditure system. Specifically, the gradient method of Hall and Hall's TSP program (Chap. 6) is used to obtain maximum likelihood parameter estimates for the models. In another study (Green et al. 1978), a program developed by Wegge (1969a, 1969b) was used, but it would not obtain convergence for the most general linear habit formulation model with autocorrelation in the present problem. The TSP program attained convergence and was used to generate these results.

8.4 EMPIRICAL RESULTS

Annual time series data from Statistics Canada (1976) for 1947-1972 are employed to estimate the model specified in (8.3) and (8.12) and also are used for the various hypotheses tests. Consumer expenditure data for three aggregate commodity groups are used: durables and semidurables, nondurables, and services. For computational reasons, the three commodity classification is used instead of the four commodity classification that generated the results in Chap. 7. Convergence problems encountered with full information maximum likelihood methods prohibited a less aggregated commodity grouping.

The major emphasis of analysis of these empirical results is the tests of restrictions afforded by the comparisons of models formulated under alternative habit formation and serial correlation hypotheses. Before presenting the results of these tests, structural parameter estimates and implied elasticities are examined for six models: (1) static LES assuming no autocorrelation, (2) static LES assuming a first-order autoregressive scheme, (3) LES with a proportional habit scheme and assuming no autocorrelation, (4) LES with a proportional habit scheme and assuming a first order autoregressive error process, (5) LES with a linear habit formation scheme assuming no autocorrelation, and (6) LES with a linear habit scheme and assuming a first order autoregressive error process.

8.4.1 Structural Estimates

Estimates of the structural parameters for the six different versions of the linear expenditure system are presented in Table 8.1. To evaluate these results, observe that the marginal budget shares μ_i are all positive, are less than one, sum to one for each of the model specifications, and significantly different from 0 in every case. The only statistically significant borderline values are for the linear habit models with and without autocorrelation and for nondurable commodities. The calculated t values are slightly larger than 2 for the estimated μ_i, even in these situations.

TABLE 8.1 Maximum likelihood estimates of structural parameters for linear expenditure systems, 1947-1972[a]

	CASE 1		CASE 2		CASE 3		CASE 4		CASE 5			CASE 6		
	No Autocorrelation $\rho = 0$		Autocorrelation $\rho \neq 0$		Proportional Habit Formation with No Autocorrelation $\gamma_{it} = \beta_i q_{it-1}$ $\rho = 0$		Proportional Habit Formation with Autocorrelation $\gamma_{it} = \beta_i q_{it-1}$ $\rho \neq 0$		Linear Habit Formation with No Autocorrelation $\gamma_{it} = \gamma_i^* + \beta_i q_{it-1}$ $\rho = 0$			Linear Habit Formation with Autocorrelation $\gamma_{it} = \gamma_i^* + \beta_i q_{it-1}$ $\rho \neq 0$		
	μ_i	γ_i^*	μ_i	γ_i^*	μ_i	β_i	μ_i	β_i	μ_i	γ_i^*	β_i	μ_i	γ_i^*	β_i
Durables and	0.297[b]	208.627	0.292	163.278	0.651	0.332	0.647	0.049	0.574	-75.039	-0.023	0.550	-93.523	-0.190
semidurables	(0.032)	(225.291)	(0.050)	(312.659)	(0.066)	(0.239)	(0.054)	(0.296)	(0.089)	(811.534)	(0.512)	(0.068)	(817.720)	(0.739)
Nondurables	0.253	428.458	0.251	335.126	0.207	0.841	0.201	0.773	0.207	21.987	0.638	0.218	31.617	0.523
	(0.026)	(145.371)	(0.023)	(291.419)	(0.054)	(0.043)	(0.053)	(0.077)	(0.102)	(315.054)	(0.276)	(0.091)	(405.460)	(0.493)
Services	0.450	359.909	0.457	152.695	0.142	0.916	0.152	0.859	0.219	-148.563	0.869	0.232	-192.092	0.824
	(0.041)	(387.033)	(0.070)	(769.586)	(0.045)	(0.043)	(0.053)	(0.087)	(0.060)	(554.518)	(0.313)	(0.005)	(616.925)	(0.393)
ρ	0		0.569		0		0.350		0			0.319		
			(0.266)				(0.314)					(0.304)		
$-2 \ln \lambda$	78.378		42.962		15.772		38.310		22.084			52.226		
$\chi^2_{.05}$, restr.	7.815		23.685		7.815		23.685		12.592			35.173		
	(3 restr.)		(14 restr.)		(3 restr.)		(14 restr.)		(6 restr.)			(23 restr.)		

[a]See Green et al. (1978) for a partial comparison of these results using TSP with the full information maximum likelihood results using a package by Wegge (1969).
[b]Estimated standard errors in parentheses.

TABLE 8.2 Income and price elasticity estimates, Cases 1-6, for linear expenditure models[a]

Commodity Group	Average Expenditure Proportions	Income Elasticity						Direct Price Elasticity[b]					
		1	2	3	4	5	6	1	2	3	4	5	6
Durables and semidurables	0.2810	1.06	1.04	2.32	2.30	2.04	1.96	-0.71	-0.77	-0.82	-0.92	-1.01	-1.37
Nondurables	0.3446	0.73	0.73	0.60	0.58	0.60	0.63	-0.49	-0.60	-0.30	-0.35	-0.44	-0.53
Services	0.3744	1.20	1.22	0.38	0.41	0.58	0.62	-0.79	-0.91	-0.21	-0.27	-0.44	-0.53

[a]For the habit models, the short-run elasticities are reported.
[b]Uncompensated.

The coefficients γ_i interpreted as minimum required quantities are all positive except for the durables and semidurables in the linear habit formation model. However, they are not significantly different from zero for any of the models. This may be symptomatic of a multicollinearity arising from a misspecification of persistence relationships and/or insufficient variation in the sample data. The presence of lagged consumption effect is apparently confounded with the minimum required quantities effect, since in Cases 5 and 6 for services and in Case 5 for nondurables, the β_i are statistically significant.

For the proportional habit formation systems, Cases 3 and 4, the β_i are significantly different from zero for nondurables and services. The exception occurs in Cases 3 and 4 for the durables and semidurables, suggesting that persistence in consumption patterns is present in the Canadian data. This claim is more systematically investigated later by using a test for habit effects based on the likelihood ratio.

Comparisons across models provide several interesting insights. First, consider Cases 1 and 2, the static LES with and without an autocorrelated error scheme. The autocorrelation coefficient is significantly different from zero in Case 2. The value of ρ is 0.569 with an estimated asymptotic standard error of 0.266. The estimated marginal budget shares differ very little in Cases 1 and 2, but the subsistence quantities are appreciably smaller when the autocorrelation parameter is not constrained to zero.

The maximum likelihood estimation methods of Wegge (1969a, 1969b and Green et al. 1978) gave more encouraging results for Cases 1 and 2. Specifically, the estimated mean values for μ_i and γ_i^* were approximately the same as those reported in Table 8.1 but the estimated standard errors for the γ_i^* were much smaller. For durables and semidurables, nondurables, and services, the values of γ_i^* (with standard errors in parentheses) were, for Case 1, 208.63 (95.26), 428.46 (82.54), and 359.91 (223.69) and for Case 2, 213.56 (103.88), 384.69 (88.59), and 289.04 (236.73), respectively. The gradient method of Hall and Hall was employed for the full set of results, since it would converge for the most general case, Case 6.

The habit formation versions of the LES reveal the β_i are higher for the proportional structures (Cases 3, 4) than for the linear structures (Cases 5, 6). When the autocorrelation parameter is not constrained to zero it is estimated at 0.319 with a standard error of 0.304 for the linear habit model and 0.350 with a standard error of 0.314 for proportional habit formation. In both instances the autocorrelation parameter is not significantly different from zero. Values of parameters defining the marginal budget shares are similar for the two habit formation versions of the LES. The estimated values for μ_i are similar for the linear habit models with and without autocorrelation (Cases 5, 6), and for the proportional habit models with and without autocorrelation (Cases 3, 4).

For the minimum subsistence quantities γ_i, the implied values (incorporating the habit framework) are less than the observed consumption levels for every commodity and time period. For the static versions these minimum quantity estimates are larger than observed consumption levels for some commodities for the first few observations in the time series. Similar results have been obtained by Pollak and Wales (1969).

8.4.2 Elasticities

Price and income elasticities calculated using the structural parameters and the sample means are presented in Table 8.2. Comparing the income elasticities for the six cases shows that quite similar results are obtained for the nondurables. For the durables and semidurables, the income elasticities nearly double from the static models (Cases 1, 2) to the models incorporating a structure for habitual behavior (Cases 3-6). The reverse is true for services.

Except for durables and semidurables, the uncompensated direct price elasticities are generally larger for the static models than for the models with structures admitting persistence. The larger elasticity variations are for services. The lower price elasticities and low income elasticities are observed for this group if the static structure is modified to allow for persistence in consumption behavior, better reflecting the secular growth in expenditures on this commodity group. Converse but less pronounced results are obtained from the durables and semidurables in which inventories are of obvious importance in influencing expenditure decisions. The most general model, Case 6, shows for durables and semidurables lower income elasticities and higher price elasticities than for other models in which the persistence hypothesis is implemented through either the systematic component or the error structure of the model.

8.4.3 Tests of Restrictions

To test for habit effects, autocorrelation, and the validity of the restrictions implied by the models, a likelihood ratio test is used where

$$\lambda = \max_w L / \max_W L \tag{8.13}$$

That is, the statistic in (8.13) is the ratio of the maximum value of the likelihood function L subject to restrictions to the maximum value of the likelihood function without restrictions. Note that

$$-2 \ln \lambda = T(\ln|\hat{\Sigma}_w| - \ln|\hat{\Sigma}_W|) \qquad (8.14)$$

under the null hypothesis is distributed asymptotically as chi-square with the number of degrees of freedom equal to the number of restrictions to be tested, where $\hat{\Sigma}_w$ is the restricted estimator of the covariance matrix and $\hat{\Sigma}_W$ is the unrestricted estimator (Theil 1971, pp. 396-97).

The test approach is to use the general form of the expenditure function (8.3) plus autocorrelation (8.12) or, equivalently, Case 6, defined in Table 8.1 as the general model. Then the following null hypotheses are tested:

H_1: $\beta_i = 0$, $\rho = 0$ (no habit persistence and autocorrelation)

H_2: $\beta_i = 0$ (no habit persistence)

H_3: $\rho = 0$ (no autocorrelation)

The organization of these nested hypotheses tests is indicated in Fig. 8.2. If H_1 is rejected, there would be empirical

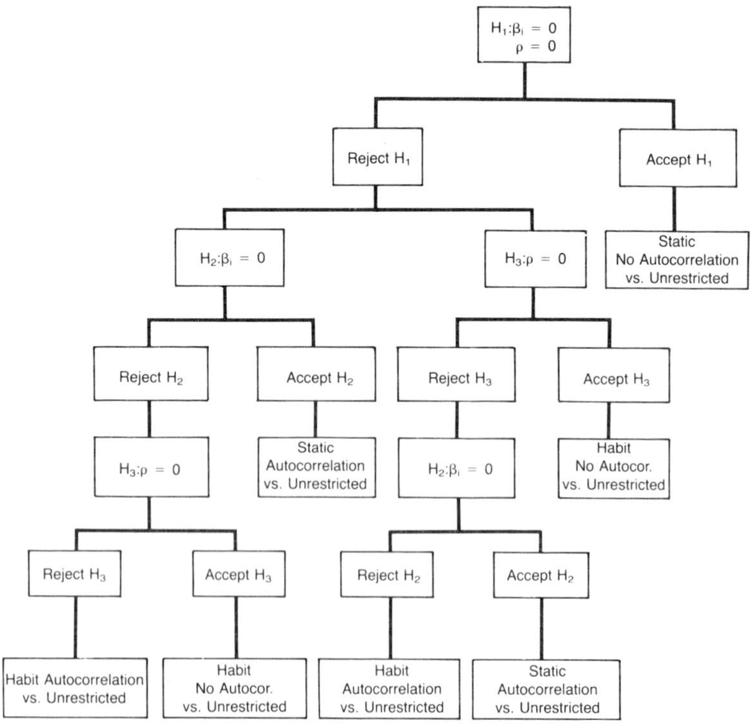

FIG 8.2. Tests for habits, autocorrelation, and theoretical restrictions.

support for either habit persistence and/or autocorrelation. The next steps consist of testing for habit persistence and autocorrelation. Assuming H_1, H_2, and H_3 are all rejected, the appropriate maintained hypothesis for testing the theoretical restrictions would again be as specified in (8.3) and (8.12).

To test for habit persistence, the likelihood ratio test is applied to models as indicated above. The static models are restricted forms, $\beta_i = 0$, of the linear habit persistence model specified in (8.3) and (8.12). The computed value of $-2 \ell n \lambda$ is 25.03 for Case 6 versus Case 2 (Table 8.3), which is larger than the chi-square value, $\chi^2_{.05,3} = 7.815$. (Note that there are 3 restrictions and thus 3 degrees of freedom; see Table 8.1.) Similar results are obtained for Case 5 versus Case 1 with $-2 \ell n \lambda = 9.01$. Therefore, the null hypothesis is rejected and habit persistence assumed present.

To test which structure better fits the habit formation data, the linear habit model or the proportional habit case, likelihood ratio tests are performed. Cases 3 and 4 are restricted versions of Cases 5 and 6, respectively, where $\gamma_i^* = 0$. The value of $-2 \ell n \lambda$ of 14.16 for Case 6 versus Case 4 is greater than $\chi^2_{.05,3} = 7.815$, thus indicating a rejection of the null hypothesis; that is, the linear habit formation model appears to describe the data better than the proportional version. Also, a value of $-2 \ell n \lambda = 14.45$ for Case 5 versus Case 3 is greater than $\chi^2_{.05,3} = 7.815$, again indicating the same result, but with γ_i^* set to zero; that is, the linear habit model is preferred over the proportional formulation.

To test whether autocorrelation is present, the likelihood ratio is again used, but with 1 degree of freedom it is equivalent to an asymptotic t test. For the static model (Case 2) the autocorrelation parameter is significantly different from zero. When autocorrelation is not constrained to zero in the linear habit model (Case 6) and the proportional habit model (Case 4), it is not significantly different from zero. As added evidence, the more general comparison, Case 6 versus Case 5, is reported in Table 8.3 with $-2 \ell n \lambda = 2.44$. Apparently, the habit formation structures were accounting for autocorrelation or persistence in residuals observed with the static LES and within the systematic components of the models.

Two more general tests of the composite habit formation and autocorrelation formulations are presented in Table 8.3. The comparison of the static model with no autocorrelation (Case 1) with the most general formulation (Case 6), gives a very large value for the test statistic, as expected from the previous results. A less pronounced difference, although still statistically significant, is obtained by comparing Cases 6 and 3.

TABLE 8.3 Computed values of $-2 \ln \lambda$ used in hypothesis tests across the six LES models

Test Statistics	Case 6 vs. Case 1	Case 6 vs. Case 2	Case 6 vs. Case 3	Case 6 vs. Case 4	Case 6 vs. Case 5
	Hypotheses Tests				
$-2 \ln \lambda$	100.44	25.03	16.89	14.16	2.44
$\chi^2_{.05}$, restr.	9.49 (4 restr.)	7.81 (3 restr.)	9.49 (4 restr.)	7.81 (3 restr.)	3.84 (1 restr.)
$\ln L$[a]	-199.96[b] (Case 1)	-167.25 (Case 2)	-158.19 (Case 3)	-156.82 (Case 4)	-150.96 (Case 5)

[a]Represents the value, excluding irrelevant constants, of the log likelihood functions for the six demand systems. The value of ln L for Case 6 is 149.741.

[b]In order to obtain $-2 \ln \lambda$ for each combination of the various hypotheses tests, just take the difference of the ln L and multiply by two. Also note that Case 2 is not a nested version of Case 4, nor is Case 1 a nested version of Case 3, so the likelihood ratio procedure cannot be used to test these cases.

To test for the full set of restrictions implied by each version of the LES, the models are compared with the unrestricted reduced forms. Degrees of freedom are calculated as the difference between unrestricted reduced form parameters and those required to specify the various versions of the LES model. Note that the "restrictions implied by the theory" are determined by the imposition of the LES parameter restrictions (see Chap. 4). As indicated by the values of the likelihood ratio statistics at the bottom of Table 8.1, in each case the restrictions implied by the theory are rejected. These conclusions are not surprising; other researchers have obtained similar results. These results imply that standard applied theory of consumption may be a poor guide to specification of aggregate expenditure models even when they incorporate simple structures to reflect persistence in consumption behavior, either in the structure of the demand systems or in the disturbance terms.

8.4.4 Comparison of Results with Other Studies

Our results are compared with other studies in Table 8.4. In most cases the autocorrelation coefficient has a high estimated value. The estimated values for the studies shown were -0.30, 0.65, 0.85, and 0.99, so for the static LES, autocorrelation appears to be present. When habits are introduced into the models, the autocorrelation coefficient becomes insignificant (see Cases 4, 6; Table 8.1). The estimated values for the autocorrelation coefficient was negative and significantly different from zero for the Howe et al. (1979) model. Clearly, a more thorough treatment of habit effects and autocorrelation is needed. Sometimes the inclusion of a time trend works about as well as lagged quantities to describe changes in tastes (Pollak and Wales 1969).

TABLE 8.4 Comparison of results with other LES studies

Study	Time Period/ Country	Demand System	Commodity Group	Elasticity Price	Elasticity Income
				(in 1961)	
MacKinnon (1976)	1927-1940	LES static,	food	-0.48	0.60
	1948-1971	$\rho = 0$	clothing	-0.59	0.81
	Canada		shelter	-0.81	1.07
			transportation	-0.89	1.27
			recreation	-0.87	1.23
			miscellaneous	-0.67	0.94
				(in 1961)	
MacKinnon (1976)	1927-1940	LES static,	food	-0.17	0.29
	1948-1971	$\rho \neq 0$	clothing	-0.66	1.07
	Canada	(r = 0.9948)	shelter	-0.76	0.97
			transportation	-0.77	1.35
			recreation	-0.89	1.60
			miscellaneous	-0.50	0.81
				(at mean values)	
Lluch & Williams (1975)	1930-1972 U.S.A.	LES static,	food	-0.275	
		$\rho \neq 0$	clothing	-0.478	
		(r = 0.85)	housing	-0.612	
			durables	-0.825	
			other	-0.742	
				(at mean values)	
Green, Hassan, & Johnson (1978)	1947-1972 Canada	LES static, $\rho = 0$	durables and semidurables	-0.63	1.07
			nondurables	-0.49	0.73
			services	-0.74	1.20
				(at mean values)	
Green, Hassan, & Johnson (1978)	1947-1972 Canada	LES static,	durables and semidurables	-0.71	1.08
		$\rho \neq 0$			
		(r = 0.65)	nondurables	-0.55	0.74
			services	-0.79	1.17
				(in 1960)	
Howe, Pollak, & Wales (1977)	1929-1941	LES linear	food	-0.38	
	1947-1975	habits,	clothing	-0.25	
	U.S.A.	$\rho \neq 0$	shelter	-0.17	
		(r = -0.30)	miscellaneous	-0.21	

Income and price elasticities obtained here appear to be consistent with those from other studies. For example, for durables and semidurables, our estimate of the uncompensated price elasticity is -0.71 compared with a value of -0.825 for durables found by Lluch and Williams (1975).

8.5 CONCLUSIONS

Several ways of incorporating endogenous tastes or habits into demand systems analyses exist. The one considered here is a linear habit formation scheme, stating that habits depend only on consumption in the previous period or periods. A limitation of this approach for the LES is that habits have a restrictive impact on short-run price elasticities; but these restrictions can be relaxed by considering more generalized expenditure or demand systems such as the quadratic expenditure system.

When autoregressive disturbances are assumed in the presence of habit formation, misspecification errors can be reduced. For example, it is well known that the omission of more complicated autoregressive stochastic structures in dynamic simultaneous equations systems can result in serious prediction problems. To avoid these specification errors, a more generalized error structure can be included as part of the model hypothesis. Then the added parameters can be evaluated statistically.

Finally, the various habit schemes and autocorrelation processes can be tested empirically using likelihood ratio methods. The empirical results presented in this chapter demonstrate that the demand system parameter estimates are not robust with respect to the different stochastic specifications. Thus, models that employ alternative habit formation schemes should be evaluated in relation to more generalized stochastic specifications involving autocorrelation. Results for habit formation hypotheses are not yet complete enough that one can assume models incorporating them will perform better than those with persistence reflected by introducing an autocorrelation structure for the disturbances.

EXERCISES

1. State several reasons other than habit formation that may explain the inclusion of lagged dependent variables in demand models. Is it possible to empirically distinguish among these various interpretations or theories?
2. In the linear expenditure system provide a plausible justification for allowing the marginal budget shares μ_i to vary over time. Could habit formation schemes be introduced into the LES by this approach? Explain.
3. In the stochastic specification for the LES we assume the following first order autoregressive error process:

   $$\varepsilon_t = R\varepsilon_{t-1} + v_t$$

   where R is diagonal. Suppose R is not diagonal.
   (a) Give an economic example explaining why the nondiagonal elements of R may be nonzero.
   (b) Given that the sum of expenditures (dependent variable) equals total expenditures (explanatory variable) and R is diagonal, prove that these conditions imply that autocorrelation coefficients must be the same for each equation.
   (c) Given the same conditions in (b), show that this implies that the contemporaneous variance covariance matrix is singular.
4. Estimate the LES in (8.2) with a first order autoregressive process by

(a) assigning values to μ_i over the region 0.1 to 0.5 in increments of 0.1
(b) assigning values to ρ, the autocorrelation coefficient, over the region 0.0 to 0.8 in increments of 0.1

Use the data given in the appendix and apply ordinary least squares to search over the above regions for μ_i and ρ. Choose those parameter estimates that correspond to the minimization of the error sum of squares over the μ_i, ρ space.

5. Can standard errors for the μ_i and ρ be obtained from the procedure used in Ex. 4? Explain.

*6. Use the data in the appendix and estimate the LES with habits and a first order autoregressive process by a full information maximum likelihood program.

*7. Use the likelihood ratio procedure to test for autocorrelation and habit persistence in the LES.

8. In testing for autocorrelation, one additional restriction relates to the case of no autocorrelation. In this situation, how do the results from the likelihood ratio procedure compare with the test results that are based on the asymptotic t values associated with the estimated value of ρ?

9. Examine the sensitivity of (8.11) and (8.12) to changes in the habit parameters β_i and γ_i^*.

REFERENCES

Barten, A. P. 1969. Maximum likelihood estimation of a complete system of demand equations. European Economic Review 1 (Fall):7-73.

Berndt, E. R., and Savin, N. E. 1975. Estimation and hypothesis testing in singular equation systems with autoregressive disturbances. Econometrica 43 (Sept.-Nov.):937-57.

Berndt, E. R.; Hall, B. H.; Hall, R. E.; and Hausman, J. A. 1974. Estimation and inference in nonlinear structural models. Annals of Economic and Social Measurement 3 (Oct.):653-65.

Box, G. E. P., and Jenkins, G. 1970. Time Series Analysis, Forecasting, and Control. San Francisco: Holden Day.

Cox, D. R. 1961. Tests of separate families of hypotheses. Proceedings of the Fourth Berkeley Symposium 1, pp.

El-Safty, A. 1976. Adaptive behavior, demand, and preferences. Journal of Economic Theory 13 (Oct.):229-318.

Gaver, K., and Geisel, M. 1974. Discriminating among alternative models: Bayesian and non-Bayesian methods. Frontiers of Econometrics, ed. P. Zarembka, pp. 49-77. New York:

---

*More difficult.

Academic Press.

Goldberger, A. S. 1964. Econometric Theory. New York: John Wiley.

Green, R.; Hassan, Z.; and Johnson, S. R. 1978. Maximum likelihood estimation of linear expenditure systems with serially correlated errors: An application. European Economic Review 11 (Aug.):207-19.

———. 1980. Testing for habit formation, autocorrelation and theoretical restrictions in linear expenditure systems. Southern Economic Journal 47 (Oct.):433-43.

Hall, B., and Hall, R. 1979. Time series processor, version 3.3 for the Burroughs 6700/7700: User's manual, March.

Hammond, P. 1976. Endogenous tastes and stable long-run choice. Journal of Economic Theory 13 (Oct.):329-40.

Hendry, D. 1974. Stochastic specification in an aggregate demand model of the United Kingdom. Econometrica 42 (May):559-78.

Houthakker, H. S., and Taylor, L. D. 1970. Consumer Demand in the United States, 2d ed. Cambridge, Mass.: Harvard University Press.

Howe, H.; Pollak, R.; and Wales, T. J. 1979. Theory and time series estimation of the quadratic expenditure system. Econometrica 47 (Oct.):1231-48.

Klijn, N. 1977. Expenditure, savings and habit formation: A comment. International Economic Review 18 (Oct.):771-78.

Lluch, C. 1974. Expenditure, savings and habit formation. International Economic Review 15 (Oct.):786-97.

Lluch, C., and Williams, R. 1975. Consumer demand systems and aggregate consumption in the USA: An application of the extended linear expenditure system. Canadian Journal of Economics 8 (Feb.):49-66.

MacKinnon, J. 1976. Estimating the linear expenditure system and its generalizations. In Studies in Nonlinear Estimation, ed. S. Goldfeld and R. Quandt, pp. 143-66. Cambridge: Ballinger.

Manser, M. 1976. Elasticities of demand for food: An analysis using non-additive utility functions allowing for habit formation. Southern Economic Journal 43 (July):879-91.

Pesaran, M. 1974. On the general problem of model selection. Review of Economic Studies 41 (Apr.):153-70.

Pesaran, M., and Deaton, A. 1978. Testing non-nested nonlinear regression models. Econometrica 46 (May):677-94.

Phlips, L. 1974. Applied Consumption Analysis. Amsterdam: North Holland.

Pollak, R. A. 1970. Habit formation and dynamic demand functions. Journal of Political Economy 78 (July/Aug.):745-62.

———. 1976. Habit formation and long-run utility functions. Journal of Economic Theory 13 (Oct.):272-97.

———. 1978. Endogenous tastes in demand and welfare analysis. Discussion Paper No. 393, University of Pennsylvania, Department of Economics.

Pollak, R. A., and Wales, T. J. 1969. Estimation of the linear expenditure system. Econometrica 37 (Oct.):629-750.

Statistics Canada. 1976. National Income and Expenditure Accounts, Vol. 1, Catalogue 13-531, Ottawa.

Stigler, G., and Becker, G. S. 1977. De gustibus non est disputandum. American Economic Review 67 (Mar.):76-90.

Stone, R. 1954. Linear expenditure systems and demand analysis: An application to the patterns of British demand. Economic Journal 64 (Sept.):511-27.

Theil, H. 1971. Principles of Econometrics. New York: John Wiley.

Wegge, L. 1969a. A family of functional iterations and the solution of maximum likelihood estimating equations. Econometrica 37 (Jan.):122-30.

———. 1969b. Full information quasi-maximum likelihood estimators. Discussion Paper, University of California-Davis, Economics Department.

9 • Past and Future

This book presents available demand systems results and evaluates alternative formulations in an applied context. These demand systems models feature strong separability assumptions about underlying preference orderings for the consumers represented. Full systems models are estimated from existing data series and, in general, the parameter estimates satisfy the set of basic conditions following from curvature of the utility function and structure of the consumer optimization problem: Engel aggregation, Cournot aggregation, homogeneity in prices and income, and symmetry of substitution relationships between commodities. Thus, the systems afford the possibility of examining in an empirical setting the consequences of the major maintained hypotheses from the theory.

The cost of specifying these tractable demand systems models is the restrictiveness of separability assumptions. Behaviorally, these conditions provide strong restrictions on the preferences of consumers. In general, it is presumed that consumption levels of one commodity or group are highly restrictive or have no impact on the marginal rates of substitution for the consumption of other commodities or groups. The interrelationships in the demand specifications then follow from the levels of the commodity-by-commodity or group-by-group utilities and their competition for income through the budget constraint. This assumption can only be rationalized for highly aggregated commodity groups.

Empirical application of demand systems in Canadian aggregate time series data reveals a major problem associated with the specifications. Since they are static, they do not adequately reflect important consumption pattern persistencies exhibited at high levels of commodity aggregation in the time series data. Knowing the past period's consumption levels for the commodities is likely as valuable for forecasting the next period's consumption levels as is knowledge of the estimated parameters for the demand systems. Of course, this could be because prices and incomes do not change rapidly between periods, but it is also apparent that consumers' choice behavior is highly conditioned by habits and inventories of durables. The empirical application indicates this important limitation of static systems for representating consumption patterns in aggregate time series data.

This observation is not unique and has occurred in other contexts. In fact, it is largely responsible for the extensions of the static demand systems reviewed in Chaps. 5 and 8. Generalizations of static to dynamic demand systems take two forms. Ad hoc adjustments in the specifications of the demand systems have been made, including the introduction of trend terms, lagged dependent variables, and other pragmatic methods for incorporating persistence in models based on static separability hypotheses. Unfortunately, these model adaptations do not leave the optimization structure and the connection to the theory intact. Hence, hypothesis tests are less general and the prior restrictions are more specialized or appropriate to the current problem. This limitation has motivated approaches generating hypotheses that accommodate persistence within the context of the theory.

The more fully dynamic demand systems models emerge as refinements of ad hoc specifications and from general representations of the consumer allocation problem. In the former case the dynamic linear expenditure models (Phlips 1974) and the quadratic dynamic models (Houthakker and Taylor 1970), under specialized conditions, retain the restrictions from static theory and separability assumptions. The second model reviewed is the control theoretic formulation of Lluch (1974), but work in this area is in its most elementary stages. Solidly justified theoretical specifications with foundations in intertemporal preference structures that are defined in terms of general primitives are not yet formulated.

Although the theory is limited for representing persistence in consumption behavior, a number of interesting possibilities for empirical testing and validation originate from the flexible functional forms for utility and applications of autocorrelation structures in systems contexts. Tests with the translog specification are directed more toward the maintained hypotheses for most of the traditional demand systems, that is, tests of theoretical propositions that follow from assumptions on the utility functions (Christensen et al. 1975). These include homogeneity, symmetry, summability (additivity), nonnegativity, and monotonicity. The tests are not conclusive and are limited by the approximation provided by the flexible functional form (translog expression).

Tests involving autocorrelation are interesting because they juxtapose the existing expressions for characterizing persistence structurally against an hypothesis to accommodate them in the residuals or error terms. These tests were greatly advanced and clarified by the work on autocorrelation and systems specifications of Berndt and Savin (1975). Since then several complete sets of tests for autocorrelation, habit or persistence structures in the demand systems, and theory restrictions have been conducted (Green et al. 1979b, 1980; Howe et al. 1979). Results of these tests generally support the earlier observation about the theory; that is, they raise sufficient questions to suggest that added theoretical developments are necessary before we can better understand the dynamics of consumption behavior. Still, from a conceptual viewpoint, these developments are encouraging because there is continuing interchange between the theoretical and applied results.

A number of possibilities for additional work on demand systems are indicated from the results obtained and summarized here: persistence, aggregation, experimental and statistical control, and policy. The objective of our speculations in these areas is to share insights gained from assembling material for this book and add to perspective for current demand systems results.

9.1 PERSISTENCE

Extensions to accommodate the observed persistence in aggregate consumption behavior are discussed first because some important points have already been anticipated in the preceding discussion. Habit formation and dynamic systems results presented and synthesized here are at the forefront of present knowledge on applications and tests of the theory. Three aspects of these dynamic models and tests identify potentially fertile areas for future developments and the limitations of our ex ante results.

Until now, theoretical works have addressed the problem of generalizing the assumptions on preference orderings to dynamic settings by using results developed in static contexts, pieced together by various time discounting mechanisms. The source of discounting mechanisms and whether preferences are, in fact, more integrally defined over future and existing consumption bundles are questions to be answered. Life cycle consumption patterns, acquisitions of durable goods, savings, and intergenerational transfers are all apparent from casual observation of consumption behavior. A modest amount of introspection results in ample evidence of the importance of these aspects of consumption behavior.

The models here, however, treat persistence of consumption patterns in highly mechanical ways and may be useful to summarize consumption behavior at an aggregate level and to generate important policy parameters to deal with the aggregate system. But it is difficult to justify the assertion that demand systems work is motivated by policy concerns. If the objective is to better understand consumer behavior and test the present theory, then these observations about the theoretical structure and how it compares observed consumption patterns and simple introspection suggest important areas for additional investigation.

Models that include persistence and a dynamic structure for consumption behavior also need to incorporate uncertainty into their structures. Consumption decisions viewed dynamically depend upon anticipated prices and incomes that are not known with certainty. Thus, an important factor in the determination of consumption behavior is expectation of future prices and incomes. Dynamic models that characterize consumption over time and habits or inventories do not at present reflect this consumption decision problem. Habits and durables purchases may not be altered in one period with a relative price change if the change is regarded as transitory. Thus expectations formations, rationality, information costs, and persistence in consumption patterns are all closely intertwined. To study persistence without directly addressing these other aspects of behavior is to study only part of the dynamic consumption decision.

The final feature of observed persistence in consumption patterns is called structure. Consumption patterns are greatly influenced by the circumstances for individual consumption decisions. For this reason, comparisons over time and between countries are hazardous, and the results of demand systems estimation must be interpreted with caution in this context. For example, the price of locks in a safe city may be the same as their price in a nonsafe city. Consumers in the nonsafe city buy locks, but this does not necessarily say anything about different consumption preferences. It is more likely that the circumstances of the consumption decision are different. This may be all right for demand systems estimation if the structure remains constant, but it shows that in applied demand work we are measuring a number of uncontrollable or uncontrolled factors in addition to preferences and responses to prices.

9.2 AGGREGATION

Important aggregation decisions have been based in applying the Canadian demand systems and on other applications (see Chap. 7 for examples). These aggregation decisions relate to commodity groups and to consumers. The limited numbers of commodity groups are used in systems are justified on the basis of separability hypotheses. The composition of these groups is given little attention; they are frequently determined by those who construct the national accounts, often for purposes different from those required for their inclusion in demand models. From the separability assumptions, these groups should be composed of commodities that consumers consider independent from those in other groups.

The delineation of commodity groups is an area for additional demand systems research. Various approaches are possible, ranging from empirical cluster analysis methods to more detailed investigations of the consistency of consumption behavior for components of existing groups. The results of Bieri and deJanvry (1972) only begin to solve this problem. Perhaps commodities should be grouped on the basis of characteristics (Lancaster 1971), but so far the important grouping decision has received little attention. As demand systems methods are contemplated or tried on a more disaggregated basis, these problems will be more difficult to leave unsolved.

Estimates of aggregation effects across consumers can be made using available socioeconomic partitions in the sample data. In addition, recent work on almost ideal demand systems provides a potentially useful way to treat the aggregation problem (Deaton and Muellbauer 1980a, 1980b). This model gives an arbitrary first order approximation to any demand system, permits exact aggregation over consumers with different incomes, and satisfies the usual restrictions for the consumer allocation problem. It is interesting that the Deaton and Muellbauer model is developed from a cost function, taking advantage of alternatives for representing the consumer optimization problem provided by duality concepts.

It is clear that for applied work higher disaggregation is desirable for demand systems estimates. Until now, researchers have been limited by the availability of computer algorithms for nonlinear demand systems estimation problems. But the technology for solving nonlinear estimation problems is improving, making it possible to estimate systems models with added commodity groups, hierarchical orderings (Hassan et al. 1973), block systems, and other approaches consistent with more plausible behavioral assumptions will need further refinement.

9.3 EXPERIMENTAL AND STATISTICAL CONTROL

Demand systems methods are applied without recognizing the supply conditions prevailing during the sample period. In commodity market models, the supply and demand parameter estimates are obtained in a simultaneous equations framework. Unless very specialized supply conditions occur (i.e., supply is perfectly inelastic), the demand parameters estimated in a single equation context reflect supply response also.

This result also holds for demand systems parameters and supply functions for aggregated commodity groups are not perfectly inelastic. Thus, the demand systems parameter estimates can, in principle, be improved by specifying a supply structure. Those who estimate demand systems parameters elect not to use the market equilibrium framework because of the problems of how to specify the supply structure and whether or not to include in it the same separability hypotheses as for the demand systems.

Still, the estimation of demand systems parameters in an equilibrium model is a promising possibility. It is clear that the annual sample periods for these systems are of sufficient length that substantial supply shifts can occur, even at highly aggregated levels. The equilibrium specification should be considered as an approach to the introduction of statistical control in the estimation process. It is applied successfully in commodity market modeling to support different types of policy analysis and forecasting exercises.

Experimental control of demand systems estimation can be introduced by studying longitudinal sample or panel data, conditioning on socioeconomic characteristics and estimation at less aggregated levels for consumers. Possibilities exist to expand available data bases significantly through use of computerized labeling and scanning devices in retail outlets. Large data bases of considerable detail keyed to households can be generated with this technology and will permit considerable refinement in the estimation of demand parameters for different consumer groups. This alternative is more attractive if an improved approach to disaggregating demand systems from a commodity viewpoint can be developed.

Inclusion of socioeconomic factors as conditioning variables can increase the value of demand systems estimates from forecasting and policy viewpoints. Household production approaches can be used to rationalize their inclusion. Scenarios constructed using the socioeconomic variables and demand responses can be evaluated. Use of socioeconomic conditioning variables can help to obtain more resolution on the systems parameter estimates. Generally, their inclusion should not lead to problems of estimability, given the length of available sample series. These same variables probably would be required for identification in estimating the demand systems parameters within an equilibrium framework.

Another alternative is to pool time series and cross section data. For the linear expenditure system, this approach has been used to estimate demand systems parameters in cross section data alone (Howe 1977; Green et al. 1979a). These methods can be extended to the pooling of time series and cross section data. For example, consider the persistence problems of Sec. 9.1, where estimation using cross section data helps to introduce experimental control, giving insights on how estimated habits and structure affect consumption patterns. Without an improved theory, this approach is attractive as a means of obtaining a better explanation of persistence in consumption patterns.

9.4 POLICY ANALYSIS AND FORECASTING

Until now, the estimated demand systems have been employed mostly in academic contexts. Tests of the theory, estimation problems, and comparisons across similar representations have been the focus of applied work. While these objectives of empirical investigations have merit, ultimate interest in these models and the empirical results must be motivated by more practical concerns. We are attempting to understand consumption behavior and improve the theory for an ultimate purpose: useful results for decision analysis and forecasting.

Specialization of these demand systems models to particular policy and forecasting problems is another area for future study. This orientation is needed to unite alternatives for representing persistence, aggregation, and options for statistical and experimental control. Clearly, choices in these areas depend upon the ultimate use of the model. Guidelines for use of the results then give structure to model design problems in demand systems estimation.

These same observations are important for the theory. We have achieved a reasonable level of familiarity with existing demand systems representations. Moreover, applications yielded relatively consistent results. But the next developments should concentrate on adapting the specifications to particular economic policy and forecasting problems. Growth, trade, and income redistribution program impact analysis seem logical possibilities for these specializations. The characteristics of systems estimates evaluated in the context of policy priorities are important for both applied and theoretical work. Some sacrifices of theoretical niceties may be necessary to provide a way to deal with the apparent impasse of the current separability requirements for disaggregated systems specifications.

REFERENCES

Berndt, E. R., and Savin, N. E. 1975. Estimation and hypothesis testing in singular equation systems with autoregressive disturbances. Econometrica 43 (Sept.-Nov.):937-57.

Bieri, J., and deJanvry, A. 1972. Empirical Analysis of Demand under Consumer Budgeting. Giannini Monograph 30, University of California, Berkeley.

Christensen, L. R.; Jorgenson, D. N.; and Lau, L. J. 1975. Transcendental logarithmic utilty functions. American Economic Review 65 (Jan.):37-54.

Deaton, A., and Muellbauer, J. 1980a. Economics of Consumer Behavior. Cambridge University Press.

———. 1980b. An almost ideal demand system. American Economic Review 70 (June):312-26.

Green, R.; Hassan, Z.; and S.R. Johnson. 1979a. Price elasticity estimates from family expenditure data: An application of the extended linear expenditure system. Canadian Journal of Agricultural Economics 27 (Feb.):41-52.

. 1979b. Maximum likelihood estimation of linear expenditure systems with autocorrelated errors: An application. European Economic Review 11 (Aug.):207-19.

———. 1980. Testing for habit formation, autocorrelation and

theoretical restrictions in linear expenditure systems. Southern Economic Journal 47 (Oct.):433-43.
Hassan, Z.; Finley, R. M.; and Johnson, S. R. 1973. The Demand for food in the United States. Applied Economics 5 (Dec.):233-48.
Houthakker, H. S., and Taylor, L. D. 1970. Consumer Demand in the United States, 2d ed. Cambridge, Mass: Harvard University Press.
Howe, H. 1977. Cross-section application of linear expenditure systems: responses to sociodemographic effects. American Journal of Agricultural Economics 59 (Feb.):141-48.
Howe, H.; Pollak, R.; and Wales, T. J. 1979. Theory and time series estimation of the quadratic expenditure system. Econometrica 47 (Oct.):1231-48.
Lancaster, K. 1971. Consumer Demand: A New Approach. New York: Columbia University Press.
Lluch, C. 1974. Expenditure, savings, and habit formation. International Economic Review 15 (Oct.):786-97.
Phlips, L. 1974. Applied Consumption Analysis. Amsterdam: North Holland.

Appendix

The data series used to estimate the demand systems models contained in this Appendix are for the models that include four commodity groups and nine commodity groups. Tables 1-5 cover the period 1947-1972 and are used to estimate the models from the results presented in Chaps. 7 and 8. Tables 6-9 contain data consistently for 1971-1980. They overlap because of changes in the definitions during the most recent revision of the data series. These data can be employed to generate our results or to estimate the systems models for other time periods.

TABLE 1 Personal expenditure on durables, semidurables, and nondurables, and services in current dollars (millions), 1947-1972

Year	Durables	Semidurables	Nondurables	Services	Total
1947	911	1779	3871	2801	9362
48	987	1946	4375	3062	10370
49	1258	2071	4545	3491	11365
50	1576	2162	4896	3848	12482
51	1651	2338	5497	4371	13857
52	1867	2518	5836	4941	15162
53	2116	2634	6004	5427	16181
54	2070	2657	6312	5895	16934
55	2440	2834	6691	6423	18388
56	2731	3075	7234	7050	20090
57	2775	3183	7832	7702	21492
58	2898	3346	8241	8360	22845
59	3176	3501	8651	9062	24390
60	3236	3577	9002	9664	25479
61	3365	3698	9220	9647	25930
62	3729	3892	9691	10140	27452
63	4127	4086	10213	10799	29225
64	4560	4388	10798	11643	31389
65	5085	4671	11526	12665	33947
66	5490	5054	12364	13982	36890
67	5915	5539	13219	15299	39972
68	6494	5953	14019	17238	43704
69	6975	6426	15073	19018	47492
70	6799	6645	16186	20697	50327
71	7762	7224	17357	22125	54468
72	8984	8108	19354	24134	60580

Source: Statistics Canada, National Income and Expenditure Accounts, Vol. 1, Catalogue 13-531, March 1976.

TABLE 2 Personal expenditure on durables, semidurables, nondurables, and services in constant (1971) dollars (millions), 1947-1972

Year	Durables	Semidurables	Nondurables	Services	Total
1947	1406	3493	6815	6818	18546
48	1375	3227	6649	6900	18099
49	1703	3270	6758	7487	19138
50	2087	3390	7114	7798	20394
51	1936	3289	7176	8281	20546
52	2144	3506	7558	8939	21984
53	2450	3680	8018	9498	23512
54	2417	3736	8431	9979	24375
55	2988	3996	8940	10635	26456
56	3309	4276	9569	11366	28440
57	3203	4385	10036	12028	29504
58	3285	4505	10326	12635	30562
59	3534	4701	10795	13434	32264
60	3594	4760	11194	14087	33392
61	3787	4861	11399	13885	33761
62	4215	5031	11827	14316	35272
63	4642	5142	12301	15003	36992
64	5180	5418	12869	15817	39218
65	5769	5676	13469	16716	41606
66	6169	5922	13878	17859	43778
67	6428	6197	14616	18676	45863
68	6876	6435	14855	20069	48138
69	7254	6744	15520	20927	50353
70	6865	6784	16414	21635	51526
71	7762	7224	17357	22125	54468
72	8847	7875	1834	23018	58083

Source: Statistics Canada, National Income and Expenditure Accounts, Vol. 1, Catalogue 13-531, March 1976.

TABLE 3 Estimated population of Canada, June 1 (thousands), 1947-1972

Year	Population	Year	Population
1947	12,551	1960	17,870
48	12,823	61	18,238
49	13,447	62	18,583
50	13,712	63	18,931
51	14,009	64	19,290
52	14,459	65	19,644
53	14,845	66	20,105
54	15,287	67	20,378
55	15,698	68	20,701
56	16,081	69	21,001
57	16,610	70	21,297
58	17,080	71	21,569
59	17,483	72	21,821

Source: Statistics Canada, _Estimate Population of Canada by Providence_, Catalogue No. 91-201.

TABLE 4 Personal expenditure on consumer goods and services in current dollars (millions), 1947-1959

Commodity Group	1947	1948	1949	1950	1951	1952	1953	1954	1955	1956	1957	1958	1959
Food and nonalcoholic bev. (ND)	2,133	2,479	2,514	2,742	3,176	3,280	3,333	3,516	3,666	3,936	4,242	4,453	4,589
Alcoholic bev. (ND)	449	474	504	531	579	659	676	672	711	759	808	840	885
Tobacco products (ND)	359	391	417	437	438	476	467	486	524	560	609	657	726
Clothing and footwear	1,121	1,265	1,316	1,331	1,452	1,567	1,618	1,624	1,716	1,855	1,926	2,016	2,107
Gross rent, fuel, and power	1,295	1,422	1,585	1,804	2,039	2,284	2,538	2,841	3,097	3,322	3,658	3,928	4,271
Furniture, furnishings, household equipment, and operation	1,159	1,269	1,413	1,534	1,568	1,748	1,870	1,922	2,102	2,297	2,357	2,473	2,604
Medical care and health services	400	449	494	537	606	701	772	853	923	1,061	1,182	1,329	1,466
Drugs and sundries (ND)	118	132	140	152	174	188	201	205	220	244	276	289	307
Transportation and communication	936	1,024	1,270	1,554	1,697	1,850	2,091	2,059	2,400	2,690	2,814	2,969	3,246
Recreation, entertainment, education, and cultural services	497	531	576	625	691	781	851	915	999	1,089	1,179	1,287	1,397
Personal goods and services	1,107	1,218	1,382	1,456	1,620	1,766	1,918	1,981	2,143	2,373	2,572	2,719	2,916
Net expenditure abroad (S)	-94	-152	-106	-69	-9	50	47	65	107	148	145	174	183

Source: Statistics Canada, National Income and Expenditure Accounts, Vol. 1, Catalogue 13-531, March 1976.

TABLE 4 (continued) 1960-1972

Commodity Group	1960	1961	1962	1963	1964	1965	1966	1967	1968	1969	1970	1971	1972
Food and nonalcoholic bev. (ND)	4,776	4,811	5,009	5,257	5,564	5,885	6,274	6,645	6,925	7,445	7,923	8,442	9,545
Alcoholic bev. (ND)	918	960	1,016	1,078	1,133	1,252	1,357	1,482	1,591	1,742	1,898	2,129	2,382
Tobacco products (ND)	743	790	836	855	884	960	1,040	1,113	1,223	1,284	1,396	1,455	1,547
Clothing and footwear	2,184	2,260	2,384	2,499	2,682	2,855	3,067	3,364	3,617	3,908	4,034	4,382	4,868
Gross rent, fuel, and power	4,510	4,785	5,081	5,464	5,747	6,064	6,573	7,247	7,960	8,742	9,861	10,592	11,402
Furniture, furnishings, household equipment, and operation	2,609	2,703	2,838	2,976	3,196	3,426	3,743	4,024	4,322	4,658	4,785	5,211	5,936
Medical care and health services	1,622	1,131	1,201	1,289	1,391	1,516	1,652	1,789	1,902	1,912	1,758	1,679	1,866
Drugs and sundries (ND)	320	334	356	381	417	461	516	565	602	658	697	754	836
Transportation and communication	3,349	3,467	3,822	4,169	4,563	5,114	5,479	5,940	6,458	6,863	6,946	7,775	8,741
Recreation, entertainment, education, and cultural services	1,492	1,600	1,740	1,916	2,150	2,400	2,787	3,334	3,682	4,104	4,467	5,041	5,696
Personal goods and services	3,097	3,288	3,501	3,761	4,060	4,460	4,898	5,497	6,034	6,683	7,133	7,667	8,468
Net expenditure abroad (S)	179	135	24	-39	19	15	20	-463	-10	151	126	95	129

TABLE 5 Personal expenditure on consumer goods and services in constant (1971) dollars (millions), 1947-1959

Commodity Group	1947	1948	1949	1950	1951	1952	1953	1954	1955	1956	1957	1958	1959
Food and nonalcoholic bev. (ND)	4,099	3,892	3,877	4,143	4,198	4,329	4,595	4,850	5,058	5,368	5,545	5,596	5,818
Alcoholic bev. (ND)	685	705	753	774	780	886	910	901	952	1,013	1,048	1,075	1,112
Tobacco products (ND)	586	607	634	648	591	626	695	735	790	843	917	989	1,024
Clothing and footwear	2,025	1,890	1,882	1,901	1,869	1,990	2,074	2,103	2,246	2,415	2,511	2,603	2,722
Gross rent, fuel, and power	2,396	2,484	2,656	2,808	3,022	3,230	3,481	3,808	4,083	4,314	4,679	4,987	5,386
Furniture, furnishing, household equipment, and operation	2,235	2,163	2,235	2,372	2,153	2,336	2,482	2,559	2,798	2,993	2,985	3,064	3,202
Medical care and health services	922	919	967	1,035	1,070	1,142	1,214	1,283	1,352	1,504	1,590	1,722	1,845
Drugs and sundries (ND)	150	151	157	169	182	196	207	210	223	247	273	280	285
Transportation and communication	1,720	1,749	2,070	2,403	2,389	2,520	2,817	2,751	3,298	3,598	3,542	3,690	3,934
Recreation, entertainment, education, and cultural services	1,159	1,177	1,232	1,300	1,336	1,428	1,496	1,560	1,661	1,776	1,875	1,911	2,034
Personal goods and services	3,225	3,189	3,426	3,507	3,592	3,772	4,013	4,033	4,248	4,529	4,692	4,774	4,998
Net expenditure abroad (S)	-178	-224	-158	-127	-46	39	30	55	99	144	155	176	189

Source: Statistics Canada, National Income and Expenditure Accounts, Vol. 1, Catalogue 13-531, March 1976.

TABLE 5 (continued) 1960-1972

Commodity Group	1960	1961	1962	1963	1964	1965	1966	1967	1968	1969	1970	1971	1972
Food and nonalcoholic bev. (ND)	6,036	6,025	6,139	6,252	6,554	6,741	6,773	7,150	7,196	7,535	7,954	8,442	8,820
Alcoholic bev. (ND)	1,142	1,185	1,229	1,300	1,329	1,457	1,558	1,675	1,674	1,774	1,918	2,129	2,266
Tobacco products (ND)	1,029	1,092	1,151	1,177	1,204	1,268	1,318	1,354	1,329	1,331	1,426	1,455	1,508
Clothing and footwear	2,793	2,855	2,982	3,043	3,188	3,337	3,457	3,620	3,792	3,990	4,061	4,382	4,758
Gross rent, fuel, and power	5,673	6,020	6,389	6,868	7,227	7,599	8,149	8,737	9,256	9,654	10,323	10,592	10,887
Furniture, furnishings, household equipment, and operation	3,200	3,315	3,424	3,549	3,779	3,989	4,237	4,383	4,593	4,853	4,856	5,211	5,771
Medical care and health services	2,006	1,393	1,453	1,538	1,628	1,730	1,835	1,904	1,985	1,930	1,741	1,679	1,801
Drugs and sundries (ND)	293	323	348	380	415	450	508	554	611	653	687	754	832
Transportation and communication	4,034	4,190	4,615	5,017	5,495	6,101	6,438	6,735	7,100	7,348	7,112	7,775	8,524
Recreation, entertainment, education, and cultural services	2,140	2,266	2,421	2,618	2,887	3,153	3,530	3,989	4,170	4,435	4,609	5,041	5,628
Personal goods and services	5,177	5,353	5,575	5,811	6,014	6,293	6,521	6,874	7,107	7,397	7,470	7,667	7,953
Net expenditure abroad (S)	174	130	-14	-74	-18	-17	5	-568	-26	131	105	95	167

TABLE 6 Personal expenditure on durables, semidurables, nondurables, and services in current dollars (millions), 1971-1980

Year	Durables	Semidurables	Nondurables	Services	Total
1971	7,883	7,133	17,521	23,079	55,616
72	9,440	7,962	19,432	25,374	62,208
73	11,481	9,059	22,302	28,436	71,278
74	13,139	11,184	26,218	32,847	83,388
75	15,320	12,428	30,422	38,825	96,995
76	17,021	14,176	33,967	45,722	110,886
77	18,335	15,374	37,383	51,438	122,530
78	19,998	16,710	41,689	56,874	135,271
79	22,593	18,709	46,451	62,864	150,617
80	24,154	20,554	52,422	71,016	168,146

Source: Statistics Canada, _National Income and Expenditure Accounts_, Catalogue 13-201, annual.

TABLE 7 Personal expenditure on durables, semidurables, nondurables, and services in constant (1971) dollars (millions), 1971-1980

Year	Durables	Semidurables	Nondurables	Services	Total
1971	7,883	7,133	17,521	23,079	55,616
72	9,285	7,731	18,464	24,361	59,841
73	11,051	8,318	19,210	25,300	63,879
74	11,606	9,306	20,070	26,178	67,160
75	12,377	9,778	20,735	27,755	70,645
76	13,025	10,543	21,943	29,740	75,251
77	13,385	10,779	22,187	31,065	77,416
78	13,892	11,210	22,376	32,073	79,550
79	14,502	11,314	22,637	32,683	81,136
80	14,271	11,178	22,766	33,740	81,955

Source: Statistics Canada, _National Income and Expenditure Accounts_, Catalogue 13-201, annual.

TABLE 8 Estimated population of Canada, June 1 (thousands), 1971-1980

Year	Population
1971	21,569
72	21,821
73	22,095
74	22,446
75	22,800
76	22,973
77	23,258
78	23,476
79	23,671
80	23,914

Source: Statistics Canada, _Estimate Population of Canada by Providence_, Catalogue No. 91-201.

TABLE 9 Personal expenditure on consumer goods and services in current dollars (millions), 1971-1979

Commodity Group	1971	1972	1973	1974	1975	1976	1977	1978	1979	1980
Food and nonalcoholic bev (ND)	8,554	9,499	11,078	12,936	15,206	16,567	18,041	20,358	22,862	25,339
Alcoholic bev. (ND)	2,139	2,391	2,653	3,027	3,501	3,779	4,133	4,487	4,838	5,518
Tobacco products (ND)	1,455	1,547	1,664	1,799	2,050	2,333	2,582	2,810	3,082	3,524
Clothing and footwear	4,143	4,550	5,120	6,412	7,155	8,132	8,773	9,508	10,621	11,600
Gross rent, fuel, and power	10,581	11,412	12,506	14,271	16,445	19,146	21,850	24,374	27,235	31,046
Furniture, furnishings, household equipment, and operation	5,295	6,135	7,304	8,652	9,884	11,117	12,016	12,976	14,281	15,508
Medical care and health services	1,618	1,804	2,054	2,466	2,896	3,465	3,829	4,272	4,755	5,266
Drugs and sundries (ND)	667	753	880	1,130	1,279	1,474	1,626	1,804	2,034	2,301
Transportation and communication	8,014	9,030	10,551	12,161	14,292	16,390	17,957	19,606	22,395	24,843
Recreation, entertainment, education, and cultural services	5,364	6,288	7,265	8,655	9,972	11,554	12,691	13,854	15,383	17,055
Personal goods and services	8,357	9,423	10,912	12,870	15,062	17,463	19,308	21,636	24,390	27,569
Net expenditure abroad (S)	96	129	171	139	532	940	1,350	1,390	775	878

Source: Statistics Canada, National Income and Expenditure Accounts, Catalogue 13-201, annual.

TABLE 10 Personal expenditure on consumer goods and services in constant (1971) dollars (millions), 1971-1979

Commodity Group	1971	1972	1973	1974	1975	1976	1977	1978	1979	1980
Food and nonalcoholic bev. (ND)	8,554	8,779	8,825	8,895	9,350	10,063	9,983	9,825	9,827	9,789
Alcoholic bev. (ND)	2,139	2,314	2,497	2,692	2,782	2,843	2,943	3,030	3,044	3,087
Tobacco products (ND)	1,455	1,508	1,563	1,608	1,649	1,716	1,758	1,749	1,822	1,877
Clothing and footwear	4,143	4,447	4,772	5,514	5,913	6,400	6,510	6,830	6,995	6,989
Gross rent, fuel, and power	10,581	11,017	11,359	11,891	12,367	12,915	13,365	13,866	14,329	14,808
Furniture, furnishings, household equipment, and operation	5,295	5,957	6,723	7,048	7,305	7,650	7,793	8,024	8,109	8,041
Medical care and health services	1,618	1,744	1,880	2,082	2,169	2,352	2,431	2,534	2,587	2,611
Drugs and sundries (ND)	667	750	856	1,047	1,072	1,146	1,213	1,269	1,303	1,342
Transportation and communication	8,014	8,807	9,999	10,452	11,141	11,741	12,039	12,401	12,994	12,858
Recreation, entertainment, education, and cultural services	5,364	6,039	6,642	7,329	7,535	8,111	8,271	8,605	8,929	9,180
Personal goods and services	8,357	9,062	9,387	9,371	987	10,526	11,309	11,874	12,164	12,371
Net expenditure abroad (S)	96	167	232	278	563	934	1,014	811	336	344

Source: Statistics Canada, National Income and Expenditure Accounts, Catalogue 13-201, annual.

Index